Company's
Coming
Millennium®
E D I T I O N

Front Cover Photo:
1. Berry Spectacular, page 114
2. Parsley Pesto Pasta, page 127
3. Margo's Rosemary Chicken, page 99

First Printing September 1999

Canadian Cataloguing in Publication Data

Paré, Jean
    Company's Coming: everyday recipes for changing times.

    Millennium ed.
    Includes index.
    Written by Jean Paré
    ISBN 1-896891-11-X

    1. Holiday cookery.   2. Cookery   3. Millennium celebrations (Year 2000)
I. Title   II. Title: Everyday recipes for changing times.
TX715.6.P37 1999   641.5'68   C99-900575-8

Published also in French under title: Jean Paré fête le millénaire
ISBN 1-896891-13-6

Published simultaneously in
Canada and the United States of America by
THE RECIPE FACTORY INC.
in conjunction with
COMPANY'S COMING PUBLISHING LIMITED
2311 - 96 Street
Edmonton, Alberta, Canada T6N 1G3
Tel: (780) 450-6223   Fax: (780) 450-1857

Company's Coming is a registered trademark owned by
Company's Coming Publishing Limited

Color separations, printing, and binding by Friesens, Altona, Manitoba, Canada
Printed in Canada

"Here's to the tastes and trends of today. May they become our traditions of tomorrow."

"I would like to say a special thank you to my long-time friends in Vermilion and area who shared their memories, recipes and old cookbooks when I was doing the research for this book. These ladies are near and dear to me and have been a source of support and inspiration for many years."

Jean Paré

Millennium Edition was created thanks to the dedicated efforts of the people and organizations listed below.

COMPANY'S COMING PUBLISHING LIMITED

Author	Jean Paré
President	Grant Lovig
Vice President, Product Development	Kathy Knowles
Design Manager	Derrick Sorochan
Designer	Jaclyn Draker
Assistant Designer	Denise Hodgins
Typesetter	Marlene Crosbie
Copywriter	Debbie Dixon

THE RECIPE FACTORY INC.

Research & Development Manager	Nora Prokop
Editor	Stephanie Amodio
Proofreader	Mimi Tindall
Test Kitchen Supervisor	Lynda Elsenheimer
Test Kitchen Staff	Ellen Bunjevac
	Allison Dosman
	Jacquie Elton
	Linda Feniak
	Carol McLeod
	Marg Steeden
	Audrey Thomas
	Pat Yukes
Photographer	Stephe Tate Photo
Food Stylist	Suzanne Hartman
Prop Stylist	Gabriele McEleney
Nutrition Analyst	Margaret Ng, B.Sc., M.A., R.D.

Our special thanks to the following businesses for providing extensive props for photography.

Bombay Company	La Cache
Call The Kettle Black	Le Gnome
Cheesecakes and more	Left Brain Productions
Chintz & Company	Mystique Pottery & Gifts
Clays Handmade Ceramic Tile & Stone	Scona Clayworks
	Stokes
Creations By Design	The Basket House
Dansk Gifts	The Bay
Eaton's	The Royal Doulton Store
From Times Past Ltd.- Antiques & Interiors	Tile Town Ltd.

Special thanks to all staff who provided family heirloom pieces.

Table of Contents

Bean Salad, page 151

Fruit Shake, page 57

Peach Shake, page 56

Garlic Dip, page 40

Chocolate Crisps, page 90

Foreword

Millennium!
What comes to mind
when you hear that word?
Celebration? Changing times?
Memories of days gone by?
One thing is certain—witnessing the
dawning of a new millennium is a
once-in-a-lifetime experience. After all,
it only happens once in about
every 30 generations!

A lot has happened over
the past millennium, and the
world certainly has gone through
huge changes. Empires have been built
up, and torn down; new countries have
been created and old ones dissolved;
and destructive wars have
encompassed the globe
not once but twice.

Much has changed in the way
we live too. Technological advances
made in the last 100 years alone have
altered how we do practically everything.
Just take a peek into the kitchen. Fresh
produce once was only available if
grown in domestic gardens. The
invention of refrigeration, combined
with improved transportation and
roads, mean that we have a much
greater variety of fresh produce in
grocery bins than ever before.

Metal cans and plastic
packaging have brought convenience
foods into our cupboards. Immigration and
integration have introduced new tastes and
shared cultures. And thanks to helpful
inventions such as the dishwasher,
self-cleaning oven and frost-free refrigerator,
we have more time on our hands than ever
before to be somewhere other than the
kitchen! And don't forget microwave ovens,
indoor grills, bread makers, blenders and
all kinds of kitchen gadgets—they offer
us the chance to explore new
and different ways to prepare
our favorite recipes.

In celebration of this start
to the next 1000 years, now is a
great time to reflect and remember, or
take a moment and talk to your parents and
grandparents. How were their lives different
in the first half of this past century? What was it
like to prepare a meal in their kitchen? They will
probably tell you about how they hauled coal or
wood to heat their stoves and struggled to keep
food cool in ice chests during summer months.
They might recount the challenge
of food rationing during World Wars I and II,
or how they endured almost no food at all
during the Great Depression. Perhaps you
remember when the only trucks allowed
on the roads on Sundays were those
carrying perishable goods.

Your parents or grandparents might also tell you about family traditions which have long since disappeared. One custom that Company's Coming would like to help you maintain, or perhaps revive, throughout these hectic lifestyle changes, is the practice of handing down recipes to our children. Generations have tried, improved upon, and then passed on, classic recipes that remain steadfast and dependable over time. And while good recipes tend to evolve down through the ages, the original substance of the recipe remains intact; they simply become more modern in their preparation. Let us take you down memory lane with a few time-honored recipes we have featured in this book, along with our modern version. You will find it fun to try both (if you can follow the often sketchy instructions in the recipes of yesteryear!).

Also included is some interesting history on everyday items in our kitchen that we have come to take for granted. Did you know that the fork was once considered sinful to use, or that Leonardo da Vinci invented the first mechanical turnspit, the forerunner to the rotisserie? You'll enjoy reading about that and more as you follow the evolution of appliances, cutlery and cooking utensils. Take a moment as well to learn about the history of nutritional guides–it offers an interesting perspective on how and why our eating habits have changed over the last 50 years.

What kind of future could we possibly imagine around the corner? For the answer, some of us might look to technology, or religion, or even the stars and beyond, for our next great adventure. But no matter what awaits us in the next millennium, it is my hope that this new era brings only the best of what life has to offer to you, your family and your friends. I invite you to join me in celebrating this special occasion with everyday recipes for changing times!

Wishing you many happy millennium memories!

Jean Paré

Celebrate the Millennium

The idea of experiencing a New Millennium Eve is much more than exciting, *it's exceptional!* We have been hearing about this big night for years and it's finally here! Bring in the new year and the new millennium with close family, good friends and delicious food.

When guests arrive to share in the festivities, offer a selection of appetizers to nibble on. Brie In Pastry presents a very special touch to the evening along with Bruschetta Pizza, certain to be a favorite among all. Your guests will also love Pot Stickers and Green Onion Cakes with the Spicy Dipping Sauce. Serve a punch such as Celebration Punch, along with the other beverages you choose—and don't forget the bubbly! When the clock strikes midnight, it's our chance to celebrate our strengths and talents, to reflect on our past, and to mark that moment in history. Cheers!

Here are some key tips to keep in mind when hosting your New Millennium celebration:

- Invite your guests well in advance. It's good to book your family and friends several months prior to this auspicious occasion. Write down your their names and check them off as they accept or decline.

- Determine if it will be a sit-down dinner, a buffet, or a night of appetizers. Choose the recipes.

- Make a list of all food, beverages and party favors you will need. Purchase any non-perishables well ahead of time.

- Determine how much time you will need to prepare the food. Note recipes that can be made ahead of time and frozen, any that can be prepared the day before and finally, those that need to be done that day.

- Do the simple, but time-consuming, chores the day before. Organize serving bowls, glasses and utensils, making certain that you have enough of everything.

- Have fun decorating the house!

- Remember to allow at least 30 minutes to relax before your guests arrive.

Celebration Punch

Pale yellow color. It will remind you of champagne.

Frozen concentrated lemonade, thawed	12½ oz.	355 mL
White grape juice	10 cups	2.5 L
Ginger ale	4 cups	1 L
Club soda	6 cups	1.5 L
Ice ring (or cubes)		
Fresh strawberries (or other fruit), for garnish		

Pour concentrated lemonade into punch bowl. Add grape juice. Stir. Chill.

Add ginger ale and club soda shortly before serving. Stir lightly. Add ice ring.

Garnish with strawberries. Makes 21 cups (5.2 L) punch.

1 cup (250 mL) punch: 117 Calories; trace Protein; trace Total Fat; 30 g Carbohydrate; 21 mg Sodium; 0 g Dietary Fiber

Pictured on page 10.

Brie In Pastry

Bruschetta Pizza
Served in appetizer-size wedges. Very colorful. Such a winner!

Pizza Crust:		
All-purpose flour	2 cups	500 mL
Baking powder	4 tsp.	20 mL
Granulated sugar (optional)	1 tsp.	5 mL
Salt	½ tsp.	2 mL
Cooking oil	⅓ cup	75 mL
Milk	¾ cup	175 mL
Topping:		
Cooking oil	2 tsp.	10 mL
Garlic powder	½ tsp.	2 mL
Light salad dressing (or mayonnaise)	½ cup	125 mL
Grated Parmesan cheese	¼ cup	60 mL
Grated part-skim mozzarella cheese	1 cup	250 mL
Seeded and diced tomato	2 cups	500 mL
Dried sweet basil	1 tsp.	5 mL
Garlic salt	½ tsp.	2 mL

Pizza Crust: Measure first 4 ingredients into medium bowl. Stir.

Add cooking oil and milk. Stir to form soft ball. Turn out onto lightly floured surface. Knead 8 times. Divide dough into 3 equal portions. Roll out or press each portion into 7 inch (18 cm) circle. Poke with fork. Place on ungreased baking sheet. Bake in 400°F (205°C) oven for about 15 minutes until golden.

Topping: Combine cooking oil and garlic powder in small cup. Brush over pizza crusts.

Mix remaining 6 ingredients lightly in small bowl. Spread ⅓ of cheese mixture over each crust. Place on ungreased baking sheet. Bake in 400°F (205°C) oven for about 15 minutes until hot and cheese is melted. Let stand for 5 minutes. Each pizza cuts into 8 wedges.

1 wedge: 336 Calories; 10 g Protein; 18.8 g Total Fat; 32 g Carbohydrate; 491 mg Sodium; 1 g Dietary Fiber

Pictured on page 10 and 11.

Brie In Pastry
Fruit with hot cheese makes a great appetizer. Brie can be wrapped in pastry, frozen, then thawed and baked just before serving.

Frozen puff pastry patty shells (from 10¾ oz., 300 g, package of 6), thawed (see Note)	2	2
Small round Brie cheese	4 oz.	125 g
Large egg, fork-beaten	1	1
Medium red apples, cut into thin wedges	2	2

Roll 1 shell out on lightly floured surface into 5½ to 6 inch (14 to 15 cm) circle.

Place Brie cheese in middle of pastry. Bring up sides, pleating dough around edge. Roll out second pastry shell. Using Brie tin, cut circle to fit top. Crimp and seal edges together. Make decorative shapes from scraps of dough. Place on top.

Brush with egg. Place on greased baking sheet. Bake in 450°F (230°C) oven for 15 minutes. Reduce heat to 350°F (175°C). Bake for about 5 minutes until golden brown. Place apple wedges around cheese. Serves 6.

1 serving: 167 Calories; 7 g Protein; 10.1 g Total Fat; 13 g Carbohydrate; 278 mg Sodium; 1 g Dietary Fiber

Pictured above.

Note: All 6 shells may be used to make 3 Brie packets. Simply triple the recipe. Allow 5 to 10 minutes more baking time at 350°F (175°C).

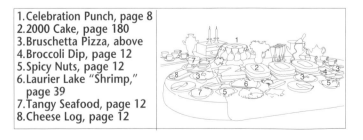

Spicy Nuts

Lots of different shapes for both crispy and crunchy textures. Made without added salt, though you may salt them if desired.

Cooking oil	⅓ cup	75 mL
Worcestershire sauce	1 tbsp.	15 mL
Curry powder	2 tsp.	10 mL
Cayenne pepper	¼ tsp.	1 mL
Paprika	1 tsp.	5 mL
Corn and rice squares cereal (such as Crispix)	2 cups	500 mL
Mixed nuts (such as peanuts, pecans, walnuts, hazelnuts and almonds)	1½ cups	375 mL
Rice crackers (found in the Asian section of grocery store)	3.6 oz.	100 g
Raisins	1½ cups	375 mL

Stir first 5 ingredients together in small cup.

Mix remaining 4 ingredients in small roaster. Drizzle with cooking oil mixture. Stir well to coat. Bake, uncovered, in 300°F (150°C) oven for 15 minutes. Stir well. Bake for about 15 minutes. Cool. Makes 6 cups (1.5 L) nuts.

¼ cup (60 mL) nuts: 145 Calories; 3 g Protein; 9.1 g Total Fat; 15 g Carbohydrate; 139 mg Sodium; 1 g Dietary Fiber

Pictured on page 10 and 11.

Broccoli Dip

Not your usual dip. A hint of garlic with a lot of cheese flavor. Very good. Serve warm with assorted chips or vegetables.

Hard margarine (or butter)	1½ tsp.	7 mL
Chopped onion	1 cup	250 mL
Frozen chopped broccoli	2 cups	500 mL
Boiling water	½ cup	125 mL
Condensed cream of mushroom soup	10 oz.	284 mL
Canned sliced mushrooms, drained and chopped	10 oz.	284 mL
Grated medium Cheddar cheese	2 cups	500 mL
Garlic powder	½ tsp.	2 mL

Melt margarine in non-stick frying pan. Add onion. Sauté until golden.

Cook broccoli in boiling water in medium saucepan until tender. Drain. Chop extra fine.

Combine remaining 4 ingredients in medium saucepan. Heat and stir until cheese is melted. Stir in onion and broccoli. Makes 4 cups (1 L) dip.

2 tbsp. (30 mL) dip: 46 Calories; 2 g Protein; 3.3 g Total Fat; 2 g Carbohydrate; 141 mg Sodium; 1 g Dietary Fiber

Pictured on page 11.

Tangy Seafood

Marinating for hours in such a tangy sauce is the secret to these delicious appetizers. Supply cocktail forks or picks.

Apple cider vinegar	½ cup	125 mL
Cooking oil	¼ cup	60 mL
Chopped fresh parsley (or 1 tbsp., 15 mL, flakes)	¼ cup	60 mL
Jar of pimientos, with liquid	2 oz.	57 mL
Medium dill pickle, cut up	1	1
Garlic clove (or ¼ tsp., 1 mL, powder)	1	1
Salt	1 tsp.	5 mL
Drops of hot pepper sauce	6	6
Variety of bite-size seafood (such as cooked large shrimp, scallops, lobster or crab)	2 lbs.	900 g

Combine first 8 ingredients in blender. Process until almost smooth. Pour into deep bowl or sealable plastic bag.

Add seafood. Stir to coat. Cover bowl or seal bag. Refrigerate for about 8 hours or overnight, stirring or turning several times. Remove seafood with slotted spoon to serving dish. Discard marinade. Serves 12.

1 serving: 96 Calories; 15 g Protein; 3.1 g Total Fat; 2 g Carbohydrate; 528 mg Sodium; trace Dietary Fiber

Pictured on page 10.

Cheese Log

Serve with spreading knife for crackers or in toast points.

Light cream cheese, softened	8 oz.	250 g
Blue cheese, packed	¼ cup	60 mL
Light cream cheese, softened	4 oz.	125 g
Prepared mustard	1 tsp.	5 mL
Soy sauce	1 tsp.	5 mL
Onion powder	¼ tsp.	1 mL
Sweet pickle relish	1 tsp.	5 mL
Canned flakes of ham, drained and mashed	6½ oz.	184 g
Chopped fresh parsley	⅓ cup	75 mL

Mash first amount of cream cheese and blue cheese together in small bowl. Spray waxed paper, 12 inches (30 cm) long, with no-stick cooking spray. Pat cheese mixture evenly into 8 x 12 inch (20 x 30 cm) rectangle on rectangle. Chill well.

Mash next 6 ingredients together in medium bowl. Mix well. Spread over first cheese layer. Chill well. Gently roll as for jelly roll from short side, removing waxed paper as you roll. Chill well.

Sprinkle parsley on working surface. Lay cheese log on top. Roll to cover. Makes 2½ cups (625 mL) cheese log.

2 tbsp. (30 mL) cheese log: 65 Calories; 4 g Protein; 5.2 g Total Fat; 1 g Carbohydrate; 338 mg Sodium; trace Dietary Fiber

Pictured on page 10.

Top Left: Soy Fire Dip, page 40
Bottom Left: Green Onion Cakes, below

Top Center: Spicy Dipping Sauce, this page
Bottom Right: Pot Stickers, this page

Green Onion Cakes

Impress your friends and family with this very easy well-known Oriental appetizer. Serve with Spicy Dipping Sauce, this page, or Soy Fire Dip, page 40.

All-purpose flour	2 cups	500 mL
Salt	1/2 tsp.	2 mL
Very hot water	3/4 cup	175 mL
Thinly sliced green onion	3/4 cup	175 mL
Cooking oil	2 tbsp.	30 mL
Salt, sprinkle		

Measure flour and salt into food processor.

With lid in place and machine running, pour very hot water slowly into food chute until dough starts to form a ball. Knead on lightly floured surface until smooth. Cover with plastic wrap. Let stand for at least 30 minutes. Shape into long roll. Divide into 12 pieces.

Put onion into shallow bowl. Flatten 1 piece of dough slightly between your palms. Press each side into onion. Knead onion into dough. Shape once more into flattened circle. Roll out with greased rolling pin on lightly greased surface into 4 1/2 inch (11 cm) circle. Repeat with remaining dough, keeping covered with plastic wrap as you make more.

Heat 1 1/2 tsp. (7 mL) cooking oil in non-stick frying pan. Arrange 4 onion cakes in pan. Cook over medium-high, flattening down with lifter, until brown patches appear on both sides. Do not overcook. They should be soft, pliable and chewy. Drain on paper towels while frying remaining onion cakes. Cut into 2 or 4 pieces each. Makes 12 green onion cakes.

1 green onion cake: 103 Calories; 2 g Protein; 2.5 g Total Fat; 17 g Carbohydrate; 115 mg Sodium; 1 g Dietary Fiber

Pictured above.

Pot Stickers

Allow extra time to make these—but they're worth it! They will disappear in no time. Serve with Spicy Dipping Sauce, this page.

Grated cabbage	3/4 cup	175 mL
Lean ground pork	6 oz.	170 g
Chopped fresh (or frozen) cooked shrimp	5 oz.	140 g
Finely chopped green onion	3 tbsp.	50 mL
Soy sauce	1 tbsp.	15 mL
Cornstarch	1 tsp.	5 mL
Ground ginger	1/4 tsp.	1 mL
Garlic powder	1/4 tsp.	1 mL
Salt	1/4 tsp.	1 mL
Round wonton wrappers	36	36
Boiling water	3 qts.	3 L
Hard margarine (or butter)	2 tsp.	10 mL

Place first 9 ingredients in medium bowl. Mix well.

Put 2 1/2 tsp. (12 mL) pork mixture onto center of each wonton wrapper. Dampen edge with water. Fold over. Press to seal. Repeat. Keep covered with damp tea towel to prevent drying out.

Have boiling water in large uncovered pot or Dutch oven. Add up to 1/3 of pot stickers. Return to a boil. Boil for 5 minutes. Remove with slotted spoon. Rinse with cold water. Repeat until all are cooked.

Melt margarine in non-stick frying pan. Arrange pot stickers close together in frying pan. Cook on 1 side only until well browned. Makes 36 pot stickers.

1 pot sticker: 19 Calories; 2 g Protein; 0.5 g Total Fat; 1 g Carbohydrate; 70 mg Sodium; trace Dietary Fiber

Pictured on this page.

Spicy Dipping Sauce

With a bite that lingers! Serve with Pot Stickers, above, or Green Onion Cakes, this page.

Apple juice	1/2 cup	125 mL
Soy sauce	2 tbsp.	30 mL
Red wine vinegar	2 tbsp.	30 mL
Chili sauce	1 tbsp.	15 mL
Garlic cloves, minced (or 1/2 tsp., 2 mL, powder)	2	2
Dried crushed chilies, finely crushed	1 tsp.	5 mL
Granulated sugar	1/4 tsp.	1 mL
Pepper	1/16 tsp.	0.5 mL

Combine all 8 ingredients in small saucepan. Heat until simmering. Cover. Simmer for 10 minutes. Serve at room temperature. Makes 1/3 cup (75 mL) sauce.

1 tbsp. (15 mL) sauce: 23 Calories; 1 g Protein; 0.1 g Total Fat; 5 g Carbohydrate; 425 mg Sodium; trace Dietary Fiber

Pictured on this page.

Midnight Buffet

Around 11 o'clock, after an evening of appetizers, serve your guests the following buffet that includes a refreshing Italian Garden Salad and a hearty Turkey Stroganoff. Everyone's tummies should be full for the 12 o'clock countdown and a flute of champagne! After midnight, bring out dessert to start the new Millennium on a sweet note. We recommend a delicious Mocha Fondue and a plate of Mince Tarts. If you have a very large group, our 2000 Cake can be made well ahead and frozen. See pages 180 and 181 for instructions.

Turkey Stroganoff

Uses leftover turkey in the best way.
Serve with rice, noodles or as a snack on toast.

Hard margarine (or butter)	¼ cup	60 mL
Chopped onion	¾ cup	175 mL
All-purpose flour	¼ cup	60 mL
Milk	2 cups	500 mL
Canned sliced mushrooms, with liquid	10 oz.	284 mL
Hot water	½ cup	125 mL
Chicken bouillon powder	2 tbsp.	30 mL
Parsley flakes	2 tsp.	10 mL
Paprika	½ tsp.	2 mL
Salt	1 tsp.	5 mL
Pepper	¼ tsp.	1 mL
Chopped cooked turkey	4 cups	1 L
Light sour cream	1 cup	250 mL

Melt margarine in large saucepan. Add onion. Sauté until clear and soft.

Mix in flour. Stir in milk until mixture is boiling and thickened.

Add next 7 ingredients. Simmer for 3 to 4 minutes.

Add turkey and sour cream. Stir. Heat through. Makes 6 cups (1.5 L) stroganoff.

1 cup (250 mL) stroganoff: 325 Calories; 36 g Protein; 13.4 g Total Fat; 14 g Carbohydrate; 1412 mg Sodium; 1 g Dietary Fiber

Pictured on page 15.

Italian Garden Salad

Colorful with green, red, purple and orange.
Serve with grated Parmesan cheese.

Dressing:

White vinegar	½ cup	125 mL
Water	⅓ cup	75 mL
Cooking oil	⅓ cup	75 mL
Corn syrup	¼ cup	60 mL
Grated Parmesan cheese	2 tbsp.	30 mL
Pectin crystals	2 tbsp.	30 mL
Large egg (optional)	1	1
Salt	1½ tsp.	7 mL
Lemon juice	1 tsp.	5 mL
Small garlic clove (or ¼ tsp., 1 mL, powder)	1	1
Parsley flakes	½ tsp.	2 mL
Dried whole oregano	⅛ tsp.	0.5 mL
Dried crushed chilies, finely crushed, just a pinch		

Salad:

Cut or torn head of iceberg lettuce	5 cups	1.25 L
Shredded red cabbage	1 cup	250 mL
Thinly sliced red pepper	½ cup	125 mL
Julienned carrot	½ cup	125 mL
Thinly sliced cucumber	½ cup	125 mL
Roma tomatoes, halved and sliced ¼ inch (6 mm) thick	2	2
Whole pitted ripe olives	25	25

Dressing: Measure all 13 ingredients into blender. Process until smooth. Chill overnight to blend flavors. Makes 1½ cups (375 mL) dressing.

Salad: Combine all 7 ingredients in large bowl. Pour ½ cup (125 mL) dressing over top. Toss well. Makes 8 cups (2 L) salad.

1 cup (250 mL) salad with dressing: 76 Calories; 1 g Protein; 4.7 g Total Fat; 8 g Carbohydrate; 279 mg Sodium; 2 g Dietary Fiber

Pictured on page 15.

Note: Keep remaining dressing refrigerated and use within three to four days if made with egg, or up to one week if not.

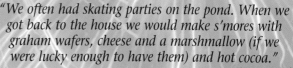

"We often had skating parties on the pond. When we got back to the house we would make s'mores with graham wafers, cheese and a marshmallow (if we were lucky enough to have them) and hot cocoa."

Jean Paré

Left: Champagne Salad, below   Top Right: Italian Garden Salad, page 14   Bottom Right: Turkey Stroganoff, page 14

Champagne Salad

*And not a drop of champagne in it! Very delicate
in both appearance and flavor. Great as a party salad
or as a palate cleanser between dinner courses.*

First Layer:

Envelope unflavored gelatin	1 × ¼ oz.	1 × 7 g
Water	½ cup	125 mL
Granulated sugar	2 tbsp.	30 mL
White grape juice	½ cup	125 mL
Frozen concentrated lemonade, thawed	⅓ cup	75 mL
Water	⅓ cup	75 mL

Second Layer:

Envelope unflavored gelatin	1 × ¼ oz.	1 × 7 g
Water	¼ cup	60 mL
Granulated sugar	2 tbsp.	30 mL
White grape juice	½ cup	125 mL
Frozen concentrated lemonade	⅔ cup	150 mL
Envelope dessert topping (prepared according to package directions)	1	1

First Layer: Sprinkle gelatin over first amount of water in small saucepan. Let stand for 1 minute. Heat and stir until dissolved. Remove from heat.

Stir in sugar until dissolved. Add grape juice, concentrated lemonade and second amount of water. Stir. Pour into 6 cup (1.5 L) jelly mold. Chill while making second layer.

Second Layer: Sprinkle gelatin over water in small saucepan. Let stand for 1 minute. Heat and stir until dissolved. Remove from heat.

Stir in sugar until dissolved. Add grape juice and concentrated lemonade. Chill, stirring and scraping down sides often until thickened.

Fold in dessert topping. Turn into jelly mold over jellied first layer. Chill. Makes 6 cups (1.5 L) salad.

½ cup (125 mL) salad: 104 Calories; 2 g Protein; 1.8 g Total Fat; 21 g Carbohydrate; 12 mg Sodium; 0 g Dietary Fiber

Pictured above.

Mocha Fondue

Arrange an assortment of fruit, marshmallows and pound cake or doughnut chunks on a plate within reach of everyone.

Whipping cream	1 cup	250 mL
Semisweet chocolate chips	2 cups	500 mL
Instant coffee granules	1 tbsp.	15 mL

Heat whipping cream, chocolate chips and coffee granules in small saucepan over low. Stir often as chocolate melts. Pour into fondue pot over low flame. Makes 2 cups (500 mL) fondue.

2 tbsp. (30 mL) fondue: 131 Calories; 2 g Protein; 11.9 g Total Fat; 9 g Carbohydrate; 6 mg Sodium; 0 g Dietary Fiber

Pictured below.

> *"Gram made cakes with cream instead of butter–and then, poured cream over the finished cake. Oh, the cholesterol–but they sure were delicious!"*
>
> Jean Paré

Mince Tarts

These have been a favorite of mine for many years, especially with their "lids." Eat warm, topped with a small dollop of ice cream. Keep a good supply in the freezer for your family to enjoy all year round. Filling will keep for months in refrigerator to make tarts when desired.

Mincemeat, processed in blender	2 cups	500 mL
Applesauce	¾ cup	175 mL
Minute tapioca	1½ tbsp.	25 mL
Pastry, enough to make three, 9 inch (22 cm) pies (your own or a mix)		
Granulated sugar	1 tsp.	5 mL

Combine mincemeat, applesauce and tapioca in small bowl. Mix well.

Roll out pastry. Divide pastry in half. Cut into 15 circles to fit in 15 ungreased muffin cups. Spoon mincemeat mixture into shells, about ¾ full. Roll out remaining half of pastry. Cut out 15 circles to fit tops. Dampen edge of pastry all around. Place top crusts on top of tarts. Press around edges to seal. Cut 3 or 4 small vents in top of each one.

Sprinkle with sugar. Bake on bottom rack in 400°F (205°C) oven for about 15 minutes until browned. Makes 15 tarts.

1 tart: 210 Calories; 2 g Protein; 9.1 g Total Fat; 31 g Carbohydrate; 228 mg Sodium; 1 g Dietary Fiber

Pictured below.

Mocha Fondue

Mince Tarts

New Year's Day

The first day of the new year is a special one, so celebrate it with good people and good food. This is the perfect opportunity to gather family and friends around the dining room table for a festive meal. Choose to make it as formal or casual as you like. You may prefer to have your celebration meal in the afternoon or early evening so that you have plenty of time to enjoy each other's company. French Onion Soup will warm their insides as a starter. Chicken By Cracky provides a satisfying entrée. We have included our favorite Cranberry Pie as a delightful end to this superb meal.

Green And White Dish

An all-in-one vegetable dish that is colorful and tasty.

Frozen cauliflower	2 cups	500 mL
Frozen cut broccoli	2 cups	500 mL
Canned whole mushrooms, drained	10 oz.	284 mL
Condensed cream of mushroom soup	10 oz.	284 mL
Grated medium Cheddar cheese	1 cup	250 mL
Onion flakes	2 tbsp.	30 mL

Combine cauliflower, broccoli and mushrooms in ungreased 1½ quart (1.5 L) casserole. Arrange evenly.

Stir soup vigorously in medium bowl. Add cheese and onion flakes. Stir. Pour over vegetable mixture, spreading to cover all. Cover. Bake in 350°F (175°C) oven for about 20 minutes. Remove cover. Bake for 20 to 30 minutes until desired tenderness is reached. Serves 6.

1 serving: 170 Calories; 9 g Protein; 10.8 g Total Fat; 12 g Carbohydrate; 655 mg Sodium; 4 g Dietary Fiber

Pictured on this page.

Chicken By Cracky

Prepare in the morning and chill until ready to bake. Line baking sheet with greased foil, if desired, for faster, easier cleanup.

Light (not non-fat) sour cream	¼ cup	60 mL
Milk	1 tbsp.	15 mL
Fine cracker crumbs (such as Breton or Ritz)	1 cup	250 mL
Salt	¾ tsp.	4 mL
Pepper	⅛ tsp.	0.5 mL
Boneless, skinless chicken breast halves (about 1½ lbs., 680 g)	6	6
Hard margarine (or butter), melted	2 tbsp.	30 mL

Stir sour cream and milk together in small bowl.

Mix cracker crumbs, salt and pepper in separate small bowl.

Pat chicken dry with paper towel. Dip chicken into sour cream to cover, then dip into crumbs to coat. Arrange on greased baking sheet. (May be refrigerated at this point until about 1 hour before serving.)

Drizzle 1 tsp. (5 mL) margarine over each chicken breast half. Bake in 350°F (175°C) oven for about 45 minutes until tender. Serves 6.

1 serving: 237 Calories; 29 g Protein; 8.3 g Total Fat; 10 g Carbohydrate; 618 mg Sodium; trace Dietary Fiber

Pictured below.

Green And White Dish

Chicken By Cracky

Shrimp Spread

A touch of sherry makes all the difference.
Serve with assorted crackers.

Hard margarine (or butter)	¼ cup	60 mL
All-purpose flour	¼ cup	60 mL
Paprika	¼ tsp.	1 mL
Salt	¼ tsp.	1 mL
Pepper	⅛ tsp.	0.5 mL
Milk	1 cup	250 mL
Canned mushroom stems and pieces, drained and finely chopped	10 oz.	284 mL
Chopped fresh chives (or 1 tsp., 5 mL, dried)	1 tbsp.	15 mL
Parsley flakes	1 tsp.	5 mL
Onion powder	¼ tsp.	1 mL
Cooked fresh (or frozen, thawed) shrimp, chopped (or 2 cans 4 oz.,113 g, each, drained and chopped)	8 oz.	225 g
Sherry (or alcohol-free sherry)	2 tbsp.	30 mL

Melt margarine in small saucepan. Mix in flour, paprika, salt and pepper. Gradually stir in milk until boiling and thickened.

Add remaining 6 ingredients. Stir. Chill. Makes 2½ cups (625 mL) spread.

2 tbsp. (30 mL) spread: 47 Calories; 3 g Protein; 2.7 g Total Fat; 2 g Carbohydrate; 112 mg Sodium; trace Dietary Fiber

Pictured below.

French Onion Soup

Outstanding flavor. A good starter to a sit-down dinner.

Cooking oil	3 tbsp.	50 mL
Thinly sliced onion	4 cups	1 L
Water	4 cups	1 L
Vegetable bouillon powder	1½ tbsp.	25 mL
Garlic powder	⅛ tsp.	0.5 mL
Soy sauce	1 tsp.	5 mL
Salt	1 tsp.	5 mL
Pepper	⅛ tsp.	0.5 mL
Croutons	1½ cups	375 mL
Grated part-skim mozzarella cheese	1 cup	250 mL

Heat cooking oil in large saucepan. Add onion. Sauté until soft and golden.

Add next 6 ingredients. Bring to a boil, stirring often. Cover. Boil gently to cook onions until tender. Divide among 4 onion soup or other ovenproof bowls.

Add croutons to each bowl. Top with cheese. Bake in 450°F (230°C) oven for about 3 minutes until cheese is melted. Serves 4.

1 serving: 286 Calories; 12 g Protein; 16.5 g Total Fat; 24 g Carbohydrate; 1692 mg Sodium; 2 g Dietary Fiber

Pictured below.

Top Left and Top Right: Cranberry Pie, page 19   Bottom Center: Shrimp Spread, this page   Top Center: French Onion Soup, above

Curry Dip

*Great for fresh vegetables, chicken wings,
ham balls and tiny meatballs. A snap to make.*

Light salad dressing (or mayonnaise)	2 cups	500 mL
Onion flakes	2 tsp.	10 mL
Garlic powder	¼ tsp.	1 mL
Ketchup	3 tbsp.	50 mL
White vinegar	½ tsp.	2 mL
Cayenne pepper	¼ tsp.	1 mL
Curry powder	1 tbsp.	15 mL
Granulated sugar	½ tsp.	2 mL

Measure all 8 ingredients into small bowl. Stir well. Makes 2 cups (500 mL) dip.

2 tbsp. (30 mL) dip: 92 Calories; trace Protein; 7.7 g Total Fat; 6 g Carbohydrate; 267 mg Sodium; trace Dietary Fiber

Pictured below.

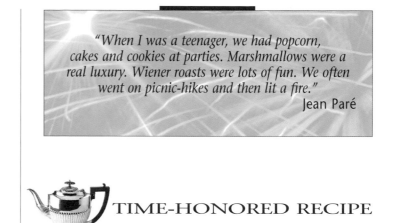

TIME-HONORED RECIPE

Cranberry Pie

*My aunt made this often for New Year's Day.
Real whipped cream was the clincher. Nowadays,
frozen whipped topping is just as good.*

Granulated sugar	¾ cup	175 mL
All-purpose flour	1½ tbsp.	25 mL
Boiling water	½ cup	125 mL
Salt	¼ tsp.	1 mL
Fresh (or frozen) cranberries	1½ cups	375 mL
Raisins	1 cup	250 mL
Unbaked 9 inch (22 cm) pie shell	1	1
Whipping cream	1 cup	250 mL
Granulated sugar	2 tsp.	10 mL
Vanilla	½ tsp.	2 mL

Stir first amount of sugar and flour together in medium bowl. Add boiling water and salt. Mix.

Grind cranberries and raisins. Add to sugar mixture. Stir. If you have a food processor all 6 ingredients can be put in and ground and mixed at the same time.

Pour filling into pie shell. Bake on bottom rack in 400°F (205°C) oven for about 20 minutes until set. Cool.

Beat whipping cream, second amount of sugar and vanilla together in small bowl until thickened. Spoon over pie. Chill. Cuts into 8 wedges.

1 wedge: 361 Calories; 3 g Protein; 17.8 g Total Fat; 50 g Carbohydrate; 237 mg Sodium; 2 g Dietary Fiber

Pictured on page 18 and 19.

Bottom Right: Curry Dip, above

Do You Remember?

Here are some moments from the past 100 years that will bring back memories for some and give insight for others.

1900 - 1909

Barrels of molasses and wheels of Cheddar at the general store

First Canada-produced milk powder

Baking powder made by the local druggist

Victor "talking machines"

Homemade yeast from hops

First machine-made ice cream cones

Jell-0® becomes popular

First horseless carriage (ex. 1907 McLaughlin)

Calories, protein, fat, carbohydrates and minerals identified and, along with water, considered the five basics for essential health. (Note: vitamins were still unknown)

Proper food and nutrition seen as treatment or cure, not prevention

Turn of the Century

1900 Meat-packing, butter and cheese processing, bread baking, sugar refining were among Canada's top 10 industries (all related to agriculture whether cattle, dairy or crop)

1900 Sugar spun into cotton candy

1901 Canada Fruit Marks Act - first Canadian food grading

1903 Canned tuna

1904 Burgers on a bun, ice cream cones, iced tea, popcorn, peanut butter, puffed rice—all introduced at St. Louis World's Fair

1904 Campbell's® cans Pork & Beans; "Campbell's® Kids" debut

1904 Tea bag invented

1905 America's first pizzeria in New York's "Little Italy"

1906 Kellogg's Corn Flakes®

1906 First graduates in nutrition and dietetics at University of Toronto

1907 Meat Inspection and Canned Food Act implemented for factories

1907 Hershey's® Kisses

1908 Dixie Cups

1909 Canada's first airplane flight at Baddeck, Nova Scotia

Culinary Journey

The consumption of food has been recognized as a necessity of life from the beginning of man's existence, as evidenced by the simple drawings of cave dwellers depicting the killing of animals. The relationship between man and food has, in many ways, shaped how man has evolved. Food has played an important role in bringing man and his neighbor together, thus creating the beginnings of communal living and the larger societies that we have today.

What food we eat, how we eat the food, in what form we eat the food and what we make and serve the food in, is a fascinating look back in history. Come with us as we journey through time, looking at the evolution of cooking methods, cooking appliances and cooking utensils. When did nutrition come into vogue? How has our increased knowledge of what foods do to our minds and bodies impacted our day-to-day food choices? And be sure to spend some time reading the Do You Remember? timelines. Did you realize that the Oreo® cookie has been around since 1912? Do you remember what you were doing when Neil Armstrong stepped foot on the moon? Enjoy these memorable moments in history!

The History of Nutrition and Food Guides

In Canada: Canada has had some form of nutrition guidelines for over 50 years.

As you might expect, the guide we use today is a result of an evolutionary process, reflecting changes we have made to our eating habits and lifestyles over the years. It has also been impacted by the findings and implementations of food guides in the United States, which occurred earlier. In addition, newer methods of food processing, storage and transportation, advances in knowledge of dietary requirements and nutrition education techniques, have all affected the look and feel of this helpful document.

1942: Wartime food rations and an economic recession, coupled with a physically active Canadian lifestyle, led to a country of people with relatively poor eating habits. It seemed necessary to develop a practical, easy-to-follow food guide, and so Canada's first nutrition guidelines were introduced, named *Canada's Official Food Rules*. In 1944 the name was changed to *Canada's Food Rules*.

1949: After the War, living standards began to rise in North America and Western Europe. The public found themselves exercising less and eating more. Alarmingly, incidence of chronic degenerative diseases such as diabetes, heart disease and cancer began to rise. Although only a few years old, changes already had to be made to *Canada's Food Rules* to reflect the new dietary needs of a country in the midst of growth. This change, made in 1949, was just the first of many to come.

The Great War

1910-1919

In Flanders Field by Canadian poet John McCrae

World War I: 1914 - 1918

Jam made for the war effort

Oven temperature determined by how long piece of white paper took to turn brown

Canada's first commercial radio station broadcast - Montreal

First boxes of granulated sugar

Dieticians upset that toast and coffee considered good breakfast by most people

Preserving with glass jars, rubber rings and metal screw-ring lids

Copper boiler used for boiling water bath container, as well as bathing

Cookies became firmer during WWI so that they could be sent overseas

Tango and fox trot were popular dances of the day

Band concerts, social debuts and fancy dinners in cities

Church picnics, softball games and sleigh rides in rural communities

Pound Cake - pound of sugar, pound of butter, pound of eggs and pound of flour

Wartime Cake - eggless, milkless, butterless; kept well and transported well; used in both WWI and WWII

1910   First 5 cent candy bar

1910   **Heinz® ketchup production begins in Leamington, Ontario**

1911   **Proctor & Gamble develops hydrogenated vegetable shortening - Crisco®**

1911   **Electric skillets, grills, percs, toasters and waffle irons—all introduced at New York Electric Exhibition**

1912   **Oreo® cookie debuts**

1912   **Free-flowing table salt introduced by Morton's®**

1912   **Vitamins identified and added to list of dietary essentials**

1915   **Corning® introduces Pyrex® to the baking world**

1918   Armistice ends WWI at the 11th hour of the 11th day of the 11th month

1918   **Canned Fruit and Vegetable Act introduces grading to commercial food canning processes**

1919   Group of Seven (painters) formed

1920 - 1929

Dried fruits, such as dates and raisins, as well as honey were staple ingredients

Lemon curd popular for use in tarts, pies, as a cake filling or for a spread on toast, scones or biscuits

 Penny candy at the general store

Cream pies, molded desserts using gelatin or the brand new flavored jelly powders, and rice, tapioca and sago basis for many desserts

Motion picture "talkies"

Chicken á la King in patty shells, Boston Cream Pie and Washington Pie

The Edmonton Grads, Canadian Women's Basketball Champions for 18 years

Oysters popular, especially at Christmas (ex. Oyster Stew)

Processed Kraft® cheese, Sheriff®'s new "flavor bud" in jelly powders, and Rice Krispies®

Refrigerators, wringer-washers, hot-water heaters, toasters, vacuum cleaners—all available

More women working outside the home, particularly in journalism and politics

1920 League of Nations formed

1920 **Food and Drug Act to protect Canadians against health hazards and fraud from sale of food, drugs, cosmetics and medical devices**

1921 **Quaker Oats® Company introduces quick-cooking oatmeal (one of first "convenience" foods)**

1921 **Betty Crocker® "born"**

1921 Schooner Bluenose launched in Nova Scotia

1921 **to 1926 - Four more vitamins identified: cod liver oil recommended for children as vitamin D supplement**

1922 Insulin discovered by Banting and Best

1923 **Kellogg®'s develops first "test kitchen"**

1924 Popsicle patented

1925 **First "Green Giant®" character appears**

1928 Fleming discovers penicillin

1929 Canadian women legally declared "persons"

1929 Wall Street stock crash

1959: At this point the name of the guide was changed to the now familiar title, *Canada's Food Guide*, to reflect the flexibility with which Canadians could apply the advice.

1977: By 1977, clear evidence showed a link between food habits and the risk of developing certain diseases. To combat this problem, scientists and health professionals wanted a guideline which would allow people to choose a diet that provided adequate protein, vitamins and minerals and to control body weight and reduce the risk of developing nutrition-related problems. The guide in its current state was not up to this task, and so changes were again made.

1982: In 1982, Health and Welfare Canada again made revisions to *Canada's Food Guide* and three major principles emerged: 1) variety in food choices and eating patterns; 2) moderation in the use of fat, sugar, salt and alcohol; and 3) balance between energy intake and energy expenditure.

1990: More research was done on the Canadian diet, and in 1990, a report emerged. This technical report became the basis for the creation of a distinct set of statements for the general public called *Canada's Guide for Healthy Eating*. The clear, simple messages intended to promote healthy eating in a general way. As a result, health-conscious consumers began to demand more substantial information on nutrition, and so the guide was again revised to reflect information available from both the previous version of *Canada's Food Guide* and *Canada's Guidelines for Healthy Eating*. The goal of this new food guide was to be simple, positive, clear, adaptable and acceptable to the consumers. Even the look changed from a sun/circle to a rainbow.

In the United States: There has been an official nutrition "standard," based on scientific information, in the United States for the past 100 years. Much of the nutrition of the first 50 years was impacted by the World Wars and the lack of food products, or the lack of money to purchase food wisely.

1941: The first *Recommended Dietary Allowances* were released that listed specific recommended intakes for calories and nine essential nutrients.

1943: The *Basic Seven* food guide was issued in 1943. It gave alternative food choices rather than recommending number of servings because of the limited supplies of certain food during the War.

1946: The *Basic Seven* was revised to the *National Food Guide* and did recommend number of servings. The complexity of determining serving size was tolerated by the general public for ten years.

1956: A new food guide was published that contained only four food groups. Its recommended number of servings was easier to understand. This more simplistic guide was the basis for American nutrition for over 20 years.

1977: *Dietary Goals for the United States* was issued which set quantitative goals for intakes of essential nutrients. It attempted to establish limits so as to avoid excessive intakes that many diets promoted. However, its feasibility and accuracy was questioned and the program did not receive general support.

1980: It wasn't until 1980 that a set of guidelines was published aimed at healthy Americans. These *Dietary Guidelines For Americans* were based on up-to-date information and have been revised several times since then. Today's guidelines address the issues of body weight and fat intake. To help implement an education program in schools the visual pyramid graphic was designed.

1930 - 1939

The Great Depression - frugal foods (macaroni chipped beef, salmon loaf, meatloaf, casseroles)

Pasteurized milk available only in larger communities

Synthetics available - nylon, rayon and imitation rubber

Eggs highly valued; available to people on relief only if sick

Nutritionists advocate use of whole grain or lightly milled flours rather than refined (sound familiar?)

Lemons, bananas and oranges were luxury items, especially in the Prairies and Midwest

Shirley Temple sings "On the Good Ship Lollipop"

In the early '30s reasonable and adequate diet for family of five in Toronto was about $7.65 per week

Horse-drawn delivery wagons for ice, bread and milk, milk bottles by back door with frozen "top hats"

The "boarding house reach"

Elbow macaroni, spaghetti and alphabet shapes for soup

Feves au lard (pork and beans) often made with maple syrup in Quebec, otherwise made with molasses. Often baked overnight for Friday breakfast in Quebec, or soaked overnight in preparation for Saturday Night Special elsewhere

Yeast cakes (fresh or dry) used to make bread

1931 First edition of *Joy of Cooking Cookbook©*

1934 Alberta first province to grade creamy butter

1934 Ritz® crackers

1934 Campbell's® Chicken Noodle Soup and Cream of Mushroom Soup

1934 The Dionne Quintuplets born

1934 Girl Scout Troop 129 in Philadelphia bake and sell first Girl Guide cookies to raise funds

1937 Kraft® Dinner

1939 Start of World War II

The Dirty Thirties

Banana bread recipes very common in church cookbooks

Angel food cake, Daffodil Cake, Sunshine Cake

Dates Squares in the East, Matrimonial Cake in the West

Pressure cookers developed for military use but soon into homes

1940 - 1949

Proper diet helped keep men healthy for war service, and industrial production up, by preventing time lost through illness

Nutrition and health education introduced to schools

War Savings Stamps and Bonds

Prime rib roast - $1

Ganong®'s ribbon candy and chicken bones; Coke® Floats

"Don't say bread, say McGavin's®"

Spanish Rice, "creole" everything, tube steaks, canned salmon

Apple juice fortified with vitamin C; vitamin D added to evaporated milk to prevent rickets in children

Shipwreck one of first all-in-one casserole meals

Pressure cookers start "cook in a hurry" pattern; pressure canners used for canning vegetables, meat and fish

Cabbage rolls bring Polish and Ukrainian influence into Canadian homes

Victory gardens were a way to help offset the food shortages; pickling and preserving became even more popular

Jams and jellies produced for overseas as well as home; sugar rations increased for those who made jams and jellies

1940 Pre cut, pre-packaged meats in cellophane

1942 Food rationing begins

1942 Alaska Highway opens

1947 Oil strike at Leduc, Alberta

1947 End of food rationing

1948 Vitamin B12 discovered

1949 Adding iodine to table salt becomes mandatory

1949 Pillsbury®'s Grand National Recipe and Baking Contest, forerunner to its biennial Bake-Off Cooking and Baking Contest

Fast-rising granulated yeast replaces yeast cakes; faster straight dough method replaced sponge method

Fruit cakes kept well, traveled well so were used for overseas and weddings

Chiffon cakes from California

Icings made with corn syrup rather than rationed sugar

World War II

The History of Cooking Appliances

 Blender - The invention of the blender goes back to 1922. At this time blenders were only used for bartending or for blending malts. In 1936, the blender was redesigned for domestic use. By 1955, they were produced in designer colors to get the attention of the housewife and to increase sales.

Bread Machine - The electric bread machine, which turned raw ingredients into hot cooked loaves, was invented in 1990.

Can Opener - The tin can was first introduced in 1810 in England. Unfortunately there was no simple way to open it, so British soldiers resorted to using pocket knives, bayonets or their guns to shoot them open. It wasn't until 1858 that the first can opener was invented and it did not gain widespread use because it was not yet safe. In 1925, a serrated rotation wheel was added. The electric can opener appeared in 1931.

Coffeepot - It wasn't until 1800 that coffee preparation was made simpler by boiling ground beans in water until it smelled good, and then pouring the water through a filter. This was done in a French invention called the biggin which consisted of two slender metal containers, separated by a plate containing holes, which acted as the filter. In 1873, the biggin was patented in America. In 1939, a heat-tempered glass chemistry pot was modified to include a top with a filter.

Dishwasher - In 1880, a wealthy housewife was determined to invent a dishwasher because she was tired of her servants breaking expensive dishes. She came up with a design that worked to the benefit mainly of hotels and restaurants, and patented it in 1886. By 1914, her company was offering smaller machines for the average American home, but at that time hot water and electricity were not abundant in homes, making them inefficient and impractical. In 1949, the first home electric dishwasher was introduced.

The Nifty Fifties

1950-1959

Food Processor - The first food processor was marketed in 1947. It was equipped with a juice squeezer, pasta wheel, flour mill, can opener, slicer, shredder, mixer, mincer, and centrifuge. In 1963, a model with a cylindrical tank, and an inner knife revolving close to the bottom and walls, quickly became popular with chefs. By 1973, food processors had better slicing and shredding discs and were safer. In 1977, half a million food processors were bought for Mother's Day in New York City alone.

Garbage Disposal - The garbage disposal arrived in home sinks in 1941.

Microwave Oven - In 1946, an engineer was testing a magnetron tube when he discovered that the candy bar in his pocket had melted. He was so intrigued that he placed a bag of popcorn kernels near the tube and within minutes, the kernels were popping. He realized that microwaves created enough vibration within food that friction heat was produced and the food cooked, melted or heated. The first microwave oven was made for commercial use only. The first home model was introduced in 1955.

Outdoor Barbecue - It's almost impossible to accurately trace the history of outdoor cooking. The Louisiana Acadians and the Texans both claim to have introduced barbecuing into the American cuisine. According to the Acadians, the word barbecue comes from the French "barbe queue," meaning "from whiskers to tail" (meaning to cook the entire animal). The Texans give credit to the Spaniards who were the first to learn about barbecue cookery from the Carib Indians. The Indians smoke-dried fish, fowl and game on a green wood lattice over open fire or heated stones. The Spaniards named this lattice "barbacoa," which was later translated to "barbecue."

Oven - Until the late 1700s, a turnspit (the forerunner of the rotisserie) was the most valued tool in the kitchen. The spit was hand-cranked over the fire until the meat was done. A rope and pulley mechanism was added, which led to a drum-shaped wooden cage mounted on the wall. A small dog was locked in the cage and as the dog ran, the cage revolved and cranked the spit. Leonardo da Vinci invented a more humane mechanical self-turning spit, powered by heat rising through the chimney. The first electric stove (a combination of the oven and range) was invented in 1890. Heat control was a definite problem making the unit unreliable. It wasn't until the 1920s that a heat-controlled range became a popular appliance in the kitchen. The first self-cleaning oven arrived in homes in 1963.

World War II veterans' appetite for sushi, sukiyaki, pizza and beef Bourguignon heightens interest in foreign food

Chickens begin to be sold in "parts" but not a big market

Ottawa teenager Paul Anka sings "Diana"

Food stamps - Lucky Green, Pinky, Domino and Gold Bond

Polio epidemic

Weight control rather than weight reduction stressed; recognition that heart disease related to diet

Jellied salads - chicken, ham, tuna, salmon, vegetables, fruit

"Kraft® Television Theatre" begins

Fast and easy mixes - cake mixes, pudding mixes

Rice Krispies® Squares and Nanaimo Bars; Lipton® Onion Soup Dip, nuts and bolts, canned luncheon meats

Saddle shoes and circle skirts

Cream cheese was indispensable for appetizers and cheese balls

North American version of Chinese food becomes popular

Dr. Benjamin Spock

Outdoor barbecuing in summer; "oven barbecuing" in winter

- **1952** Dow produces Saran Wrap®
- **1953** Vitamin A added to margarine; vitamin D added to milk
- **1954** Butterball self-basting turkeys
- **1954** General Electric offers appliances in decorator colors
- **1954** Swanson®'s frozen TV dinners
- **1955** Tappan®'s home-size microwave oven goes on sale
- **1956** U.S. Department of Agriculture reduces the *Basic Seven Food Groups* to *The Basic Four*
- **1956** Colonel Sander's Kentucky Fried Chicken®
- **1957** Saccharin arrives on tables in little pink packets
- **1957** Soviet Union launches first satellite in space, Sputnik I
- **1959** St. Lawrence Seaway opens

The Psychedelic Years

1960-1969

Uncooked freezer jam a popular recipe

Corning Ware® casseroles with cornflower pattern; Teflon®

Obesity control even stronger; fad diets popular

The Twist; listening to the hi-fi

Back-to-nature movement - organic and health foods flourished; vegetarian and macrobiotic diets in vogue

Deluge of snack and nibbler recipes including pâtés

Teased hair, beehives and white lipstick

Cheese fondue; Spinach salad; Brownies; frozen ready-made pizzas

Italian-style main dishes (Chicken Cacciatore, Lasagne)

"Gourmet" became more common (stroganoff, sherry in sauces, wine in cooking)

No-knead or casserole breads were a big hit

Cake mixes and pudding mixes became only part of the recipe (Dump Cake, Friendship Cake, Sex-In-A-Pan)

Flaming desserts were the rage (Cherries Jubilee, Crêpes Suzette)

Cheesecake in many variations; parfait pies using jelly powder

Sweetened condensed milk became popular ingredient in desserts

---

1960 Native women given right to vote in Canada

1963 Assassination of U.S. President John F. Kennedy

1964 **Nachos introduced at Dallas State Fair**

1964 **Chicken parts sales soar**

1964 **Buffalo Chicken Wings created at bar in Buffalo, NY**

1964 Northern Dancer wins Kentucky Derby

1965 Canada adopts the red and white maple leaf flag

1965 **General Foods® launches Tang®**

1965 **Pillsbury®'s "Poppin' Fresh" Dough Boy®**

1969 Neil Armstrong becomes first man on the moon

1969 - Canada bans use of DDT

1969 **22% of food dollar spent away from home; concern by nutritionists about quality of fast food**

Pressure Cooker - In 1679 a French inventor developed the steam digester, a machine consisting of a metal container with a safety valve and tightly fitting lid. Its function was to increase internal steam pressure, in turn raising the cooking liquid's boiling point. Although the idea was sound, the steam digester caused many accidents because of an unreliable safety valve. In 1810, a safer pressure cooker was designed on orders of French emperor Napoleon Bonaparte, who wanted preserved food available for his army troops.

Range (Stove top) - The concept of using a stove-top cooking method came in 1630 with the development of a large metal closed-top, coal-powered range. This unusual concept of cooking above an enclosed fire was slow to catch on because cooking time was slower than that of the turnspit. In 1802, a cast-iron even-heating range with a modern flue was patented as well as the gas range.

Refrigerator - Ice caves and ice chests were commonly used in the 1800s to keep food cold, but only for short periods of time because of the continual need to add more ice as it melted. The first refrigerator for domestic use was designed in 1882. It wasn't until the 1920s and '30s that a practical model became available.

Toaster - Toasting bread dates back to around 2600 B.C., when Egyptians toasted bread to slow the molding process. For over 4000 years people throughout the world toasted their bread, like the Egyptians, over an open fire. In 1910 the first electric toaster was invented, but the bread had to be watched carefully and flipped manually from side to side. In 1919, springs and a variable timer were incorporated. 1926 saw the first pop-up toaster for use in the home.

Slow Cooker - In 1971, the electric slow cooker made its way into North American kitchens. Off to a good start, it declined in popularity until a huge resurgence in the 1990s.

Whistling Tea Kettle - A retired cookware executive from New York invented a tea kettle in 1921 that whistled when the water came to a boil.

The History of Cutlery and other Kitchen Items

Aluminum Foil - R. S. Reynolds worked for his uncle's tobacco company in Kentucky. Loose tobacco needed to be tightly wrapped in thin sheets of tin and lead to keep out moisture. In 1919 he started his own company, supplying tin-lead wraps to tobacco and candy manufacturers. In 1947, Reynolds developed paper-thin aluminum foil.

Bundt Pan - In 1950, a group of Minneapolis women asked the owner of Nordic Products if he could make an aluminum version of the cast-iron kugelhupf pan, common in Europe. Ten years later the *Good Housekeeping Cookbook* showed a pound cake that had been made in that pan, and a demand was suddenly created. The bundt pan became very popular after a bundt cake made the finals in the 1966 Pillsbury® Bake-Off Contest.

Chinese Chopsticks - For centuries, the Chinese thought it was quite uncouth and barbaric to serve a large piece of meat that in any way resembled the original animal. Their philosophy was that food had to be diced, not at the table, but in the kitchen before it was served, which hints at the eating utensils required - chopsticks.

Fork - Prior to the invention of the fork, people ate with their hands. In the 1530s, it was proper to use only three fingers of the hand to eat; using all five fingers was considered indecent. The word "fork" comes from the Latin word "furka," which is a "farmer's pitch fork." Small examples of these ancient tools date back to the fourth millennium B.C., but were probably not used for tableware. Small forks (used for eating) date back to the eleventh century. It was not until the eighteenth century that the fork became fashionable.

1970 - 1979

One-half of adult Canadians overweight; new wave of health conscious eating

Pocket calculators, tape cassettes, digital watches

Spicy cuisine abounds

Canadians discover yogurt

Microwave ovens are in more and more households; fish particularly popular

First UPCs and scanners in stores

Tupperware® parties

Roasting bags and cooking film; self-basting turkeys

Formulated foods appear on market (instant breakfasts, meal replacements)

Food presentation more important and plates became more colorful with larger borders

Quiche becomes a luncheon favorite

PCBs, PVCs, mercury, asbestos, flurocarbons - all big ban issues

Sit-down dinner parties; influx of make-ahead recipes such as layered salads

Fancy drinks and liqueurs were a part of home (Harvey Wallbanger Cake, Brandy Alexander Pie, Grasshopper Pie)

Carrot cake was a healthy alternative to other desserts and for those who didn't like fruit cake

1970 Canadian Metric Commission formed

1971 Salad bars arrive in restaurants

1972 Paul Henderson's "shot heard 'round the world" in Canada-Russia World Hockey Championship

1973 Cuisinart® Food Processor unveiled at Chicago housewares show

1974 Recognition of impact of diet on cardiovascular disease

1975 International Women's Year

1975 French becomes Quebec's official language

1975 Per serving calorie counts begin to show up in cookbooks

1976 T. Eaton Co. ends mail-order catalogue

1977 Revised *Canada's Food Guide* had some 30 changes including going from the five food groups to four

1978 International Association of Culinary Professionals (IACP)

1979 Baby food manufacturers stop adding sugar and salt

The Diet Decade

THE YUPPIE YEARS

1980 -1989

Fast-food chains sell 200 hamburgers per second in the U.S.

Garnishing becomes an art form

Cabbage Patch® dolls

Array of international breads gain popularity (focaccia, crostini, pita bread, flatbreads, tortillas)

International appetizers take off - tapas, dips, hummus, nachos, caponata

Crêpes become creative and lead to new "wrappers" - tortillas, egg rolls, rice papers, pitas, frozen puff pastry, phyllo

Italian cooking continues with fresh basil, home-made pasta and pasta-making machines, pasta salads

Microwave cooking finally finds a comfortable acceptance

Rice appears in more varieties (arborio, basmati, brown, wild)

Salad greens became more varied - radicchio, Belgian endive, arugula, fresh herbs, edible flowers

Vinaigrette salad dressings using flavored oils or olive oil; topping salad off with hot meat - chicken, shrimp

Salsas become common chip dip; pesto shows up in pasta sauces, vinaigrettes

Stir-fry appeals to healthy eating trend - fast, flexible too

Mega muffins

1980 "O Canada" replaces "God Save The Queen" as national anthem

1981 Jean Paré publishes first cookbook *Company's Coming® 150 Delicious Squares*

1981 U.S. Food and Drug Administration approves aspartame as artificial sweetener

1982 *Canada's Food Guide* revised again to stress variety, balance and moderation

1982 Canada "brings home" the Constitution

1984 "Blackened" cooking has its beginnings

1988 Free Trade Agreement between Canada and U.S.

1989 U.S. pasta consumption soars to 18 lbs. per man, woman and child per year

Zucchini garden overflow - recipes for every possible use

"Decadent" desserts (but served in smaller portions); designer desserts in upscale restaurants

Popular food and nutrition issues: reducing fat intake, cholesterol, oat bran, calcium, osteoporosis

---

Knife - The first stone knives were invented 1½ million years ago in Africa and Asia, and were used for butchering prey. Since that time, knives have been an important part of man's weaponry and cutlery. The word knife is from the Anglo-Saxon word "cnif." For many centuries men owned just one knife. Only the nobility could afford separate knives for weapons and eating. Knives had pointed tips up until 1630 when the table knife became rounded for polite table practice: only steak knives retained their pointed tips.

Non-Stick Coating - The world's first non-stick frying pan was invented in France in 1954, and had captured the American market by 1961.

Place Setting - Full place settings that included the fork, knife and spoon took ages to come together at the table. Around 200 years ago, most inns throughout North America and Europe served the meal with one or two of the utensils but never all three. Wealthy people often brought their own utensils when dining out. With the advent of the place setting came all the rules of table etiquette such as which utensil to use for which food, how to set the table and where to place each utensil before, during and after eating.

Plastic Containers - In the 1930s, Earl Tupper had a dream of shaping plastics into various bowls and containers. His first invention, a 7 ounce (200 mL) bathroom tumbler (plastic water glass) appeared in 1945. His next development was polyethylene bowls with snug fitting lids. Tupperware® Home Parties Inc. was formed in 1951 and the operation went on to become a multimillion-dollar business.

Pots and Pans - Cast-iron pots invented in 1642, had a 1 quart (1 L) capacity, a coarse exterior and were three-legged with a lid. The first enameled cast-iron pot with the now-familiar shimmering white finish, appeared in 1778. In 1886, lightweight, durable and easy-to-clean cookware made of aluminum was produced. But it wasn't until 1903 when aluminum cookware became all the rage.

Spoon - The spoon was invented 20,000 years ago in Asia. Spoons of wood, ivory, stone and gold have been found in ancient Egyptian tombs. The shape of the spoon is from the Anglo-Saxon word "spon," meaning "chip," and was very much accepted, especially for eating liquids. In Italy during the fifteenth century, spoons with a figure of an apostle on the handle were very treasured, especially a baptismal gift. But they were also very expensive. Thus the saying, "a privileged child is born with a silver spoon in his mouth."

Stainless Steel Cutlery - Before the invention of stainless steel, forks, knives, and spoons were made of a compound of carbon and steel which made them very durable but incredibly hard to keep clean. They discolored extremely quickly and required constant work to keep them shiny. The first stainless steel dinnerware was produced 1920.

Steel Wool Scouring Pads - In 1917, a San Francisco man sold aluminum cookware door to door, but found it hard to get into kitchens to demonstrate his product. He decided to offer a free gift for every in-home demonstration. Knowing that the biggest frustration with cookware was when food stuck to pans, he developed square steel-wool pads which had been dipped into a soapy solution. They became such a success, he stopped selling pots and pans and spent all his time manufacturing soap pads. His wife named the soap pads, SOS® Pads, which meant "save our saucepans."

1990-1999

North Americans begin obsessing about amount of fat in food so learn to count fat grams, compute % of calories from fat

Electric bread machines become a must-have

Food companies produce "low-fat" "no-fat" dairy and dairy-type products

Fresh and organically grown foods are stressed

Cross-cultural cooking takes off; East-meets-West cuisine (spring rolls, noodle salads, curries, peanut dipping sauce, hot and sour soup)

Renewed interest in classic "comfort" foods - but streamlined

Mediterranean flavors more popular than ever (olive oils, Greek salads)

Fat-reduced baking products (often using honey in place of sugar, getting rid of added nuts, using part whole grain flour)

1990 Blended fruit juices (fruit "smoothies") enriched with "healing" extracts debut in California

1990 Health and Welfare Canada publishes Canada's *Guidelines for Healthy Eating*

1991 Canadians spend 31% of food dollar in restaurants

1992 32% of household budget used for some form of home-based business

1992 New guide called *Canada's Food Guide to Health Eating* places greater emphasis on grains, fruits and vegetables

1994 New Canadian food labeling laws go into effect

1995 Betty Crocker® starts on-line hot line to answer cooks' questions

1995 Pillsbury raises grand prize for Bake-Off Cooking and Baking Contest to $1 million dollars

1996 A man wins the Pillsbury® Bake-Off for first time

1997 100th anniversary of Jell-O®

1999 Jean Paré publishes 50th cookbook title *Company's Coming® Low-fat Pasta*

Baby Boomers Meet Generation X

Menu Suggestions

Do You Remember When?

(nibblies for 8)

Cheese Tarts, page 33
Fluffy Salmon Spread, page 41
Cheese Log, page 12
Apple Brie Pizza, page 43
Sesame Wings, page 37
Cranberry Meatballs, page 39
Tangy Seafood, page 12
Marmalade Tarts, page 141
New Magic Squares, page 169

Quiet Dinner

(dinner for 4)

Crab Bisque, page 163
Springtime Salad, page 155
Lobster Newburg, page 126
(in patty shells)
Mocha Fondue, page 16

Sleigh Ride Get-Together

(buffet for 12)

White Bread, page 61
Chili Modern, page 48
Noodle Casserole, page 46
Tomato Mushroom Salad, page 153
Orange Lettuce Salad, page 154
Cranberry Perc, page 57
Lemon Rum Cake, page 79

Quilters' Luncheon

(light lunch for 6)

Bran Buns, page 59
Salmon Casserole, page 125
Broccoli Salad, page 151
Matrimonial Squares, page 169

Brunch

(for 8)

Apricot Bran Muffins, page 63
Turkey Strata, page 68
Apple Scallop, page 71
Swedish Tea Ring, page 72
Baked Pancake, page 74
Maple-Flavored Syrup, page 74

The Big Band Sound

(dinner for 6)

Dilled Onions, page 152
Elegant Squash, page 177
Baked Chops And Stuffing, page 148
Dainty Queen Cakes, page 83
Impossible Pie, page 143

Housewarming

(buffet for 12)

Brie In Pastry, page 9
Parmesan Appies, page 42
Mushroom Canapés, page 34
Spicy Nuts, page 12
Italian Garden Salad, page 14
Noodle Slaw, page 152
Sweet And Sour Ribs, page 144
Four Cheese Lasagne, page 128
Turtle Cheesecake, page 114

Sit-Down Sunday Dinner

(dinner for 6)

Roast And Gravy, page 50
Corn Scallop, page 178
Tomato Dumplings, page 175
Bean Salad, page 151
Chow Chow Maritime, page 106
Fruit Cobbler, page 120

Millennium Celebration For The Teens

(munchies for 16)

Chili Con Queso, page 36
Teriyaki Chicken Wings, page 36
Spicy Cheddar Popcorn, page 94
Turkey Sandwiches, page 69
Cheese Bites, page 32
Pink Sunrise Punch, page 56
Circus Cookies, page 109
Brownies, page 168
Double-Decker Fudge, page 92

Intimate Dinner

(dinner for 2)

French Onion Soup, page 18
Elegant Chicken Phyllo, page 104
Noodles With Herbs, page 129
Truffles, page 92

Retirement Gathering

(buffet for 20)

Shrimp Spread, page 18
Relish Cheese Ball, page 41
Ginger-Sauced Meatballs, page 38
Pesto-Sauced Salad, page 150
Champagne Salad, page 15
Mustard Ham Balls, page 38
Chicken With Ginger, page 102
Nut Smacks, page 170
Caramel Chocolate Squares, page 172

Ladies' Bridge Club

(lunch for 4)

Bran Buns, page 59
Cuke Spread 'R Dip, page 40
(with vegetables)
Niçoise Pasta Salad, page 70
Chocolate Goodies, page 172

Monday Night Football

(for 6 men)

Chili Popcorn, page 94
Short Rib Magic, page 45
Lazy Ravioli, page 53
Brown Bread, page 59
Dark Chocolate Cake, page 80
Chocolate Mocha Icing, page 80

Hot Tub Party

(munchies for 6)

Green Onion Cakes, page 13
Pot Stickers, page 13
Spicy Dipping Sauce, page 13
Curry Dip, page 19
(with vegetables)
Mushroom Toasties, page 34
Guacamole Mold, page 36
Salami Rolls, page 42
(with assorted crackers)

Team Wind-Up Party

(buffet for 12)

Caesar-Dressed Salad, page 155
Bacon And Pea Salad, page 152
Chicken Fried Rice, page 96
Casserole Lasagne, page 130
Chicken Express, page 97
Strawberries And Cream, page 118
Piña Colada Cake, page 78

Appetizers

Appetizers and finger foods became the fashion in the early twentieth century. Prior to then, they appeared more simply in the form of soup, seafood on the half shell, and dainty open-faced sandwiches. Cocktail appetizers evolved from free samples set out for the patrons in public bars and from more people hosting home cocktail parties. In the late 1930s, the first catering shop opened, dedicated specifically to buffet and cocktail food. Today, we wouldn't consider having a special get-together or party without appetizers. Here are a variety of hot and cold appetizers to choose from for your next gathering of family and friends.

Cheese Bites

Crispy on the outside—soft on the inside.
May be frozen untoasted. Bake an extra two
minutes from frozen state. Serve as is or with cocktail picks.

Hard margarine (or butter), softened	2 tbsp.	30 mL
Light salad dressing (or mayonnaise)	2 tbsp.	30 mL
Grated sharp Cheddar cheese	¾ cup	175 mL
Finely grated onion	2 tbsp.	30 mL
Finely chopped pimiento	1½ tsp.	7 mL
Cayenne pepper, sprinkle		
Sandwich loaf bread slices, crusts removed, flattened with rolling pin	8	8

Paprika, sprinkle (optional)

Mix first 6 ingredients in small bowl.

Spread each bread slice with about 1 tbsp. (15 mL) cheese mixture. Roll up like jelly roll.

Sprinkle with paprika. Place on ungreased baking sheet. Toast in 350°F (175°C) oven for about 10 minutes. Cuts into 4 pieces each. Makes 32 appetizers.

1 appetizer: 38 Calories; 1 g Protein; 2.1 g Total Fat; 3 g Carbohydrate; 65 mg Sodium; trace Dietary Fiber

Pictured on page 33.

Mushroom Turnovers, page 33

Top: Cheese Tarts, this page   Bottom: Cheese Bites, page 32

Mushroom Turnovers

Cute little duffers. A winner to be sure. These freeze well.

Cream Cheese Pastry:

Light cream cheese, softened	8 oz.	250 g
Hard margarine (or butter), softened	1/2 cup	125 mL
Milk	1/4 cup	60 mL
All-purpose flour	2 cups	500 mL
Salt	1/2 tsp.	2 mL

Filling:

Canned sliced mushrooms, drained and chopped	10 oz.	284 mL
Finely chopped onion	1/2 cup	125 mL
Hard margarine (or butter)	2 tsp.	10 mL
Lemon juice	1 tsp.	5 mL
Seasoned salt	1/2 tsp.	2 mL
Salt	1/4 tsp.	1 mL
Pepper	1/4 tsp.	1 mL
Milk	1/2 cup	125 mL
All-purpose flour	4 tsp.	20 mL
Sherry (or alcohol-free sherry)	1 tbsp.	15 mL

Cream Cheese Pastry: Beat cream cheese and margarine well in medium bowl. Mix in milk, flour and salt. Shape into ball. Cover and chill for at least 1 hour.

Filling: Sauté mushrooms and onion in margarine in non-stick frying pan until onion is soft.

Stir in lemon juice, seasoned salt, salt and pepper.

Gradually whisk milk into flour in small bowl until smooth. Add sherry. Stir into mushroom mixture until boiling and thickened. Cool thoroughly. Roll out dough about 1/8 inch (3 mm) thick. Cut into 3 inch (7.5 cm) rounds. Place 1 1/2 tsp. (7 mL) mushroom filling in center of each. Moisten edge. Fold over. Press to seal. Arrange on ungreased baking sheet. Cut tiny slits in top of each. Bake in 425°F (220°C) oven for 11 to 13 minutes. Makes 48 turnovers.

1 turnover: 55 Calories; 1 g Protein; 3.2 g Total Fat; 5 g Carbohydrate; 147 mg Sodium; trace Dietary Fiber

Pictured on page 32.

Note: To freeze uncooked turnovers, place on baking sheet and freeze. Pack frozen turnovers in plastic containers. Bake from frozen state in 350°F (175°C) oven for 20 to 25 minutes until browned. If baked and frozen, heat in 325°F (160°C) oven for 15 to 20 minutes.

Cheese Tarts

Pastry appetizers always are the first to go.
Make ahead, reheat and serve.

Grated medium Cheddar cheese (see Note)	1 cup	250 mL
Unbaked mini tart shells	24	24
Large egg, fork-beaten	1	1
Skim evaporated milk	1/2 cup	125 mL
Dill weed	1/2 tsp.	2 mL
Onion powder	1/4 tsp.	1 mL
Pepper	1/8 tsp.	0.5 mL

Divide cheese among tart shells.

Combine egg, evaporated milk, dill weed, onion powder and pepper in small bowl. Spoon over cheese. Bake in 350°F (175°C) oven for 20 to 25 minutes until set. Makes 24 tarts.

1 tart: 63 Calories; 2 g Protein; 4.2 g Total Fat; 4 g Carbohydrate; 83 mg Sodium; trace Dietary Fiber

Pictured on this page.

Note: Cheese and last 5 ingredients can be processed in blender and poured into each tart shell. Much faster.

"We would always make five or six pies on Saturday. What we didn't use Sunday for company, we would eat the rest of the week."

Jean Paré

Mushroom Toasties

These hot appetizers go fast.

Hard margarine (or butter), softened	½ cup	125 mL
Light cream cheese, softened	4 oz.	125 g
Onion powder	¼ tsp.	1 mL
Garlic salt	¼ tsp.	1 mL
Canned sliced mushrooms, drained and chopped	10 oz.	284 mL
Chopped fresh chives (or 1 tsp., 5 mL, dried)	1 tbsp.	15 mL
White (or brown) bread slices, crusts removed, cut into 4 squares each	10	10

Beat margarine, cream cheese, onion powder and garlic salt together in medium bowl.

Add mushrooms and chives. Stir.

Arrange bread on broiler tray. Broil 1 side on top rack in oven until toasted. Turn bread over. Spread each square with 2 tsp. (10 mL) mushroom mixture. Broil on center rack until bubbly hot. Makes 40 appetizers.

1 appetizer: 46 Calories; 1 g Protein; 3.2 g Total Fat; 4 g Carbohydrate; 114 mg Sodium; trace Dietary Fiber

Pictured on page 35.

Mushroom Canapés

Both creamy and cheesy. Serve hot.

Sausage meat	½ lb.	225 g
Chopped green onion	¼ cup	60 mL
Light salad dressing (or mayonnaise)	¾ cup	175 mL
Baguette slices	24	24
Fresh mushrooms, sliced	24	24
Grated medium Cheddar cheese	2 cups	500 mL
Paprika, sprinkle		

Scramble-fry sausage meat in non-stick frying pan. Drain well.

Add green onion and salad dressing. Stir.

Spread 1 tbsp. (15 mL) sausage mixture on each slice of baguette. Divide mushroom slices evenly over sausage mixture. Sprinkle generous 1 tbsp. (15 mL) cheese over mushroom slices. Sprinkle each canapé with paprika. Arrange on ungreased baking sheet. Bake in 350°F (175°C) oven for 20 minutes. Cool slightly. Makes 24 canapés.

1 canapé: 140 Calories; 5 g Protein; 7.5 g Total Fat; 13 g Carbohydrate; 268 mg Sodium; 1 g Dietary Fiber

Pictured on page 35.

"During World War II, if you had a wedding coming up in your family, you had to start saving your ration coupons in order to be able to feed a large group of 50 or so."

Jean Paré

Mushroom Surprise

There's a mushroom hiding in that biscuit! Then again, it might be an onion.

Refrigerator country-style biscuits (10 per tube)	12 oz.	340 g
Canned whole mushrooms, drained and liquid reserved	2 × 10 oz.	2 × 284 mL
Reserved mushroom liquid		
Grated Parmesan cheese	¾ cup	175 mL

Cut each biscuit into quarters. Press and shape each piece into flat circle large enough to cover mushroom.

Pat mushrooms dry with paper towel. Wrap in biscuit rounds. Press around mushroom, pinching together to seal.

Place reserved mushroom liquid in small bowl. Place Parmesan cheese in separate small bowl. Dip 1 at a time into mushroom liquid then into cheese to coat. Arrange on greased baking sheet. Bake in 400°F (205°C) oven for about 10 minutes until browned. Makes 40 appetizers.

1 appetizer: 4 Calories; 2 g Protein; 1.2 g Total Fat; 4 g Carbohydrate; 141 mg Sodium; trace Dietary Fiber

Pictured on page 35.

Variation: For a different flavor, substitute finely grated commercial Cheddar cheese product for Parmesan cheese.

PICKLED ONION SURPRISE: Substitute pickled onions for mushrooms.

Top: Mushroom Toasties, this page
Center: Mushroom Canapés, this page
Bottom: Mushroom Surprise, above

Guacamole Mold

Double duty. Use as a salad or as a spread for tortilla chips.

Envelopes unflavored gelatin	2 × ¼ oz.	2 × 7 g
Water	½ cup	125 mL
Lime juice	2 tbsp.	30 mL
Small ripe avocados, mashed smooth	3	3
Light sour cream	¾ cup	175 mL
Light salad dressing (or mayonnaise)	⅓ cup	75 mL
Spicy salsa, run through blender	½ cup	125 mL
Salt	½ tsp.	2 mL
Garlic powder	¼ tsp.	1 mL
Hot pepper sauce (optional)	⅛ tsp.	0.5 mL
Small cherry tomatoes, halved (optional)		

Sprinkle gelatin over water in small saucepan. Let stand for 1 minute. Heat and stir until gelatin is dissolved.

Whisk next 8 ingredients together in medium bowl. Stir in gelatin mixture.

If you have a 4 cup (1 L) mold with round indentations, place a cherry tomato half in each. Pour gelatin mixture over top. Chill for at least 2½ hours before unmolding. If you don't have a mold with indentations, decorate top and sides with tomatoes after unmolding. Makes 4 cups (1 L) guacamole.

2 tbsp. (30 mL) guacamole: 45 Calories; 1 g Protein; 3.8 g Total Fat; 3 g Carbohydrate; 123 mg Sodium; 1 Dietary Fiber

Pictured above.

Teriyaki Chicken Wings

A tasty marinade produces these delicious wings.

Commercial teriyaki sauce	½ cup	125 mL
Liquid honey	¼ cup	60 mL
Fancy molasses	1 tbsp.	15 mL
Lemon juice	1 tbsp.	15 mL
Small onion, chopped	1	1
Garlic cloves, minced (or ½ tsp., 2 mL, powder)	2	2
Grated fresh gingerroot	2 tsp.	10 mL
Dry mustard	½ tsp.	2 mL
Salt	½ tsp.	2 mL
Chicken drumettes (or whole chicken wings)	4 lbs.	1.8 kg

Stir first 9 ingredients in large bowl. Add drumettes. If using whole wings, discard wing tips and cut wings apart at joint. Stir well. Cover. Refrigerate for 5 hours or overnight, stirring occasionally.

Line large baking sheet with greased foil. Arrange drumettes on foil. Bake in 375°F (190°C) oven for 20 to 30 minutes, turning wings at half-time, until glazed and tender. Makes about 32 drumettes or 48 wing pieces.

1 drumette (with skin): 83 Calories; 6 g Protein; 4.9 g Total Fat; 4 g Carbohydrate; 247 mg Sodium; trace Dietary Fiber

Pictured on page 37.

Chili Con Queso

Pronounced CHIH-lee kon KAY-soh. No need to go south of the border to enjoy this Mexican favorite. Serve with tortilla chips or raw vegetables.

Canned stewed tomatoes, with juice, broken up	14 oz.	398 mL
Chopped onion	1 cup	250 mL
Garlic powder (or 1 clove, minced)	¼ tsp.	1 mL
Canned chopped green chilies, with liquid	4 oz.	114 mL
Process cheese loaf (such as Velveeta), cubed	1 lb.	454 g

Put tomatoes with juice, onion, garlic powder and green chilies with liquid into medium saucepan. Cook, uncovered, over medium until liquid is evaporated.

Add cheese. Stir over low until melted. Makes 4 cups (1 L) dip.

2 tbsp. (30 mL) dip: 51 Calories; 3 g Protein; 3.4 g Total Fat; 2 g Carbohydrate; 273 mg Sodium; trace Dietary Fiber

Pictured on page 37.

Sesame Wings

A nutty buttery coating makes these irresistible. Serve hot.

Sesame seeds	½ cup	125 mL
Fine dry bread crumbs	½ cup	125 mL
Paprika	1 tsp.	5 mL
Salt	1 tsp.	5 mL
Garlic powder	¼ tsp.	1 mL
Hard margarine (or butter), melted	½ cup	125 mL
Prepared mustard	1 tbsp.	15 mL
Chicken drumettes (or whole wings)	2 lbs.	900 g

Measure first 5 ingredients into small bowl. Mix well.

Stir margarine and mustard together in small dish.

Dip each drumette into margarine mixture, then into seed mixture to coat completely. If using whole wings, discard wing tips and cut wings apart at joint. Place on foil-lined baking sheet with sides. Bake in 350°F (175°C) oven for about 45 minutes until tender. Makes about 16 drumettes or 24 wing pieces.

1 drumette (with skin). 167 Calories; 7 g Protein; 13.9 g Total Fat; 3 g Carbohydrate; 304 mg Sodium; trace Dietary Fiber

Pictured below.

Jalapeño Pie

This has a fair bit of heat to it. Use the whole can of jalapeños if you dare. Serve warm.

Hard margarine (or butter)	2 tsp.	10 mL
Finely chopped onion	1 cup	250 mL
Canned jalapeño peppers, drained, seeded and chopped	½ × 4 oz.	½ × 114 mL
Grated sharp Cheddar cheese	2 cups	500 mL
Large eggs, fork-beaten	4	4
Salt	½ tsp.	2 mL
Garlic powder	¼ tsp.	1 mL

Melt margarine in non-stick frying pan. Add onion. Sauté until soft.

Scatter onion, jalapeño peppers and cheese in greased 8 × 8 inch (20 × 20 cm) pan.

Combine egg, salt and garlic powder in small bowl. Beat. Pour over top. Bake in 350°F (175°C) oven for about 30 minutes. Cuts into 25 squares.

1 square; 56 Calories; 3 g Protein; 4.3 g Total Fat; 1 g Carbohydrate; 140 mg Sodium; trace Dietary Fiber

Pictured below.

Left: Sesame Wings, above   Center: Teriyaki Chicken Wings, page 36   Top Right: Jalapeño Pie, above   Bottom Right: Chili Con Queso, page 36

Mustard Ham Balls, below   Ginger-Sauced Meatballs, below   Cranberry Meatballs, page 39

Mustard Ham Balls

Serve hot with picks. Soft and glazed.
Good choice for any get-together.

Lean ham, ground	1½ lbs.	680 g
Ground chicken	½ lb.	225 g
Milk	½ cup	125 mL
Large egg, fork-beaten	1	1
Seasoned salt	½ tsp.	2 mL
Salt	½ tsp.	2 mL
Dry bread crumbs	1½ cups	375 mL
Brown sugar, packed	1 cup	250 mL
All-purpose flour	2 tsp.	10 mL
Dry mustard	2 tsp.	10 mL
White vinegar	½ cup	125 mL
Water	½ cup	125 mL
Prepared mustard	2 tsp.	10 mL

Mix first 7 ingredients in large bowl. Shape into 1 inch (2.5 cm) balls. Arrange on greased baking sheet. Bake in 400°F (205°C) oven for 15 minutes until firmed a bit and browned. Turn into ungreased 3 quart (3 L) casserole.

Stir brown sugar, flour and dry mustard together in small bowl. Stir in vinegar, water and prepared mustard. Pour over ham balls. Bake, uncovered, in 350°F (175°C) oven, basting 2 or 3 times with sauce, for about 45 minutes. Makes about 80 ham balls.

4 ham balls (with sauce): 144 Calories; 11 g Protein; 2.7 g Total Fat; 19 g Carbohydrate; 676 mg Sodium; trace Dietary Fiber

Pictured above.

Ginger-Sauced Meatballs

Easy to double for a crowd.

Lean ground beef	½ lb.	225 g
Lean ground pork	½ lb.	225 g
Milk	¼ cup	60 mL
Large egg, fork-beaten	1	1
Dry bread crumbs	1 cup	250 mL
Worcestershire sauce	1 tsp.	5 mL
Onion flakes	1 tbsp.	15 mL
Salt	¾ tsp.	4 mL
Pepper	¼ tsp.	1 mL
Chili sauce	1 cup	250 mL
Water	¾ cup	175 mL
Gingersnap cookie crumbs (about 10 cookies)	1 cup	250 mL

Combine first 9 ingredients in large bowl. Mix well. Shape into 1 inch (2.5 cm) balls. Arrange on greased baking sheet. Bake in 375°F (190°C) oven for 15 minutes until cooked through. Makes 40 meatballs.

Stir chili sauce and water together in small saucepan. Add cookie crumbs. Heat, stirring often, until simmering. Simmer for about 1 minute. Makes 2 cups (500 mL) sauce. Serve over meatballs.

3 meatballs with sauce: 123 Calories; 9 g Protein; 4.5 g Total Fat; 11 g Carbohydrate; 381 mg Sodium; 1 g Dietary Fiber

Pictured above.

Zucchini Treats, this page

Laurier Lake "Shrimp"

A great imitation since there weren't any shrimp in Laurier Lake near where I grew up. Not only works as an appetizer but also for a meal. Even good cold. Serve with seafood sauce.

Pancake mix	2 cups	500 mL
Large egg, fork-beaten	1	1
Cooking oil	1 tbsp.	15 mL
Beer	¾ cup	175 mL
Milk	¼ cup	60 mL
Salt	1 tsp.	5 mL

Fish fillets, cut into 1 inch
(2.5 cm) squares
Oil, for deep-frying

Stir pancake mix, egg, cooking oil, beer, milk and salt in medium bowl until smooth.

Dip a few fish pieces into batter. Drop carefully into 375°F (190°C) hot oil. Cook for about 2 minutes until browned. Remove with slotted spoon to paper towel-lined baking sheet. Keep warm in 200°F (95°C) oven while cooking remaining fish. Makes 4 cups (1 L), or about 30 appetizers.

1 appetizer: 78 Calories; 7 g Protein; 2 g Total Fat; 8 g Carbohydrate; 255 mg Sodium;
trace Dietary Fiber

Pictured on page 10.

Cranberry Meatballs

*Meatballs are soft and tasty
dressed up with an exceptionally good sauce.*

Large eggs, fork-beaten	2	2
Soy sauce	2 tbsp.	30 mL
Finely chopped onion	½ cup	125 mL
Parsley flakes	1 tbsp.	15 mL
Garlic powder (or 2 cloves, minced)	½ tsp.	2 mL
Corn flake crumbs	1 cup	250 mL
Salt	2 tsp.	10 mL
Pepper	½ tsp.	2 mL
Lean ground beef	2 lbs.	900 g
Canned cranberry sauce	14 oz.	398 mL
Chili sauce	½ cup	125 mL
Ketchup	½ cup	125 mL
Brown sugar, packed	2 tbsp.	30 mL
White vinegar	1 tbsp.	15 mL

Mix first 8 ingredients in large bowl.

Add ground beef. Mix well. Shape into 1 inch (2.5 cm) balls. Arrange in greased 3 quart (3 L) casserole.

Mix remaining 5 ingredients in small bowl. Pour over meatballs. Bake, uncovered, in 350°F (175°C) oven for 45 minutes. Makes 80 meatballs.

4 meatballs (with sauce): 182 Calories; 10 g Protein; 7.4 g Total Fat; 19 g Carbohydrate;
650 mg Sodium; 1 g Dietary Fiber

Pictured on page 38/39.

Zucchini Treats

*Cut these larger if you like. Parmesan cheese
gives this its really good flavor.*

Large eggs, fork-beaten	4	4
Finely chopped onion	½ cup	125 mL
Cooking oil	½ cup	125 mL
Parsley flakes	1 tsp.	5 mL
Salt	½ tsp.	2 mL
Celery salt	½ tsp.	2 mL
Dried whole oregano	½ tsp	2 mL
Garlic powder	¼ tsp.	1 mL
Grated Parmesan cheese	½ cup	125 mL
Biscuit mix	1 cup	250 mL
Thinly sliced zucchini, with peel	3½ cups	875 mL
Grated Parmesan cheese	¼ cup	60 mL

Combine first 9 ingredients in medium bowl. Beat well.

Stir in biscuit mix and zucchini. Turn into greased 9 x 13 inch (22 x 33 cm) pan.

Sprinkle with second amount of cheese. Bake in 350°F (175°C) oven for about 30 minutes until browned. Cuts into 54 squares.

1 square: 44 Calories; 1 g Protein; 3.3 g Total Fat; 2 g Carbohydrate; 103 mg Sodium;
trace Dietary Fiber

Pictured on this page.

Garlic Dip

Make in the morning or up to two days ahead and keep refrigerated. Serve with an assortment of raw vegetables.

Light salad dressing (or mayonnaise)	¾ cup	175 mL
Non-fat sour cream	¼ cup	60 mL
Garlic cloves, minced (or ¾ tsp., 4 mL, powder)	3	3
Parsley flakes	2 tsp.	10 mL
Lemon juice	1 tsp.	5 mL

Stir all 5 ingredients together in small bowl. Cover. Chill well. Makes 1 cup (250 mL) dip.

1 tbsp. (15 mL) dip: 34 Calories; trace Protein; 2.9 g Total Fat; 2 g Carbohydrate; 88 mg Sodium; trace Dietary Fiber

Pictured below.

Relish Cheese Ball, page 41   Cuke Spread 'R Dip, below

Garlic Dip

Cuke Spread 'R Dip

This needs to be made ahead and refrigerated for at least two hours. It is thick enough to serve as a spread with small dark cocktail-size bread slices or as a dip with a selection of fresh vegetables.

Light cream cheese, softened	8 oz.	250 g
Finely chopped, peeled and seeded cucumber	2 cups	500 mL
Seasoned salt	1 tsp.	5 mL
Cayenne pepper	¹⁄₁₆ tsp.	0.5 mL

Mash cream cheese with fork. Add cucumber pieces, seasoned salt and cayenne pepper. Mix well. Chill for at least 2 hours to blend flavors. Makes 3 cups (750 mL) dip.

2 tbsp. (30 mL) dip: 22 Calories; 1 g Protein; 1.7 g Total Fat; 1 g Carbohydrate; 150 mg Sodium; trace Dietary Fiber

Pictured above.

Soy Fire Dip

Hot spicy soy flavor. Good with Pot Stickers, page 13, and Green Onion Cakes, page 13.

Soy sauce	¼ cup	60 mL
Apple cider vinegar	2 tbsp.	30 mL
Ketchup	2 tsp.	10 mL
Garlic clove (or ¼ tsp., 1 mL, powder)	1	1
Dried crushed chilies	1 tsp.	5 mL

Combine all 5 ingredients in blender. Process until smooth. Let stand for about 1 hour at room temperature to blend flavors. Makes ½ cup (125 mL) dip.

1 tbsp. (15 mL) dip: 9 Calories; 1 g Protein; 0.1 g Total Fat; 2 g Carbohydrate; 546 mg Sodium; trace Dietary Fiber

Pictured on page 13.

Relish Cheese Ball

You can make two smaller balls and freeze one for later use. Make one or two days ahead to allow flavors to mingle. Serve with assorted crackers.

Light cream cheese, softened	2 × 8 oz.	2 × 250 g
Grated medium or sharp Cheddar cheese	2 cups	500 mL
Sweet pickle relish, drained	1/2 cup	125 mL
Onion powder	1/8 tsp.	0.5 mL
Finely chopped pecans (or walnuts)	1 cup	250 mL

Measure first 4 ingredients into medium bowl. Beat on low until well mixed. Shape into ball. If too soft to shape into ball, chill for at least 1 hour.

Roll ball in pecans to coat. Chill until needed. Makes 1 cheese ball, 3½ cups (875 mL).

2 tbsp. (30 mL) cheese ball: 100 Calories; 4 g Protein; 8.5 g Total Fat; 2 g Carbohydrate; 232 mg Sodium; trace Dietary Fiber

Pictured on page 40.

Fluffy Salmon Spread

Makes a good spread for crackers or use as a filling for toast cups.

Light salad dressing (or mayonnaise)	1/2 cup	125 mL
Lemon juice	1 tbsp.	15 mL
Onion flakes	1 tbsp.	15 mL
Hot pepper sauce	1/2 tsp.	2 mL
Worcestershire sauce	1/2 tsp.	2 mL
Salt	1 tsp.	5 mL
Pepper, sprinkle		
Canned salmon, drained, skin and round bones removed, broken up (red is best for color)	2 × 4 oz.	2 × 114 g
Creamed cottage cheese	1 cup	250 mL
Frozen whipped topping (in a tub), thawed	1 cup	250 mL

Measure first 7 ingredients into medium bowl. Stir.

Add salmon. Mix well.

Stir in cottage cheese. Fold in whipped topping. Turn into pretty glass bowl. Chill for 3 to 4 hours. Makes 4 cups (1 L) mousse.

2 tbsp. (30 mL) mousse: 33 Calories; 2 g Protein; 2 g Total Fat; 2 g Carbohydrate; 171 mg Sodium; trace Dietary Fiber

Pictured on this page.

Spinach Balls

Flavorful, moist and colorful. Pretty on a plate of mixed appetizers or piled on their own plate.

Frozen chopped spinach	10 oz.	300 g
Large eggs, fork-beaten	2	2
Grated Parmesan cheese	1/4 cup	60 mL
Parsley flakes	1 tsp.	5 mL
Poultry seasoning	3/4 tsp.	4 mL
Garlic salt	1/4 tsp.	1 mL
Salt	1/4 tsp.	1 mL
Pepper	1/2 tsp.	2 mL
Very finely chopped onion	1/2 cup	125 mL
Dry bread crumbs	1 1/2 cups	375 mL
Hard margarine (or butter), melted	1/4 cup	60 mL
Hard margarine (or butter), melted	2 tbsp.	30 mL

Cook spinach according to package directions. Drain. Squeeze dry.

Combine next 7 ingredients in medium bowl. Beat to mix.

Add onion and bread crumbs. Stir. Add first amount of melted margarine and spinach. Mix well. Shape into 1 inch (2.5 cm) balls. Arrange on greased baking sheet.

Brush with second amount of melted margarine. Bake in 325°F (160°C) oven for 10 to 12 minutes. Do not overcook. If desired these may be frozen on a tray before baking, then stored in containers. Makes 48 spinach balls.

3 spinach balls: 104 Calories; 4 g Protein; 5.8 g Total Fat; 10 g Carbohydrate; 247 mg Sodium; 1 g Dietary Fiber

Pictured below.

Fluffy Salmon Spread, this page   Spinach Balls, above

Parmesan Appies

Soft and creamy topping covers baguette slices. Serve hot.

Mayonnaise (not salad dressing)	½ cup	125 mL
Grated Parmesan cheese	½ cup	125 mL
Minced onion	1 tbsp.	15 mL
Garlic powder	⅛ tsp.	0.5 mL
Baguette, cut into ½ inch (12 mm) slices	1	1

Stir mayonnaise, Parmesan cheese, onion and garlic powder together in small bowl.

Arrange bread slices on ungreased baking sheet. Broil to toast 1 side. Turn slices over. Spread 2 tsp. (10 mL) on each slice. Broil until slightly browned. Makes ¾ cup (175 mL) topping, enough for 18 slices.

1 slice: 134 Calories; 4 g Protein; 6.8 g Total Fat; 14 g Carbohydrate; 234 mg Sodium; trace Dietary Fiber

Pictured below.

Top: Salami Rolls, this page   Center: Stuffed Mushrooms, this page
Bottom: Parmesan Appies, above

Salami Rolls

Great addition to an appetizer selection. And you made it yourself! Wrap well and freeze for up to six months.

Water	1½ cups	375 mL
Quick curing salt (such as Morton's)	2 tbsp.	30 mL
Liquid smoke	1 tbsp.	15 mL
Mustard seed	2 tsp.	10 mL
Garlic salt	1½ tsp.	7 mL
Pepper	½ tsp.	2 mL
Lean ground beef	3 lbs.	1.4 kg

Stir first 6 ingredients together in large bowl.

Add ground beef. Mix well. Shape into 3 rolls, 2 × 14 inches (5 × 35 cm) long. Wrap up tightly in foil on shiny side. Chill for 24 hours. Poke holes through foil with tip of sharp knife in bottom of rolls. Pour hot water into bottom of broiler pan. Set broiler rack on top. Arrange salami rolls on rack.

Bake in 300°F (150°C) oven for 2 hours. Cool. Makes 3 rolls, 2¼ lbs. (1 kg). Cuts into about 70 pieces each.

1 piece: 30 Calories; 4 g Protein; 1.6 g Total Fat; trace Carbohydrate; 236 mg Sodium; trace Dietary Fiber

Pictured on this page.

Stuffed Mushrooms

Always a welcome flavorful appetizer. Can be made ahead and popped in the oven when needed.

Medium fresh mushrooms	26	26
Hard margarine (or butter)	2 tbsp.	30 mL
Chopped onion	1 cup	250 mL
Finely diced pepperoni (or garlic sausage)	½ cup	125 mL
Water	¼ cup	60 mL
Grated Parmesan cheese	¼ cup	60 mL
Parsley flakes	½ tsp.	2 mL
Chopped chives	1 tsp.	5 mL
Chicken bouillon powder	1 tsp.	5 mL
Dried whole oregano, crushed	¼ tsp.	1 mL
Garlic powder	¼ tsp.	1 mL
Dry bread crumbs	¾ cup	175 mL

Gently twist stems from mushrooms. Chop stems.

Melt margarine in non-stick frying pan. Add mushroom stems, onion and pepperoni. Sauté until onion is soft. Remove from heat.

Add remaining 8 ingredients. Mix well. Stuff mushroom caps. Arrange on greased baking sheet. Bake in 350°F (175°C) oven for 20 to 30 minutes. Makes about 26 stuffed mushrooms.

1 stuffed mushroom: 48 Calories; 2 g Protein; 2.7 g Total Fat; 4 g Carbohydrate; 139 mg Sodium; trace Dietary Fiber

Pictured on this page.

Apple Brie Pizza

Apple Brie Pizza

A thin, crispy appetizer. A delicious hint of sweetness from the apples. Cuts well. Easy to eat out of hand.

Pizza Crust:		
All-purpose flour	1¼ cups	300 mL
Instant yeast	1 tsp.	5 mL
Salt	¼ tsp.	1 mL
Hot water	½ cup	125 mL
Cooking oil	4 tsp.	20 mL
Cornmeal	2 tsp.	10 mL

Topping:		
Brie cheese, with rind, softened	7 oz.	200 g
Sour cream	2 tbsp.	30 mL
Dill weed	¼ tsp.	1 mL
Sherry (or alcohol-free sherry)	1 tsp.	5 mL
Medium red apple, with peel, cut into paper-thin wedges	1	1
Bacon slices, cooked crisp and crumbled (or 2 tbsp., 30 mL, real bacon bits)	3	3
Grated Parmesan cheese	2 tsp.	10 mL

Pizza Crust: Measure flour, yeast and salt into food processor.

With lid in place and machine running, pour hot water and cooking oil through food chute. Process for about 50 seconds until a ball is formed. Remove and wrap in plastic wrap. Let rest for 10 minutes.

Divide dough into 2 equal portions. Sprinkle 1 tsp. (5 mL) cornmeal on working surface. Roll 1 portion of dough over cornmeal to 10 inch (25 cm) diameter. Repeat with second portion of dough. Place on greased baking sheet. Poke holes all over dough with fork. Bake on bottom rack in 450°F (230°C) oven for about 10 minutes. You can bake these 1 at a time. Cool.

Topping: Mash Brie cheese, sour cream, dill weed and sherry with fork on large plate. No need to mash until smooth but rather to coarsely mix. Divide between crusts.

Arrange apple slices in single layer over each. Sprinkle with bacon. Sprinkle with Parmesan cheese. Bake in center of 450°F (230°C) oven for about 5 minutes until crust is crisp and surface is beginning to turn golden. Cut each pizza into 12 wedges, for a total of 24 wedges.

1 wedge: 71 Calories; 3 g Protein; 3.8 g Total Fat; 6 g Carbohydrate; 97 mg Sodium; trace Dietary Fiber

Pictured above.

Beef

Early in the twentieth century, there were very few actual recipes for meat. These early recipes mostly gave instructions for methods of cooking—broiling, braising, roasting and frying. In 1910, Campbell's® published *Helps For The Hostess,* featuring recipes that combined their soups with beef. This led to the development of many more beef recipes, and today there are unlimited ways to prepare beef. The meat section in grocery stores is filled with trendy stir-fry strips, kabobs, and specialty barbecue and rouladen cuts, as well as the traditional roasts and steaks. Recipes in this section include casseroles, chilis, steaks, stews and stir-fries.

Shipwreck

An old favorite many of us grew up with.

Large onions, thinly sliced	2	2
Salt, sprinkle		
Pepper, sprinkle		
Medium potatoes, thinly sliced	2	2
Salt, sprinkle		
Pepper, sprinkle		
Lean ground beef	1 lb.	454 g
Salt, sprinkle		
Pepper, sprinkle		
Uncooked long grain white rice	½ cup	125 mL
Chopped celery	1 cup	250 mL
Salt, sprinkle		
Pepper, sprinkle		
Condensed cream of tomato soup	10 oz.	284 mL
Soup can of boiling water	10 oz.	284 mL

Place onion in bottom of ungreased 2 quart (2 L) casserole. Sprinkle with salt and pepper. Lay potato over onion. Sprinkle with salt and pepper. Pat ground beef over potato. Sprinkle with salt and pepper. Sprinkle rice then celery over top. Sprinkle with salt and pepper.

Mix soup and boiling water in small bowl. Pour over top. Cover. Bake in 350°F (175°C) oven for 1½ to 2 hours until vegetables are tender. Serves 4.

1 serving: 463 Calories; 27 g Protein; 18.7 g Total Fat; 48 g Carbohydrate; 1312 mg Sodium; 4 g Dietary Fiber

Pictured on this page.

Short Rib Magic

Very tender, dark and delicious. Beautifully glazed. Extra tasty.

Boneless beef short ribs	3 lbs.	1.4 kg
Envelope dry onion soup mix	1 × 1½ oz.	1 × 42 g
Ketchup	¾ cup	175 mL
Brown sugar, packed	½ cup	125 mL

Arrange short ribs in medium roaster. Stir onion soup mix and sprinkle over top. Pour ketchup over soup mix. Sprinkle with brown sugar. Cover. Bake in 325°F (160°C) oven for 2½ to 3 hours until very tender. Serves 8.

1 serving: 399 Calories; 35 g Protein; 17.8 g Total Fat; 24 g Carbohydrate; 925 mg Sodium; 1 g Dietary Fiber

Pictured on page 44.

Short Rib Magic, above

Swiss Steak Casserole

Baby carrots and baby potatoes make for a most appealing dish.

Beef sirloin (or round) steak, cut into 6 serving pieces	2 lbs.	900 g
All-purpose flour	¼ cup	60 mL
Salt	1 tsp.	5 mL
Pepper	¼ tsp.	1 mL
Cooking oil	1 tbsp.	15 mL
Chili sauce	½ cup	125 mL
Water	½ cup	125 mL
Beef bouillon powder	2 tsp.	10 mL
Tomato sauce	7½ oz.	213 mL
Garlic powder	¼ tsp.	1 mL
Baby red potatoes, with peel	12	12
Peeled baby carrots	24	24
Medium onions, cut into wedges	2	2

Pound steaks well with meat mallet.

Mix flour, salt and pepper in shallow dish. Dip both sides of steak in to coat.

Heat ½ of cooking oil in non-stick frying pan. Add 3 steaks. Brown both sides well. Arrange in medium roaster. Repeat with remaining steaks.

Stir next 5 ingredients together in small bowl. Pour over steaks. Cover. Bake in 350°F (175°C) oven for 1¾ to 2 hours until tender.

Add potatoes, carrot and onion. Bake, covered, for about 1½ hours until vegetables are tender. Add a touch more water if needed. Serves 6.

1 serving: 417 Calories; 37 g Protein; 8.6 g Total Fat; 47 g Carbohydrate; 1316 mg Sodium; 6 g Dietary Fiber

Pictured below.

Top: Shipwreck, this page   Bottom: Swiss Steak Casserole, above

Noodle Casserole

*Little chunks of cheese melt in this as it bakes.
A topping of onion rings sets it off. A favorite.*

Lean ground beef	1½ lbs.	680 g
Chopped green pepper (optional)	½ cup	125 mL
Chopped onion	1 cup	250 mL
Medium noodles (8 oz., 225 g)	3⅓ cups	825 mL
Boiling water	3 qts.	3 L
Cooking oil (optional)	1 tbsp.	15 mL
Salt	2 tsp.	10 mL
Condensed cream of tomato soup	10 oz.	284 mL
Condensed cream of mushroom soup	10 oz.	284 mL
Worcestershire sauce	1 tsp.	5 mL
Salt	¾ tsp.	4 mL
Pepper	¼ tsp.	1 mL
Canned sliced mushrooms, drained	10 oz.	284 mL
Small cubed medium Cheddar cheese	1 cup	250 mL
Topping:		
Hard margarine (or butter)	1 tbsp.	15 mL
Water	1 tbsp.	15 mL
Dry bread crumbs	½ cup	125 mL
Canned french-fried onion rings	2¾ oz.	79 g

Scramble-fry ground beef, green pepper and onion in non-stick frying pan until onion is soft and beef is no longer pink. Drain.

Cook noodles in boiling water, cooking oil and first amount of salt in large uncovered pot or Dutch oven for 5 to 7 minutes until tender but firm. Drain. Return noodles to pot.

Empty both soups into medium bowl. Add Worcestershire sauce, second amount of salt and pepper. Stir vigorously. Add to noodles. Add beef mixture. Stir.

Add mushrooms and cheese. Stir. Turn into ungreased 3 quart (3 L) casserole.

Topping: Melt margarine in small saucepan. Stir in water and bread crumbs. Sprinkle over casserole. Bake, uncovered, in 350°F (175°C) oven for 25 to 30 minutes.

Top with onion rings. Bake for about 10 minutes until heated through. Serves 6.

1 serving: 593 Calories; 34 g Protein; 26.1 g Total Fat; 54 g Carbohydrate; 1537 mg Sodium; 3 g Dietary Fiber

Pictured on page 47.

Three Layer Pasta And Beef

*Great mild flavor. Layers can
be seen when it is cut into to serve.*

Fusilli pasta (8 oz., 225 g)	2⅔ cups	650 mL
Boiling water	3 qts.	3 L
Cooking oil (optional)	1 tbsp.	15 mL
Salt	2 tsp.	10 mL
Lean ground beef	1 lb.	454 g
Chopped onion	1 cup	250 mL
All-purpose flour	1 tbsp.	15 mL
Ground allspice	¼ tsp.	1 mL
Salt	½ tsp.	2 mL
Pepper	⅛-¼ tsp.	0.5-1 mL
Tomato sauce	7½ oz.	213 mL
Milk	2 cups	500 mL
All-purpose flour	¼ cup	60 mL
Salt	½ tsp.	2 mL
Pepper	⅛ tsp.	0.5 mL
Grated Parmesan cheese	⅓ cup	75 mL

Cook pasta in boiling water, cooking oil and first amount of salt in large uncovered pot or Dutch oven for 7 to 8 minutes until tender but firm. Drain. Turn pasta into ungreased 2 quart (2 L) casserole.

Scramble-fry ground beef and onion in non-stick frying pan until onion is soft and beef is no longer pink. Drain.

Mix in first amount of flour, allspice, second amount of salt and pepper. Stir in tomato sauce until boiling. Spoon over pasta.

Gradually whisk milk into second amount of flour in small saucepan until no lumps remain. Add third amount of salt and second amount of pepper. Heat and stir until boiling.

Stir in Parmesan cheese. Pour over beef. Poke here and there with knife to allow some sauce to reach bottom. Bake, uncovered, in 350°F (175°C) oven for about 40 minutes until browned. Makes 8 cups (2 L) casserole.

1½ cups (375 mL) casserole: 411 Calories; 28 g Protein; 10.9 g Total Fat; 48 g Carbohydrate; 967 mg Sodium; 2 g Dietary Fiber

Pictured on page 47.

1. Noodle Casserole, this page
2. Dairy Beef Bake, page 48
3. Chili Modern, page 48
4. Three Layer Pasta And Beef, above

Chili Modern

Contains salsa instead of tomatoes.
Add crusty bread for a complete meal.

Lean ground beef	1½ lbs.	680 g
Chopped onion	1 cup	250 mL
Canned kidney beans, with liquid	2 × 14 oz.	2 × 398 mL
Frozen kernel corn	1½ cups	375 mL
Canned chopped green chilies, with liquid	4 oz.	114 mL
Chili powder	2 tsp.	10 mL
Garlic powder	¼ tsp.	1 mL
Salt	½ tsp.	2 mL
Pepper	⅛ tsp.	0.5 mL
Medium salsa	1½ cups	375 mL

Scramble-fry ground beef and onion in large pot or Dutch oven until onion is soft and beef is no longer pink. Drain.

Add remaining 8 ingredients. Heat, stirring occasionally, until boiling. Simmer for 10 to 15 minutes. Makes 8½ cups (2.1 L) chili.

1½ cups (375 mL) chili: 399 Calories; 33 g Protein; 11 g Total Fat; 45 g Carbohydrate; 1989 mg Sodium; 12 g Dietary Fiber

Pictured on page 47.

Broiled Steak

A great time awaits when steaks are
broiled or barbecued. This has unusual flavorings.

Red wine vinegar	¼ cup	60 mL
Beef T-bone (or porterhouse) steaks (about 3 lbs., 1.4 kg)	4	4
Cooking oil	1 tbsp.	15 mL
Salt	1 tsp.	5 mL
Pepper	1 tsp.	5 mL
Dried sweet basil, crushed	1 tsp.	5 mL

Brush vinegar on both sides of each steak. Brush with cooking oil. Arrange on broiler tray.

Mix salt, pepper and basil in small cup. Sprinkle ½ over steaks. Broil for 5 minutes. Turn steaks over. Sprinkle with remaining ½ of seasoning. Broil for 5 minutes until desired degree of doneness. Serves 4.

1 serving: 603 Calories; 56 g Protein; 39.8 g Total Fat; 2 g Carbohydrate; 795 mg Sodium; trace Dietary Fiber

Pictured on this page.

BARBECUED STEAK: Instead of broiling in oven, barbecue steaks over medium for 5 minutes per side until desired degree of doneness is reached.

Dairy Beef Bake

So creamy tasting. Excellent.

Lean ground beef	1½ lbs.	680 g
Chopped onion	½ cup	125 mL
Chopped celery	¼ cup	60 mL
Broad egg noodles (8 oz., 225 g)	4 cups	1 L
Boiling water	3 qts.	3 L
Cooking oil (optional)	1 tbsp.	15 mL
Salt	2 tsp.	10 mL
Canned stewed tomatoes, with juice	14 oz.	398 mL
Chili sauce	½ cup	125 mL
Garlic powder	½ tsp.	2 mL
Salt	½ tsp.	2 mL
Pepper	⅛ tsp.	0.5 mL
Non-fat sour cream	1 cup	250 mL
Light cream cheese	4 oz.	125 g

Scramble-fry ground beef, onion and celery in non-stick frying pan until slightly browned. Drain.

Cook noodles in boiling water, cooking oil and first amount of salt in large uncovered pot or Dutch oven for 5 to 7 minutes until tender but firm. Drain. Return noodles to pot. Add beef mixture. Stir.

Add tomatoes with juice, chili sauce, garlic powder, second amount of salt and pepper. Stir.

Beat sour cream and cream cheese together well in small bowl. Add to pot. Stir gently, just to marble through. Turn into ungreased 3 quart (3 L) casserole. Cover. Bake in 350°F (175°C) oven for about 30 minutes until heated through. Makes 8 cups (2 L) casserole.

1½ cups (375 mL) casserole: 510 Calories; 36 g Protein; 19.6 g Total Fat; 47 g Carbohydrate; 1306 mg Sodium; 4 g Dietary Fiber

Pictured on page 47.

Broiled Steak, this page

Shepherd's Pie

An old favorite generally made on Monday to use up Sunday's leftover roast beef and potatoes.

Cooked roast beef, chopped	3 cups	750 mL
Small onion	1	1
Beef gravy	½-1 cup	125-250 mL
Salt	1 tsp.	5 mL
Pepper	¼ tsp.	1 mL
Leftover mashed potato	3 cups	750 mL
Paprika, sprinkle (optional)		

Put beef and onion through food chopper or processor. If you don't have either, chop with knife into very small pieces.

Add gravy. Mix well. Should be pasty enough to hold together. Pack in ungreased 9 × 9 inch (22 × 22 cm) pan. Sprinkle with salt and pepper.

Spread potato over top of beef. Sprinkle with paprika. Bake in 350°F (175°C) oven for 30 minutes until hot and potato is browned. Serves 4.

1 serving: 387 Calories; 36 g Protein; 13.7 g Total Fat; 31 g Carbohydrate; 1414 mg Sodium; 4 g Dietary Fiber

Pictured on page 50 and on back cover.

Crispy Minute Steak

Good flavor to this crispy coated tender steak.

Large egg	1	1
Water	2 tsp.	10 mL
Salt	1 tsp.	5 mL
Pepper	¼ tsp.	1 mL
Fine dry bread crumbs	¾ cup	175 mL
Hard margarine (or butter)	1½ tbsp.	25 mL
Minute steaks (tenderized beef steak)	1½ lbs.	680 g

Beat egg, water, salt and pepper in shallow bowl until smooth.

Put bread crumbs into shallow dish.

Melt margarine in non-stick frying pan. Dip minute steak into egg mixture, then into crumbs. Lay crumbed steak on waxed paper. Press with your hand to ensure crumbs stay on. Add to frying pan. Brown both sides, cooking to degree of desired doneness. Serves 4.

1 serving: 362 Calories; 41 g Protein; 13.7 g Total Fat; 16 g Carbohydrate; 1017 mg Sodium; trace Dietary Fiber

Pictured on this page.

Top: Crispy Minute Steak, this page
Bottom: Mellow Stew, below

Mellow Stew

Rich-colored sauce. Serve with mashed potato for a complete meal.

Beef stew meat, cut into 1 inch (2.5 cm) cubes	1½ lbs.	680 g
Cooking oil	2 tsp.	10 mL
Water	2 cups	500 mL
Ketchup	½ cup	125 mL
White vinegar	3 tbsp.	50 mL
Brown sugar, packed	3 tbsp.	50 mL
Sliced carrot	2 cups	500 mL
Chopped onion	1 cup	250 mL
Salt	1 tsp.	5 mL
Pepper	¼ tsp.	1 mL

Brown beef in cooking oil in large pot or Dutch oven.

Add water, ketchup, vinegar and brown sugar. Stir. Cover. Boil slowly for 1¼ hours.

Add carrot, onion, salt and pepper. Stir. Cover. Boil gently for 30 to 40 minutes until beef and vegetables are tender. Makes 4½ cups (1.1 L) stew.

1½ cups (375 mL) stew: 571 Calories; 51 g Protein; 23 g Total Fat; 40 g Carbohydrate; 1641 mg Sodium; 4 g Dietary Fiber

Pictured above.

Left: Roast And Gravy, below   Top Right: Slow Stew, page 51   Bottom: Shepherd's Pie, page 49

Roast And Gravy

This has a different twist—gravy is made using the cooked vegetables.

Boneless beef roast (such as chuck or round)	3 lbs.	1.4 kg
Medium carrot, diced	1	1
Chopped onion	½ cup	125 mL
Water	2 cups	500 mL
Garlic powder	½ tsp.	2 mL
Ground sage	½ tsp.	2 mL
Salt	½ tsp.	2 mL
Pepper	⅛ tsp.	0.5 mL
All-purpose flour	2 tbsp.	30 mL

Place roast in center of small roaster. Scatter carrot and onion around roast. Pour water over top.

Mix garlic powder, sage, salt and pepper in small cup. Sprinkle over vegetables. Cover. Bake in 350°F (175°C) oven for 2 to 2½ hours until roast is very tender. Remove roast to platter.

Process drippings and vegetables in blender to make gravy. Add flour. Process until smooth. Pour into medium saucepan. Heat and stir until boiling and thickened. Makes 3½ cups (875 mL) gravy. Serves 8.

1 serving: 402 Calories; 33 g Protein; 27.5 g Total Fat; 4 g Carbohydrate; 265 mg Sodium; trace Dietary Fiber

Pictured above and on back cover.

Slow Stew

It is so easy to double this convenient recipe either to serve more people or to have leftovers for the next day.

Beef stew meat, cut into ¾ inch (2 cm) cubes	1 lb.	454 g
Medium potatoes, cut bite size	3	3
Medium carrots, cut bite size	4	4
Cubed turnip (about ¾ inch, 2 cm, size)	1 cup	250 mL
Medium onion, cut up	1	1
Sliced celery	½ cup	125 mL
Beef bouillon powder	2 tsp.	10 mL
Boiling water	½ cup	125 mL
Canned stewed tomatoes, with juice	14 oz.	398 mL
Minute tapioca	2 tbsp.	30 mL
Granulated sugar	1 tsp.	5 mL
Salt	¾ tsp.	4 mL
Pepper	¼ tsp.	1 mL

Combine first 6 ingredients in small roaster.

Stir bouillon powder into boiling water in medium bowl.

Add remaining 5 ingredients to bouillon mixture. Pour over beef and vegetables. Cover. Bake in 300°F (150°C) oven for 3½ to 4 hours until beef is very tender. Serves 4.

1 serving: 369 Calories; 29 g Protein; 10.4 g Total Fat; 41 g Carbohydrate; 1216 mg Sodium; 6 g Dietary Fiber

Pictured on page 50 and on back cover.

Gravy Browner

There was no commercial gravy browner in the mid-1800s. This was used instead. Simply stir in small amount at a time into gravy until darkened to your liking.

Granulated sugar	2 tbsp.	30 mL
Salt, just a pinch		
Water	2 tsp.	10 mL
Water	1 cup	250 mL

Combine sugar and salt in small saucepan. Heat and stir constantly until sugar is melted. It will darken until it looks slightly burnt.

When very dark brown, add first amount of water. It will spatter. Keep stirring.

Gradually stir in second amount of water. Be sure all hard sugar syrup is dissolved. Cool. Makes 1 cup (250 mL) gravy browner.

1 tsp. (5 mL) gravy browner: 2 Calories; 0 g Protein; 0 g Total Fat; 1 g Carbohydrate; trace Sodium; 0 g Dietary Fiber

Pictured on this page.

Boiled Roast

In days long past, when the oven was being used for baking bread, a roast was often boiled. Great nowadays for those tougher cuts and always-busy ovens. Best when you want sliced or shredded cooked beef. Use leftover beef stock for a soup base or as a dip for beef sandwiches.

Boneless beef roast (such as chuck or round)	3 lbs.	1.4 kg
Boiling water, to cover		
Garlic powder (optional)	½ tsp.	2 mL
Onion powder	½ tsp.	2 mL
Celery salt	½ tsp.	2 mL
Pepper	¼ tsp.	1 mL
Chicken bouillon powder	1 tsp.	5 mL
Gravy Browner, this page	1-2 tsp.	5-10 mL

Set roast in center of large pot or Dutch oven. Cover with boiling water ¼ to ½ inch (6 to 12 mm) over top of roast.

Add remaining 6 ingredients to water. Stir. Cover. Boil gently for about 2 hours until tender. Serves 6 to 8.

⅙ recipe: 517 Calories; 43 g Protein; 36.7 g Total Fat; trace Carbohydrate; 344 mg Sodium; trace Dietary Fiber

Pictured below.

Top: Gravy Browner, this page   Bottom: Boiled Roast, above

Pacific Beef Stir-Fry

Pacific Beef Stir-Fry

If you have everything prepared ahead, this cooks up in no time.

Medium onions, sliced	2	2
Red pepper slivers	1/3 cup	75 mL
Sliced fresh mushrooms	1 cup	250 mL
Cooking oil	2 tsp.	10 mL
Frozen whole green beans	2½ cups	625 mL
Water	2 tbsp.	30 mL
Bean sprouts (large handful)	1 cup	250 mL
Cooking oil	1 tsp.	5 mL
Lean beef rump steak, cut into thin strips	1 lb.	454 g
Cooking oil	1 tsp.	5 mL
Soy sauce	3 tbsp.	50 mL
Granulated sugar	2 tsp.	10 mL
Ground ginger	1/8 tsp.	0.5 mL
Garlic powder	1/8 tsp.	0.5 mL
Cornstarch	1½ tbsp.	25 mL

Stir-fry onion, red pepper and mushrooms in first amount of cooking oil in large non-stick wok or frying pan for 5 minutes. Vegetables will be tender-crisp. Turn into medium bowl.

Combine green beans and water in wok. Cover. Cook for 4 minutes. Drain. Add bean sprouts and second amount of cooking oil to beans in wok. Stir-fry for about 4 minutes until hot. Add to vegetable mixture in bowl.

Stir-fry beef in wok in third amount of cooking oil for about 10 minutes until desired degree of doneness.

Combine remaining 5 ingredients in small cup. Stir well. Stir into beef until bubbling and thickened. Add vegetables and liquid in bowl to wok. Stir-fry until heated through. Makes 4 cups (1 L) stir-fry.

1½ cups (375 mL) stir-fry: 439 Calories; 45 g Protein; 16.3 g Total Fat; 30 g Carbohydrate; 1310 mg Sodium; 6 g Dietary Fiber

Pictured above.

Layered Meatloaf

Using a large shallow pan rather than a loaf pan gives this a different shape. Just add a vegetable and you're set for supper.

Skim evaporated milk	13½ oz.	385 mL
Finely chopped onion	3/4 cup	175 mL
Dry bread crumbs	1 cup	250 mL
Salt	1 tsp.	5 mL
Pepper	1/4 tsp.	1 mL
Lean ground beef	2 lbs.	900 g
Medium egg noodles (about 6 cups, 1.5 L)	10 oz.	285 g
Boiling water	2 qts.	2 L
Cooking oil (optional)	1 tbsp.	15 mL
Salt	2 tsp.	10 mL
Large eggs, fork-beaten	2	2
Grated Parmesan cheese	1/3 cup	75 mL
Canned chunky meatless spaghetti sauce	25 oz.	700 mL
Grated medium Cheddar cheese	1 cup	250 mL

Mix first 5 ingredients in medium bowl.

Add ground beef. Mix well. Pack in greased 9 x 13 inch (22 x 33 cm) pan. Bake in 350°F (175°C) oven for 30 to 35 minutes. Drain.

Cook noodles in boiling water, cooking oil and second amount of salt in large uncovered pot or Dutch oven for 5 to 7 minutes until tender but firm. Drain.

Combine eggs and Parmesan cheese in small bowl. Stir. Add to noodles. Mix well. Pour over beef. Spread to make even layer.

Drizzle spaghetti sauce over top. Sprinkle with Cheddar cheese. Return to oven for 15 minutes. Serves 8.

1 serving: 545 Calories; 39 g Protein; 19.8 g Total Fat; 52 g Carbohydrate; 1238 mg Sodium; 3 g Dietary Fiber

Pictured below.

Layered Meatloaf, above

Mexicali Special

Cook on top of the stove or bake, uncovered, in greased 3 quart (3 L) casserole in 325°F (160°C) oven for 1 hour.

Medium noodles	1 lb.	454 g
Boiling water	3 qts.	3 L
Salt	1 tbsp.	15 mL
Cooking oil (optional)	1 tbsp.	15 mL
Lean ground beef	2 lbs.	900 g
Chopped onion	1 cup	250 mL
Chopped celery	½ cup	125 mL
Sliced fresh mushrooms	1 cup	250 mL
Medium green pepper, chopped	1	1
Cooking oil	2 tbsp.	30 mL
Tomato juice	19 oz.	540 mL
Chili sauce	½ cup	125 mL
Canned chopped green chilies, with liquid	4 oz.	114 mL
Chili powder	1 tbsp.	15 mL
Dried whole oregano	1 tsp.	5 mL
Granulated sugar	1 tsp.	5 mL
Salt	2 tsp.	10 mL
Process cheese loaf (such as Velveeta), cut up	8 oz.	250 g

Cook noodles in boiling water and first amounts of salt and cooking oil in large uncovered pot or Dutch oven for 5 to 7 minutes until tender but firm. Drain. Set aside.

Scramble-fry ground beef, onion, celery, mushrooms and green pepper in 2 batches in second amount of cooking oil in same large pot or Dutch oven until browned. Drain. Return both batches to pot.

Add tomato juice, chili sauce, green chilies with liquid, chili powder, oregano, sugar and second amount of salt. Cover. Simmer gently, stirring occasionally, for about 30 minutes.

Add noodles and cheese. Heat and stir until cheese is melted. Serves 6.

1 serving: 756 Calories; 47 g Protein; 29 g Total Fat; 76 g Carbohydrate; 2526 mg Sodium; 5 g Dietary Fiber

Pictured below.

Top: Mexicali Special, above   Bottom: Lazy Ravioli, this page

Lazy Ravioli

This cooks and tastes better when baked in a shallow dish.

Lean ground beef	1½ lbs.	680 g
Chopped onion	1½ cups	375 mL
Coarsely chopped fresh mushrooms	1½ cups	375 mL
Garlic clove, minced (or ¼ tsp., 1 mL, powder)	1	1
Tomato paste	5½ oz.	156 mL
Tomato sauce	7½ oz.	213 mL
Hot water	1 cup	250 mL
Beef bouillon powder	1 tbsp.	15 mL
Parsley flakes	1½ tsp.	7 mL
Dried sweet basil	1½ tsp.	7 mL
Granulated sugar	¾ tsp.	4 mL
Dried whole oregano	¼ tsp.	1 mL
Dried thyme	¼ tsp.	1 mL
Salt	½ tsp.	2 mL
Pepper	¼ tsp.	1 mL
Frozen chopped spinach, cooked and drained	10 oz.	300 g
Large egg, fork-beaten	1	1
Dry bread crumbs	⅓ cup	75 mL
Parsley flakes	1 tbsp.	15 mL
Grated medium or sharp Cheddar cheese	1 cup	250 mL
Garlic salt	⅛ tsp.	0.5 mL
Ground nutmeg	⅛ tsp.	0.5 mL
Lasagne noodles, broken in half	8	8
Boiling water	4 qts.	4 L
Salt	1 tbsp.	15 mL
Cooking oil (optional)		
Grated part-skim mozzarella cheese	1 cup	250 mL

Scramble-fry ground beef, onion, mushrooms and garlic in large non-stick frying pan until beef is no longer pink. Drain. Return to frying pan.

Add next 11 ingredients. Stir. Bring to a boil. Cook, uncovered, until thickened.

Combine next 7 ingredients in small bowl. Mix.

Cook noodles in boiling water, second amount of salt and cooking oil for 14 to 16 minutes until tender but firm. Drain. Rinse with cold water. Drain well.

Arrange layers in ungreased 4 quart (4 L) casserole or small roaster as follows:

1. ½ of beef mixture
2. ½ of noodles
3. All of spinach mixture
4. ½ of noodles
5. ½ of beef mixture
6. All of mozzarella cheese

Cover. Bake in 350°F (175°C) oven for about 45 minutes. Serves 6 to 8.

⅙ recipe: 520 Calories; 40 g Protein; 21.6 g Total Fat; 42 g Carbohydrate; 1159 mg Sodium; 5 g Dietary Fiber

Pictured on this page.

Beverages

For centuries, water and milk were the most popular choices of non-alcoholic beverages. In the early 1900s, lemonade, made from crystals mixed with water, became a thirst-quenching drink. Today, the varieties of fruit juice, soda pop and ice cream available, offer us the chance to be creative in the liquid refreshments we serve. Whether it's a simple fruit ade or an ice cream shake, we can count on their diverse flavors to whet our appetite, complement a meal or quench our thirst.

1. Party Punch, below
2. Pink Sunrise Punch, below
3. Cranberry Perc, page 57
4. Orangeade, this page

Pink Sunrise Punch

A refreshing drink without being sweet.

Pink grapefruit cocktail	2 cups	500 mL
Prepared orange juice	1 cup	250 mL
Grenadine syrup	¼ cup	60 mL
Ginger ale	8 cups	2 L
Ice ring (or cubes)		
Maraschino cherries (optional)		

Combine grapefruit cocktail, orange juice and grenadine syrup in punch bowl.

Add ginger ale. Stir gently. Add ice ring. Serve in stemmed champagne glasses. Garnish each glass with a cherry. Makes 10²/₃ cups (2.75 L) punch.

1 cup (250 mL) punch: 123 Calories; trace Protein; 0.1 g Total Fat; 31 g Carbohydrate; 20 mg Sodium; trace Dietary Fiber

Pictured on page 54.

Party Punch

Pineapple and lemon-lime make a pretty party drink.

Pineapple juice	1½ qts.	1.5 L
Water	1 qt.	1 L
Envelope unsweetened lemon-lime drink powder	1 × ¼ oz.	1 × 6 g
Granulated sugar	1 cup	250 mL
Ginger ale	2 qts.	2 L
Ice ring (or cubes)		

Combine pineapple juice, water, drink powder and sugar in large container. Stir for several minutes until sugar is dissolved. Chill. Transfer to punch bowl.

Add ginger ale. Stir gently. Add ice ring. Makes 18 cups (4.5 L) punch.

1 cup (250 mL) punch: 133 Calories; trace Protein; 0.1 g Total Fat; 34 g Carbohydrate; 9 mg Sodium; trace Dietary Fiber

Pictured on page 54.

Orangeade

Vibrant orange color. Very refreshing. Good to serve for any occasion—morning through evening.

Medium oranges, with peel, cut up	12	12
Water	12 cups	3 L
Citric acid (available at drug stores), generous 3 tbsp. (50 mL)	2 oz.	57 g
Granulated sugar	3 cups	750 mL
Ice cubes		

Put orange pieces through meat grinder or food processor being sure to catch all juice. Pour into large bowl or plastic pail.

Add water and citric acid. Stir well. Cover. Chill overnight.

Strain juice into large punch bowl. Add sugar. Stir until dissolved. Serve over ice in large glasses. Makes 14 cups (3.5 L) punch.

1 cup (250 mL) punch: 228 Calories; 2 g Protein; 0.4 g Total Fat; 66 g Carbohydrate; 3 mg Sodium; 1 g Dietary Fiber

Pictured on page 55.

Peach Shake

A tasty and healthy yogurt shake.

Canned sliced peaches, with juice	14 oz.	398 mL
Lemon juice	2 tsp.	10 mL
Brown sugar, packed	1 tbsp.	15 mL
Vanilla yogurt	1 cup	250 mL
Crushed ice (or 4 ice cubes)	½ cup	125 mL

Combine all 5 ingredients in blender. Process until smooth. Makes 3½ cups (875 mL) shake.

1 cup (250 mL) shake: 115 Calories; 5 g Protein; 1.2 g Total Fat; 23 g Carbohydrate; 58 mg Sodium; 1 g Dietary Fiber

Pictured on page 57.

PEAR SHAKE: Use canned pears instead of peaches.

APRICOT SHAKE: Use canned apricots instead of peaches.

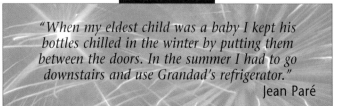

"When my eldest child was a baby I kept his bottles chilled in the winter by putting them between the doors. In the summer I had to go downstairs and use Grandad's refrigerator."

Jean Paré

Fruit Shake

Pretty pink color. Deliciously thick. Bananas and strawberries are a natural combination. Garnish with additional strawberries.

Medium bananas, cut up	2	2
Frozen whole strawberries	2 cups	500 mL
Milk	2 cups	500 mL
Granulated sugar	2 tbsp.	30 mL

Put all 4 ingredients into blender. Process until smooth. Pour into glasses. Makes 4 cups (1 L) shake.

1 cup (250 mL) shake: 156 Calories; 5 g Protein; 1.7 g Total Fat; 32 g Carbohydrate; 67 mg Sodium; 2 g Dietary Fiber

Pictured on this page.

Cranberry Perc

Spicy aroma fills the room. A warming but lively drink. Serve with whole cinnamon sticks.

Cranberry cocktail	2 qts.	2 L
Apple juice	2 qts.	2 L
Frozen concentrated orange juice, thawed	12 oz.	341 mL
Granulated sugar	½ cup	125 mL
Cinnamon sticks (3 inches, 7.5 cm, each), smashed with hammer	2	2
Whole allspice	2 tsp.	10 mL
Whole cloves	1 tsp.	5 mL

Pour cranberry cocktail, apple juice and concentrated orange juice into percolator that has been washed with vinegar and baking soda. Put stem and basket into place.

Tie remaining 4 ingredients in double-layer of cheesecloth or filter bag. Set in basket. Cover. Perk as usual. Makes 17½ cups (4.4 L) hot punch.

1 cup (250 mL) punch: 188 Calories; 1 g Protein; 0.2 g Total Fat; 47 g Carbohydrate; 9 mg Sodium; trace Dietary Fiber

Pictured on page 54 and 55.

Slow Cooker Variation: Instead of using a percolator, pour first 3 ingredients into 5 to 6 quart (5 to 6 L) slow cooker. Tie remaining 4 ingredients in cheesecloth or filter bag. Add to slow cooker. Cook on Low for at least 2 hours until hot.

Fruit Shake, this page

Peach Shake, page 56

Hot Mocha Drink

This is decadent, especially with whipped topping.

Water	2 cups	500 mL
Unsweetened chocolate	1 × 1 oz.	1 × 28 g
baking square, cut up		
Instant coffee granules	¼ cup	60 mL
Granulated sugar	2 tbsp.	30 mL
Milk	2 cups	500 mL
Vanilla	½ tsp.	2 mL
Frozen whipped topping	½ cup	125 mL
(in a tub), thawed (or		
whipped cream or tiny		
marshmallows), optional		
Chocolate curls, for garnish		
(optional)		

Stir first 6 ingredients in small saucepan. Heat slowly, stirring often, until chocolate is melted and mixture is steaming hot. Pour into mugs. Stir in a bit more sugar if desired.

Top with a dollop of whipped topping. Garnish with chocolate curls. Makes 4 cups (1 L) hot mocha.

1 cup (250 mL) hot mocha: 126 Calories; 6 g Protein; 5.1 g Total Fat; 16 g Carbohydrate; 66 mg Sodium; 1 g Dietary Fiber

Pictured below.

Rhubarb Punch, below

Rhubarb Punch

This refreshing drink can be made any time of the year. Garnish punch with pineapple rings and maraschino cherries.

Fresh (or frozen) rhubarb,	2 lbs.	900 g
cut into ½ inch (12 mm)		
lengths (about 10 cups, 2.5 L)		
Water	3 cups	750 mL
Granulated sugar	1 cup	250 mL
Prepared orange juice	1 cup	250 mL
Lemon juice	3 tbsp.	50 mL
Ginger ale (equal to above	5¼ cups	1.3 L
mixture), approximately		
Ice cubes		

Cook rhubarb in water in large pot or Dutch oven until soft and tender. Place colander over large bowl. Pour rhubarb and juice into colander. Allow 30 minutes to drain. Discard rhubarb.

Add sugar to warm juice. If too cooled, warm slightly. Stir until sugar is dissolved.

Add orange juice and lemon juice. Stir. Pour into pitcher. Cover. Chill.

When ready to serve, pour into punch bowl. Add ginger ale. Pour over ice cubes in glasses. For single serving fill glass with ½ of juice mixture and ½ of ginger ale. Makes 10½ cups (2.6 L) punch.

1 cup (250 mL) punch: 140 Calories; 1 g Protein; 0.1 g Total Fat; 36 g Carbohydrate; 11 mg Sodium; 1 g Dietary Fiber

Pictured above.

Hot Mocha Drink

Breads & Quick Breads

Prior to the 1850s, people relied on slow-growing yeast to leaven their breads. Soon after, single-acting baking powders became popular and in 1889, double-acting baking powder was introduced. In 1902, we began to see cookbooks using baking powder in recipes for biscuits, scones, muffins, waffles and batter bread. Today, there are all kinds of exciting variations to these bread and quick bread classics, made even easier with the introduction of instant yeast. For years, muffins were either bran, blueberry, corn, date, apple or oatmeal. In the 1970s and 1980s they became a trend, setting off a new generation of megamuffins, three or four times their original size and featuring ingredients such as grated carrot or zucchini, chocolate chips, nuts and streusel toppings.

Bran Buns

Sweet with light bran flavor. Fluffy texture inside, crispy outside.

Granulated sugar	1 tsp.	5 mL
Warm water	½ cup	125 mL
Envelope active dry yeast (1 scant tbsp., 15 mL)	1 × ¼ oz.	1 × 8 g
All-bran cereal (100% bran)	½ cup	125 mL
Granulated sugar	⅓ cup	75 mL
Hard margarine (or butter)	6 tbsp.	100 mL
Salt	½ tsp.	2 mL
Boiling water	½ cup	125 mL
Large egg, fork-beaten	1	1
All-purpose flour, approximately	3 cups	750 mL

Stir first amount of sugar and warm water in small bowl until sugar is dissolved. Sprinkle yeast over top. Let stand for 10 minutes. Stir until yeast is dissolved.

Combine next 5 ingredients in large bowl. Stir until margarine is melted. Cool to lukewarm. Add yeast mixture. Add egg. Mix well.

Work in flour. Turn out onto lightly floured surface. Knead for 8 to 10 minutes until smooth and elastic. Place in large greased bowl, turning once to grease top. Cover with tea towel. Let stand in oven with light on and door closed for about 50 minutes until doubled in size. Punch down dough. Shape into 18 buns. Place on greased 11 × 17 inch (28 × 43 cm) baking sheet. Cover with tea towel. Let stand in oven with light on and door closed for about 20 minutes until doubled in size. Bake in 375°F (190°C) oven for about 15 minutes until browned. Makes 18 buns.

1 bun: 141 Calories; 3 g Protein; 4.5 g Total Fat; 23 g Carbohydrate; 143 mg Sodium; 1 g Dietary Fiber

Pictured on page 60.

Brown Bread

A quick way to add hot bread to a meal.

All-purpose flour	2⅓ cups	575 mL
Natural bran	1 cup	250 mL
Granulated sugar	2 tsp.	10 mL
Baking powder	4 tsp.	20 mL
Baking soda	1 tsp.	5 mL
Salt	1 tsp.	5 mL
Hard margarine (or butter), melted	¼ cup	60 mL
Buttermilk (or reconstituted from powder)	1 cup	250 mL
Large egg, fork-beaten	1	1

Measure first 6 ingredients into medium bowl. Stir. Make a well in center. Combine margarine, buttermilk and egg in small bowl. Pour into well. Stir to make a soft ball. Turn out onto lightly floured surface. Knead 8 times. Shape into loaf. Place in greased 9 × 5 × 3 inch (22 × 12.5 × 7.5 cm) loaf pan. Bake in 350°F (175°C) oven for about 50 minutes until wooden pick inserted in center comes out clean. Turn out onto rack to cool. Cuts into 16 slices.

1 slice: 119 Calories; 4 g Protein; 3.6 g Total Fat; 19 g Carbohydrate; 314 mg Sodium; 2 g Dietary Fiber

Pictured on page 60.

White Bread

Wonderfully flavored bread. Slices well.

Milk	1 cup	250 mL
Water	½ cup	125 mL
Granulated sugar	2 tbsp.	30 mL
Hard margarine (or butter)	2 tbsp.	30 mL
Salt	2 tsp.	10 mL
Lukewarm water	½ cup	125 mL
Granulated sugar	1 tsp.	5 mL
Envelope active dry yeast (1 scant tbsp., 15 mL)	1 × ¼ oz.	1 × 8 g
All-purpose flour	2½ cups	625 mL
All-purpose flour, approximately	2¼ cups	560 mL
Hard margarine (or butter), softened	2 tsp.	10 mL

Heat milk, first amounts of water, sugar, margarine and salt in small saucepan until margarine is melted and sugar is dissolved. Pour into large bowl. Cool to lukewarm.

Stir second amounts of water and sugar in small bowl until sugar is dissolved. Sprinkle with yeast. Let stand for 10 minutes. Stir until yeast is dissolved. Add to lukewarm mixture. Stir.

Add first amount of flour. Beat well.

Work in second amount of flour until no longer sticky. Turn out onto lightly floured surface. Knead for 8 to 10 minutes until smooth and elastic. Place in large greased bowl, turning once to grease top. Cover with tea towel. Let stand in oven with light on and door closed for about 1 hour until doubled in size. Punch down dough. Divide in half. Shape into loaves. Place in 2 greased, 8 × 4 × 3 inch (20 × 10 × 7.5 cm) loaf pans. Cover with tea towel. Let stand in oven with light on and door closed for 30 to 40 minutes until doubled in size. Remove to preheat oven. Bake in 375°F (190°C) oven for about 30 minutes. Turn out onto racks to cool.

Brush warm tops with second amount of margarine. Makes 2 loaves. Each loaf cuts into 16 slices, for a total of 32 slices.

1 slice: 88 Calories; 2 g Protein; 1.3 g Total Fat; 16 g Carbohydrate; 186 mg Sodium; 1 g Dietary Fiber

Pictured on page 60.

WHOLE WHEAT BREAD: Substitute whole wheat flour for ½ of all-purpose flour.

Chelsea Buns

A pretty bun. Fluffy soft, golden brown and glistening with a glaze. Sweet, buttery and fruity.

Granulated sugar	1 tsp.	5 mL
Warm water	½ cup	125 mL
Envelope active dry yeast (1 scant tbsp., 15 mL)	1 × ¼ oz.	1 × 8 g
Hard margarine (or butter)	¼ cup	60 mL
Granulated sugar	½ cup	125 mL
Large eggs	2	2
Salt	½ tsp.	2 mL
All-purpose flour	1 cup	250 mL
Milk, heated to lukewarm	1 cup	250 mL
All-purpose flour, approximately	4 cups	1 L
Filling:		
Hard margarine (or butter), melted	¼ cup	60 mL
Raisins	¾ cup	175 mL
Chopped mixed peel	½ cup	125 mL
Brown sugar, packed	¾ cup	175 mL
Glaze:		
Liquid honey, warmed	3 tbsp.	50 mL

Stir first amount of sugar and warm water in small bowl until sugar is dissolved. Sprinkle yeast over top. Let stand for 10 minutes. Stir until yeast is dissolved.

Beat margarine and second amount of sugar in large bowl. Beat in eggs, 1 at a time. Add salt and first amount of flour. Beat on high until smooth.

Add yeast mixture. Mix well. Add milk. Stir. Work in second amount of flour until dough pulls away from sides of bowl. Turn out onto lightly floured surface. Knead for 5 to 10 minutes until smooth and elastic. Place in large greased bowl, turning once to grease top. Cover with tea towel. Let stand in oven with light on and door closed for about 1 hour until doubled in size. Punch down dough. Divide into 2 equal portions. Roll out each portion on lightly floured surface into 10 × 14 inch (25 × 35 cm) rectangle.

Filling: Brush each rectangle of dough with ½ of margarine. Sprinkle with ½ of raisins, ½ of mixed peel and ½ of brown sugar. Roll up from long side like jelly roll. Cut each roll into 12 slices. Place cut side down on greased 11 × 17 inch (28 × 43 cm) baking sheet. Cover with tea towel. Let stand in oven with light on and door closed for about 1 hour until doubled in size. Remove to preheat oven. Bake in 375°F (190°C) oven for 15 to 18 minutes.

Glaze: While still warm, dip wet brush into honey and brush tops of buns. Makes 24 buns.

1 bun: 227 Calories; 4 g Protein; 4.8 g Total Fat; 43 g Carbohydrate; 117 mg Sodium; 1 g Dietary Fiber

Pictured on page 60.

Apple Cheese Muffins

Like having a piece of cheese with apple pie.
Very moist because of the apple.

All-purpose flour	1½ cups	375 mL
Baking soda	1 tsp.	5 mL
Salt	½ tsp.	2 mL
Hard margarine (or butter), softened	½ cup	125 mL
Granulated sugar	½ cup	125 mL
Large eggs	2	2
Milk	¼ cup	60 mL
Grated cooking apple (such as McIntosh), approximately 1 large	¾ cup	175 mL
Grated sharp Cheddar cheese	¾ cup	175 mL
Ground cinnamon	½ tsp.	2 mL
Granulated sugar	1 tbsp.	15 mL

Stir flour, baking soda and salt in large bowl. Make a well in center.

Cream margarine and first amount of sugar together in separate large bowl. Beat in eggs, 1 at a time. Add milk. Beat. Stir in apple and cheese. Pour into well. Stir just to moisten. Fill greased muffin cups almost full.

Mix cinnamon and second amount of sugar in small cup. Sprinkle over muffins. Bake in 400°F (205°C) oven for about 20 minutes until wooden pick inserted in center comes out clean. Let stand for 5 minutes before removing to rack to cool. Makes 12 muffins.

1 muffin: 220 Calories; 5 g Protein; 11.7 g Total Fat; 24 g Carbohydrate; 383 mg Sodium; 1 g Dietary Fiber

Pictured below.

Banana Graham Muffins

The ultimate tender muffin. Excellent.

All-purpose flour	¾ cup	175 mL
Graham cracker crumbs	1 cup	250 mL
Brown sugar, packed	½ cup	125 mL
Baking powder	1 tsp.	5 mL
Baking soda	1 tsp.	5 mL
Salt	¼ tsp.	1 mL
Large egg, fork-beaten	1	1
Cooking oil	¼ cup	60 mL
Mashed banana (about 3 medium)	1 cup	250 mL
Chopped walnuts (optional)	⅔ cup	150 mL

Measure first 6 ingredients into large bowl. Stir together. Make a well in center.

Combine egg, cooking oil and banana in medium bowl. Beat to mix well. Stir in walnuts. Turn into well. Stir just to moisten. Fill greased muffin cups almost full. Bake in 400°F (205°C) oven for about 15 minutes until wooden pick inserted in center comes out clean. Let stand for 5 minutes before removing to rack to cool. Makes 12 muffins.

1 muffin: 171 Calories; 2 g Protein; 6.3 g Total Fat; 28 g Carbohydrate; 245 mg Sodium; 1 g Dietary Fiber

Pictured below.

Top Left: Apple Cheese Muffins, this page
Top Right: Banana Graham Muffins, this page
Bottom: Lemon Muffins, page 63

Apricot Bran Muffins

A healthy muffin. Not sweet.

All-purpose flour	1¼ cups	300 mL
Natural bran	1 cup	250 mL
Granulated sugar	½ cup	125 mL
Baking powder	4 tsp.	20 mL
Salt	½ tsp.	2 mL
Large eggs	2	2
Apricot nectar (or apricot baby food)	½ cup	125 mL
Cooking oil	½ cup	125 mL
Dried apricots, cut up	½ cup	125 mL
Ground nutmeg	¼ tsp.	1 mL

Combine first 5 ingredients in large bowl. Stir. Make a well in center.

Put remaining 5 ingredients into blender. Process until dried apricots are finely chopped. Pour into well. Stir just to moisten. Fill greased muffin cups almost full. Bake in 400°F (205°C) oven for about 15 minutes until wooden pick inserted in center comes out clean. Let stand for 5 minutes before removing to rack to cool. Makes 12 muffins.

1 muffin: 215 Calories; 4 g Protein; 10.9 g Total Fat; 28 g Carbohydrate; 131 mg Sodium; 3 g Dietary Fiber

Pictured on this page.

Lemon Muffins

Lemon flavor is mild. Can be enhanced by adding more peel.

Hard margarine (or butter), softened	⅓ cup	75 mL
Granulated sugar	½ cup	125 mL
Large egg	1	1
Lemon juice	2 tbsp.	30 mL
Grated lemon peel	1 tbsp.	15 mL
Milk	¾ cup	175 mL
Lemon flavoring (optional)	½ tsp.	2 mL
All-purpose flour	2 cups	500 mL
Baking powder	2½ tsp.	12 mL
Salt	½ tsp.	2 mL

Beat margarine, sugar and egg together well in medium bowl. Beat in lemon juice, lemon peel, milk and lemon flavoring.

Measure flour, baking powder and salt into large bowl. Stir. Make a well in center. Pour lemon batter into well. Stir just to moisten. Fill greased muffin cups almost full. Bake in 400°F (205°C) oven for about 20 minutes until wooden pick inserted in center comes out clean. Let stand for 5 minutes before removing to rack to cool. Makes 12 muffins.

1 muffin: 177 Calories; 3 g Protein; 6.2 g Total Fat; 27 g Carbohydrate; 194 mg Sodium; 1 g Dietary Fiber

Pictured on page 62.

Pineapple Muffins, below   Apricot Bran Muffins, this page

Pineapple Muffins

The pineapple makes this a particularly moist muffin.

All-purpose flour	2 cups	500 mL
Brown sugar, packed	¾ cup	175 mL
Baking powder	1½ tsp.	7 mL
Baking soda	½ tsp.	2 mL
Salt	½ tsp.	2 mL
Large egg, fork-beaten	1	1
Cooking oil	¼ cup	60 mL
Sour cream	1 cup	250 mL
Canned crushed pineapple, with juice	8 oz.	227 mL
Chopped walnuts (or pecans)	½ cup	125 mL

Combine first 5 ingredients in large bowl. Make a well in center.

Combine egg, cooking oil and sour cream in medium bowl. Beat. Stir in pineapple with juice and walnuts. Turn into well. Stir just to moisten. Fill greased muffin cups almost full. Bake in 400°F (205°C) oven for 15 to 20 minutes until wooden pick inserted in center comes out clean. Let stand for 5 minutes before removing to rack to cool. Makes 14 muffins.

1 muffin: 225 Calories; 4 g Protein; 10.1 g Total Fat; 31 g Carbohydrate; 164 mg Sodium; 1 g Dietary Fiber

Pictured above.

Variation: Add ½ cup (125 mL) toasted long thread or fancy flake coconut.

Month Of Muffins

Keep batter in the refrigerator and enjoy fresh muffins all month.

Crushed shredded wheat cereal (4-5 biscuits)	2 cups	500 mL
Quick-cooking rolled oats (not instant)	2 cups	500 mL
All-bran cereal (100% bran)	2 cups	500 mL
Hard margarine (or butter), cut up	1 cup	250 mL
Boiling water	2 cups	500 mL
Large eggs, fork-beaten	4	4
Buttermilk (or reconstituted from powder)	4 cups	1 L
All-purpose flour	5 cups	1.25 L
Granulated sugar	2 cups	500 mL
Baking powder	1 tbsp.	15 mL
Baking soda	1 tbsp.	15 mL
Salt	1 tbsp.	15 mL
Raisins (optional)	2 cups	500 mL

Measure shredded wheat cereal into large bowl. Add rolled oats, all-bran cereal, margarine and boiling water. Stir well until margarine is melted.

Mix eggs well in batter. Stir in buttermilk.

Combine remaining 6 ingredients in separate large bowl. Add to batter. Stir just to moisten. Cover. Refrigerate for up to 1 month. To bake, fill greased muffin cups almost full. Bake in 400°F (205°C) oven for about 20 minutes until wooden pick inserted in center comes out clean. Let stand for 5 minutes before removing to rack to cool. Makes 4½ dozen muffins.

1 muffin: 151 Calories; 4 g Protein; 4.6 g Total Fat; 25 g Carbohydrate; 288 mg Sodium; 2 g Dietary Fiber

Pictured below.

Coconut Muffins

Wonderful with fresh fruit.

All-purpose flour	1¾ cups	425 mL
Granulated sugar	½ cup	125 mL
Medium coconut (see Note)	1 cup	250 mL
Baking powder	1 tbsp.	15 mL
Salt	½ tsp.	2 mL
Large egg, fork-beaten	1	1
Milk	1 cup	250 mL
Cooking oil	¼ cup	60 mL
Coconut flavoring	1 tsp.	5 mL

Measure flour, sugar, coconut, baking powder and salt into large bowl. Stir. Make a well in center.

Combine egg, milk, cooking oil and coconut flavoring in small bowl. Beat slowly to mix. Pour into well. Stir just to moisten. Fill greased muffin cups almost full. Bake in 400°F (205°C) oven for 15 to 20 minutes until golden and wooden pick inserted in center comes out clean. Let stand for 5 minutes before removing to rack to cool. Makes 12 muffins.

1 muffin: 216 Calories; 4 g Protein; 10.8 g Total Fat; 27 g Carbohydrate; 137 mg Sodium; 1 g Dietary Fiber

Pictured below.

Note: Toast coconut first on ungreased baking sheet in 350°F (175°C) oven for about 5 minutes until browned for a nice flavor change.

Center Left: Coconut Muffins, this page   Center Right: French Puffins, page 65   Bottom Left: Month Of Muffins, this page   Bottom Right: Apricot Date Loaf, page 65

French Puffins

Taste like cake doughnuts. Very tender.

All-purpose flour	2 cups	500 mL
Baking powder	2½ tsp.	12 mL
Ground nutmeg	½ tsp.	2 mL
Salt	½ tsp.	2 mL
Hard margarine (or butter), softened	¼ cup	60 mL
Granulated sugar	½ cup	125 mL
Large egg	1	1
Milk	⅔ cup	150 mL
Hard margarine (or butter), melted	3 tbsp.	50 mL
Granulated sugar	¼ cup	60 mL
Ground cinnamon	½ tsp.	2 mL

Stir first 4 ingredients in large bowl. Make a well in center.

Cream first amounts of margarine and sugar in medium bowl until smooth. Beat in egg. Add milk. Beat. Pour into well in flour mixture. Stir just to mix. Fill greased muffin cups almost full. Bake in 375°F (190°C) oven for 20 to 25 minutes until wooden pick inserted in center comes out clean. Let stand for 5 minutes before removing to rack.

Brush each hot muffin top generously with second amount of margarine. Mix second amount of sugar and cinnamon in small bowl. Dip buttered top of each muffin into sugar mixture. Makes 12 muffins.

1 muffin: 206 Calories; 3 g Protein; 7.6 g Total Fat; 31 g Carbohydrate; 209 mg Sodium; 1 g Dietary Fiber

Pictured on page 64.

Apricot Date Loaf

Perfect choice for tea. Serve lightly buttered.

Hard margarine (or butter), softened	¼ cup	60 mL
Chopped dates	½ cup	125 mL
Chopped dried apricots	½ cup	125 mL
Baking soda	1 tsp.	5 mL
Boiling water	¾ cup	175 mL
Large egg, fork-beaten	1	1
Brown sugar, packed	½ cup	125 mL
Salt	½ tsp.	2 mL
Vanilla	1 tsp.	5 mL
All-purpose flour	1 cup	250 mL
Whole wheat (or all-purpose) flour	1 cup	250 mL
Baking powder	1½ tsp.	7 mL

Combine first 5 ingredients in small bowl. Let stand until cool.

Combine egg, brown sugar, salt and vanilla in large bowl. Beat. Stir in date mixture.

Add both flours and baking powder. Stir just to moisten. Turn into greased 9 x 5 x 3 inch (22 x 12.5 x 7.5 cm) loaf pan. Bake in 350°F (175°C) oven for about 1 hour. Cool in pan for 5 minutes. Remove to rack to cool completely. Cuts into 18 slices.

1 slice: 126 Calories; 2 g Protein; 3.3 g Total Fat; 23 g Carbohydrate; 191 mg Sodium; 2 g Dietary Fiber

Pictured on page 64.

Barm Brack, below

TIME-HONORED RECIPE

Barm Brack

To make this Irish loaf, it must be planned the previous evening. You will find this a moist, different loaf. Serve sliced with butter.

Cold tea	1 cup	250 mL
Raisins	1 cup	250 mL
Cut mixed peel	½ cup	125 mL
Currants	½ cup	125 mL
Granulated sugar	1 cup	250 mL
Large egg, fork-beaten	1	1
Hard margarine (or butter), melted	¼ cup	60 mL
All-purpose flour	2 cups	500 mL
Baking powder	1 tsp.	5 mL
Baking soda	¼ tsp.	1 mL
Salt	¼ tsp.	1 mL

Combine tea, raisins, mixed peel, currants and sugar in large bowl. Cover. Let stand overnight.

Stir egg and margarine into fruit mixture.

Combine remaining 4 ingredients in small bowl. Stir. Add to fruit batter. Stir until well blended. Spoon into greased 9 x 5 x 3 inch (22 x 12.5 x 7.5 cm) loaf pan. Bake in 350°F (175°C) oven for 60 to 70 minutes. Let stand for 10 minutes before removing to rack. Cuts into 18 slices.

1 slice: 180 Calories; 2 g Protein; 3 g Total Fat; 37 g Carbohydrate; 93 mg Sodium; 1 g Dietary Fiber

Pictured above.

Brunches & Lunches

At the turn of the century, mid-morning,

afternoon teas and picnics consisted mainly of

soups and sandwiches. Sandwich fillings were very

different: lettuce, sardine, anchovy, oyster, sliced

candied ginger and sliced fruit. When we think

of brunches or lunches today, we have a

vast selection of dishes from which to choose.

These can include stratas, stir-fries and pasta salads.

However, if you prefer the more traditional, serve

Baked Pancake with Maple-Flavored Syrup,

Macaroni And Cheese, or Tuna Biscuits.

Turkey Strata

It will remind you of a hot chicken salad sandwich.

White (or brown) bread slices, with crusts, trimmed to fit	6	6
Grated medium Cheddar cheese	1 cup	250 mL
Light salad dressing (or mayonnaise)	½ cup	125 mL
Sweet pickle relish	¼ cup	60 mL
Finely chopped cooked turkey	2 cups	500 mL
White (or brown) bread slices, with crusts, trimmed to fit	6	6
Large eggs	6	6
Salt	¾ tsp.	4 mL
Pepper	⅛ tsp.	0.5 mL
Milk	2¾ cups	675 mL
Sliced almonds, toasted in 350°F (175°C) oven for 5 to 8 minutes	½ cup	125 mL

Cover bottom of greased 9 x 13 inch (22 x 33 cm) pan with first amount of bread slices.

Stir next 4 ingredients together in medium bowl. Spread over bread slices. Cover with second amount of bread slices.

Beat eggs, salt and pepper in medium bowl. Stir in milk. Pour over all. Cover. Refrigerate several hours or overnight. Cover. Bake in 350°F (175°C) oven for 45 to 50 minutes. Remove cover.

Sprinkle with almonds. Bake, uncovered, for about 15 minutes. Serves 6.

1 serving: 539 Calories; 37 g Protein; 24.6 g Total Fat; 42 g Carbohydrate; 1098 mg Sodium; 2 g Dietary Fiber

Pictured below.

CHICKEN STRATA: Substitute finely chopped cooked chicken for turkey.

Macaroni And Cheese

A mainstay of many families way back when—and still today!

Elbow macaroni	2 cups	500 mL
Chopped onion	½ cup	125 mL
Boiling water	3 qts.	3 L
Cooking oil (optional)	1 tbsp.	15 mL
Salt	2 tsp.	10 mL
Milk	1¼ cups	300 mL
All-purpose flour	3 tbsp.	50 mL
Grated medium or sharp Cheddar cheese	2 cups	500 mL
Dry mustard	1 tsp.	5 mL
Salt	½ tsp.	2 mL
Pepper	⅛ tsp.	0.5 mL
Paprika, sprinkle		

Cook macaroni and onion in boiling water, cooking oil and first amount of salt in large uncovered pot or Dutch oven for 7 to 8 minutes until macaroni is tender but firm. Drain well. Return to pot.

Gradually whisk milk into flour in medium saucepan. Stir until smooth. Heat over medium, stirring continually, until thickened. Stir in cheese, dry mustard, second amount of salt and pepper. Stir to melt cheese. Pour over macaroni mixture. Stir. Pour into ungreased shallow 2 quart (2 L) casserole.

Sprinkle with paprika. Cover. Bake in 350°F (175°C) oven for about 35 minutes until thickened and bubbling. Remove cover. Bake for 10 minutes. Serves 4.

1 serving: 514 Calories; 26 g Protein; 21.9 g Total Fat; 53 g Carbohydrate; 755 mg Sodium; 2 g Dietary Fiber

Pictured below.

Turkey Strata, above   Macaroni And Cheese, above   Turkey Sandwiches, page 69

Beacon Shrimp Omelet

This is a real breakfast or brunch treat.

Seafood Sauce:

Ketchup	3 tbsp.	50 mL
Lemon juice	1½ tsp.	7 mL
Creamed horseradish	1 tsp.	5 mL
Worcestershire sauce	¼ tsp.	1 mL

Omelet:

Hard margarine (or butter)	½ tsp.	2 mL
Large eggs, fork-beaten	2	2
Light cream cheese, softened and cut up	3 tbsp.	50 mL
Chopped green onion	2 tbsp.	30 mL
Cooked fresh baby shrimp	⅓ cup	75 mL

Seafood Sauce: Combine ketchup, lemon juice, horseradish and Worcestershire sauce in small bowl. Makes 3 tbsp. (50 mL) sauce.

Omelet: Melt margarine in 8 inch (20 cm) non-stick frying pan over medium. Pour in eggs. Cover. Cook for 1 minute. Push 1 side of egg away from edge, tipping pan so some uncooked egg flows underneath. Cover. Cook for 1 minute.

Scatter cream cheese over top. Drizzle with seafood sauce. Sprinkle with green onion and shrimp. Cover. Cook over low for 1 to 2 minutes until cheese is melted and shrimp is hot. Slide onto plate, folding one half over the other. Serves 1.

1 serving: 363 Calories; 28 g Protein; 19.8 g Total Fat; 19 g Carbohydrate; 1309 mg Sodium; 1 g Dietary Fiber

Pictured on page 67.

Turkey Sandwiches

You would never know canned turkey was used.

Turkey Filling:

Canned flaked turkey, with liquid	6½ oz.	184 g
Grated medium Cheddar cheese	½ cup	125 mL
Sweet pickle relish	2 tbsp.	30 mL
Light salad dressing (or mayonnaise)	2 tbsp.	30 mL
Finely chopped celery	2 tbsp.	30 mL
Finely chopped onion (or ½ tsp., 2 mL, powder)	2 tbsp.	30 mL
Salt, sprinkle		
Pepper, sprinkle		
Bread slices (buttered, optional)	8	8

Turkey Filling: Mix first 8 ingredients well in small bowl.

Spread ¼ of filling on each of 4 bread slices. Cover with remaining 4 bread slices. Cut diagonally into quarters. Makes 16 small sandwiches, enough to serve 4.

1 serving: 302 Calories; 18 g Protein; 11 g Total Fat; 31 g Carbohydrate; 648 mg Sodium; 1 g Dietary Fiber

Pictured on page 68.

Tuna Biscuits

Tuna Biscuits

A novel way to serve a tuna sandwich.

Tuna Filling:

Canned tuna, drained and flaked	6½ oz.	184 g
Finely diced celery	⅓ cup	75 mL
Grated carrot	⅓ cup	75 mL
Light salad dressing (or mayonnaise)	⅓ cup	75 mL
Sweet pickle relish	2 tbsp.	30 mL
Lemon juice	½ tsp.	2 mL
Salt	⅛ tsp.	0.5 mL
Pepper, sprinkle		

Biscuit Dough:

All-purpose flour	2 cups	500 mL
Baking powder	4 tsp.	20 mL
Granulated sugar	1 tsp.	5 mL
Salt	1 tsp.	5 mL
Milk	¾ cup	175 mL
Cooking oil	⅓ cup	75 mL

Tuna Filling: Combine all 8 ingredients in small bowl.

Biscuit Dough: Stir flour, baking powder, sugar and salt in medium bowl.

Add milk and cooking oil. Mix to form soft ball. Knead on lightly floured surface 8 times. Roll ½ of dough ¼ inch (6 mm) thick. Cut into 6 rounds, 4 inches (10 cm) in diameter.

Place 3 tbsp. (50 mL) filling in center of each round. Roll out second ½ of dough. Cut into 6 more circles. Dampen edge of filled rounds with water. Cover with second round. Press edges to seal. Arrange on ungreased baking sheet. Bake in 375°F (190°C) oven for 15 to 20 minutes until golden. Scraps of dough may be made into biscuits and baked as well. Makes 6 filled biscuits.

1 biscuit: 376 Calories; 13 g Protein; 17.7 g Total Fat; 41 g Carbohydrate; 775 mg Sodium; 2 g Dietary Fiber

Pictured above.

Niçoise Pasta Salad

Decorative. Serve with crusty bread for a great lunch.

Tri-colored fusilli (or other medium) pasta	8 oz.	225 g
Boiling water	2 qts.	2 L
Cooking oil (optional)	1 tbsp.	15 mL
Salt	2 tsp.	10 mL
Small head of iceberg lettuce, coarsely shredded	1	1
Small red onion, sliced paper thin and separated into rings	1	1
Canned solid tuna, drained and broken into chunks	2 × 6½ oz.	2 × 184 g
Fresh (or frozen) cooked green beans, cooled, cut or french cut	1½ cups	375 mL
Whole pitted ripe olives, halved	⅓ cup	75 mL
Dressing:		
Cooking oil	⅓ cup	75 mL
Red wine vinegar	⅓ cup	75 mL
Dried sweet basil	½ tsp.	2 mL
Salt	½ tsp.	2 mL
Pepper	¼ tsp.	1 mL
Garlic powder	¼ tsp.	1 mL
Medium tomatoes, cut into wedges	2	2
Hard-boiled eggs, quartered (or sliced)	3	3

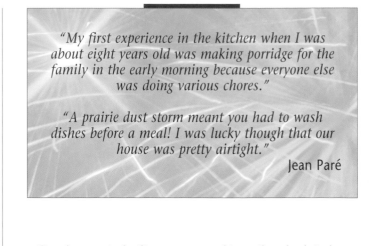

Cook pasta in boiling water, cooking oil and salt in large uncovered pot or Dutch oven for 8 to 10 minutes until tender but firm. Drain. Rinse with cold water. Drain well. Transfer to large bowl. Cool completely.

Add next 5 ingredients. Mix.

Dressing: Stir all 6 ingredients in small bowl. Pour over tuna mixture. Toss. Divide among 6 plates.

Garnish each plate with tomato and egg wedges. Serves 6.

1 serving: 397 Calories; 23 g Protein; 18.1 g Total Fat; 36 g Carbohydrate; 516 mg Sodium; 3 g Dietary Fiber

Pictured below.

Niçoise Pasta Salad

Saucy Asparagus

Baked on a tender biscuit crust. A very different presentation.

Milk	1½ cups	375 mL
All-purpose flour	3 tbsp.	50 mL
Grated medium Cheddar cheese	1 cup	250 mL
Salt	¼ tsp.	1 mL
Pepper	¼ tsp.	1 mL
Refrigerator country-style biscuits (10 per tube)	12 oz.	340 g
Canned asparagus tips, drained	12 oz.	341 mL
Sliced almonds, toasted in 350°F (175°C) oven for 5 to 8 minutes	¼ cup	60 mL

Gradually whisk milk into flour in small saucepan until smooth. Heat and stir until boiling and thickened.

Stir in cheese, salt and pepper. Heat until cheese is melted.

Press biscuits to make crust in greased 9 inch (22 cm) pie plate.

Arrange asparagus over crust. Pour sauce over asparagus. Sprinkle with almonds. Bake in 450°F (230°C) oven for about 15 minutes. Cuts into 8 wedges.

1 wedge: 236 Calories; 10 g Protein; 10.1 g Total Fat; 26 g Carbohydrate; 736 mg Sodium; 1 g Dietary Fiber

Pictured on this page.

Apple Scallop

A wonderful addition to breakfast. Double or triple the recipe for a buffet breakfast. A dollop of whipped topping finishes it nicely.

Granulated sugar	¼ cup	60 mL
All-purpose flour	1½ tbsp.	25 mL
Ground cinnamon	1 tsp.	5 mL
Medium cooking apples, (such as McIntosh), peeled and sliced	4	4
Hard margarine (or butter)	1 tbsp.	15 mL

Measure sugar, flour and cinnamon into ungreased 1½ quart (1.5 L) casserole. Stir.

Add apple. Stir well.

Dab pieces of margarine here and there. Cover. Bake in 350°F (175°C) oven for 45 to 55 minutes until tender. Serves 4.

1 serving: 164 Calories; 1 g Protein; 3.4 g Total Fat; 35 g Carbohydrate; 35 mg Sodium; 3 g Dietary Fiber

Pictured on this page.

Top: Apple Scallop, this page   Bottom: Saucy Asparagus, this page

Stir-Fry Salad

A most attractive presentation. Contains tender strips of beef.

Dressing:		
Cooking oil	¼ cup	60 mL
Brown sugar, packed	1 tbsp.	15 mL
Ground cumin	1 tsp.	5 mL
Ground coriander	1 tsp.	5 mL
Dried crushed chilies, finely crushed	1 tsp.	5 mL
Garlic powder	½ tsp.	2 mL
Lime juice	2 tbsp.	30 mL
Beef flank (or top round) steak, cut on angle across grain into very thin strips	1 lb.	454 g
Medium green pepper, slivered	1	1
Medium red pepper, slivered	1	1
Medium red onion, halved lengthwise and sliced crosswise, ¼ inch (6 mm) thick	1	1
Green jalapeño pepper, seeds and ribs removed, finely chopped	1	1
Shredded romaine lettuce	4 cups	1 L

Dressing: Combine all 6 ingredients in small cup.

Put lime juice and beef strips into medium bowl. Add 1 tbsp. (15 mL) dressing. Stir to coat well. Let stand at room temperature for 30 minutes.

Heat 1 tbsp. (15 mL) dressing in large non-stick frying pan. Add green pepper, red pepper, red onion and jalapeño pepper. Sauté until tender-crisp. Transfer vegetables and any remaining dressing into large bowl.

Add beef strips with liquid to same hot frying pan. Stir-fry for 3 to 4 minutes until desired doneness. Add to vegetables in bowl. Toss well with remaining dressing. Divide lettuce among 4 plates. Divide beef mixture over top. Serve immediately. Serves 4.

1 serving: 318 Calories; 26 g Protein; 25 g Total Fat; 11 g Carbohydrate; 85 mg Sodium; 2 g Dietary Fiber

Pictured on page 67.

Swedish Tea Ring

Sweet biscuit taste with a delicate cream cheese flavor. Very attractive. Best served warm but good either way.

Cheese Filling:

Light cream cheese, softened	4 oz.	125 g
Granulated sugar	3 tbsp.	50 mL
Vanilla	½ tsp.	2 mL

Bread:

All-purpose flour	1¾ cups	425 mL
Granulated sugar	1 tbsp.	15 mL
Baking powder	1 tbsp.	15 mL
Salt	½ tsp.	2 mL
Hard margarine (or butter)	¼ cup	60 mL
Milk	¾ cup	175 mL
Chopped glazed cherries	⅓ cup	75 mL
Raisins	¼ cup	60 mL

Glaze:

Icing (confectioner's) sugar	½ cup	125 mL
Water	1½ tsp.	7 mL
Sliced almonds, toasted in 350°F (175°C) oven for 5 to 8 minutes (optional)	¼ cup	60 mL

Cheese Filling: Beat cream cheese, sugar and vanilla in small bowl until smooth.

Bread: Measure flour, sugar, baking powder, salt and margarine into medium bowl. Cut in margarine with pastry cutter until crumbly.

Stir in milk until ball is formed. Turn out onto lightly floured surface. Knead 8 times. Roll into 8 × 16 inch (20 × 40 cm) rectangle. Spread with filling.

Sprinkle with cherries and raisins. Roll up from long side like jelly roll. Seal long edge. Place seam side down on greased baking sheet. Form into ring. Pinch ends together to seal. Using scissors, cut from outside edge toward middle, over halfway through roll at 1 inch (2.5 cm) intervals. Turn each cut section on its side. Bake in 425°F (220°C) oven for 18 to 20 minutes until golden. Cool slightly.

Glaze: Stir icing sugar and water in small bowl, adding more icing sugar or water if needed to make a barely pourable consistency. Drizzle over barely warm tea ring.

Sprinkle almonds over glaze. Cuts into 12 pieces.

1 piece: 200 Calories; 4 g Protein; 6.2 g Total Fat; 33 g Carbohydrate; 274 mg Sodium; 1 g Dietary Fiber

Pictured on page 67.

"Jam cans, Rogers® syrup pails and lard pails were used to carry school lunches in and for collecting berries. The lunches were mostly peanut butter and jam sandwiches, and fruit with cake or cookies. Sometimes there was a hard-boiled egg or a tomato."

Jean Paré

Sweet Swirl Rolls

Very decorative with a bit of red jam showing through a white glaze.

Large egg, fork-beaten	1	1
Granulated sugar	2 tbsp.	30 mL
Envelope instant yeast (1 scant tbsp., 15 mL)	1 × ¼ oz.	1 × 8 g
Warm milk	¾ cup	175 mL
Warm water	⅓ cup	75 mL
Salt	1 tsp.	5 mL
All-purpose flour	1½ cups	375 mL
All-purpose flour, approximately	2 cups	500 mL
Red jam	½ cup	125 mL

Glaze:

Icing (confectioner's) sugar	1 cup	250 mL
Milk (or water)	1 tbsp.	15 mL
Vanilla	¼ tsp.	1 mL

Combine egg, sugar and yeast in large bowl. Beat to mix. Add warm milk, warm water and salt. Mix.

Add first amount of flour. Beat well.

Stir and knead in second amount of flour until no longer sticky. Divide dough into 20 pieces. Roll each piece into 14 inch (35 cm) rope. Coil each into circle like a pinwheel on 2 greased baking sheets, pinching ends underneath to seal. Cover with tea towel. Let stand in oven with light on and door closed for about 1 hour until doubled in size.

Make indentation in center of each roll using thumb. Fill with 1 tsp. (5 mL) jam. Bake in 375°F (190°C) oven for about 15 minutes until browned. Cool.

Glaze: Stir icing sugar, milk and vanilla together in small bowl. Add more icing sugar or milk if needed to make barely pourable consistency. Drizzle over rolls. Makes 20 rolls.

1 roll: 145 Calories; 3 g Protein; 0.6 g Total Fat; 32 g Carbohydrate; 146 mg Sodium; 1 g Dietary Fiber

Pictured on page 67.

Cheese Brunch Cake

Makes two wonderful yeast coffee cakes.
Serve one warm and freeze the other.

Milk	½ cup	125 mL
Hard margarine (or butter)	6 tbsp.	100 mL
Granulated sugar	⅓ cup	75 mL
Salt	¾ tsp.	4 mL
Envelope instant yeast (1 scant tbsp., 15 mL)	1 × ¼ oz.	1 × 8 g
All-purpose flour	½ cup	125 mL
Large eggs, room temperature	3	3
Golden raisins	½ cup	125 mL
Grated lemon peel	2 tsp.	10 mL
All-purpose flour, approximately	3¼ cups	810 mL
Cheese Filling:		
Light cream cheese	8 oz.	250 g
Dry curd cottage cheese	½ cup	125 mL
Granulated sugar	¼ cup	60 mL
Large egg	1	1
Grated lemon peel	1 tsp.	5 mL
Vanilla	1 tsp.	5 mL
Ground cinnamon	¼ tsp.	1 mL
Crumb Topping:		
All-purpose flour	¼ cup	60 mL
Granulated sugar	¼ cup	60 mL
Finely chopped nuts	⅓ cup	75 mL
Ground cinnamon	¼ tsp.	1 mL
Hard margarine (or butter), softened	¼ cup	60 mL

Combine first 4 ingredients in small saucepan. Heat until margarine is melted. Pour into large bowl. Cool slightly until still very warm but not hot.

Combine yeast and first amount of flour in small bowl. Whisk into milk mixture until smooth and yeast is dissolved.

Beat eggs in medium bowl until frothy. Stir into yeast mixture. Add raisins and first amount of lemon peel. Stir.

Knead in second amount of flour until dough is elastic and no longer sticky. Place in large greased bowl, turning once to grease top. Cover with tea towel. Let stand in oven with light on and door closed for 1 hour. Punch down dough. Divide into 4 portions. Press 1 portion in greased 8 or 9 inch (20 or 22 cm) round cake pan, covering bottom and 1 inch (2.5 cm) up sides. Repeat with second portion in second cake pan. Set remaining 2 portions aside.

Cheese Filling: Beat all 7 ingredients together well in medium bowl until fairly smooth. Spread ½ over each crust in pans. Roll remaining 2 portions of dough into circles large enough to fit tops. Place over cheese filling. Pinch edges of crusts together to seal.

Crumb Topping: Mix all 5 ingredients in small bowl until crumbly. Sprinkle ½ over each coffee cake. Cover with tea towel. Let stand in oven with light on and door closed for 1 hour until doubled in size. Bake in 350°F (175°C) oven for about 30 minutes until golden. Remove from pans to racks to cool for 30 minutes before serving. Each cake cuts into 6 wedges, for a total of 12 wedges.

1 wedge: 430 Calories; 11 g Protein; 18 g Total Fat; 56 g Carbohydrate; 515 mg Sodium; 2 g Dietary Fiber

Pictured below.

Top Left: Maple-Flavored Syrup, page 74
Top Right: Cheese Brunch Cake, this page
Center Left: Marshmallow Puffs, page 74
Bottom Right: Baked Pancake, page 74

Granola Bars

Soft and chewy. Perfect for breakfast on the go or school lunches.

Quick-cooking rolled oats (not instant)	3 cups	750 mL
Brown sugar, packed	¼ cup	60 mL
Flake coconut	¼ cup	60 mL
Salt	½ tsp.	2 mL
Wheat germ	¼ cup	60 mL
Hard margarine (or butter)	½ cup	125 mL
Corn syrup	⅓ cup	75 mL
Liquid honey	⅓ cup	75 mL
Vanilla	1 tsp.	5 mL
Semisweet chocolate chips	½ cup	125 mL

Stir rolled oats, brown sugar, coconut, salt and wheat germ in large bowl. Cut in margarine until mixture is crumbly and no large pieces remain.

Add corn syrup, honey and vanilla. Stir well.

Add chocolate chips. Work in. Press firmly in greased 9 x 9 inch (22 x 22 cm) pan. Bake in 350°F (175°C) oven for 30 to 40 minutes until golden. Chill for several hours or overnight. Cuts into 24 bars.

1 bar: 159 Calories; 2 g Protein; 7.5 g Total Fat; 22 g Carbohydrate; 111 mg Sodium; 2 g Dietary Fiber

Pictured on page 66.

Baked Pancake

Feed a morning grouch this Yorkshire Pudding-like pancake and watch a transformation before your eyes. Serve with warm Maple-Flavored Syrup, below.

Large eggs	3	3
All-purpose flour	½ cup	125 mL
Milk	½ cup	125 mL
Salt	¼ tsp.	1 mL
Hard margarine (or butter), melted	2 tbsp.	30 mL

Beat all 5 ingredients together in small bowl or process in blender. Pour into greased 8 x 8 inch (20 x 20 cm) pan. Bake in 400°F (205°C) oven for about 20 minutes until lightly browned. Cuts into 4 pieces.

1 piece: 177 Calories; 8 g Protein; 9.6 g Total Fat; 15 g Carbohydrate; 296 mg Sodium; 1 g Dietary Fiber

Pictured on page 73.

Marshmallow Puffs

It's magic! The marshmallow disappears leaving delicious hollow buns. Serve warm with a fruit salad for a special brunch. A fun bun.

Refrigerator crescent-style rolls (8 per tube)	2 x 8½ oz.	2 x 235 g
Hard margarine (or butter), melted	1 tbsp.	15 mL
Finely chopped pecans (or walnuts)	3 tbsp.	50 mL
Large marshmallows	16	16
Granulated sugar	2 tbsp.	30 mL
Ground cinnamon	½ tsp.	2 mL

Separate crescent rolls into 16 triangles.

Put margarine and pecans into 2 small dishes. Dip 1 end of each marshmallow into margarine, then into pecans. Place each marshmallow on each triangle of dough.

Combine sugar and cinnamon in small cup. Sprinkle ¼ tsp. (1 mL) over each marshmallow. Pinch dough around marshmallow to seal. Gently roll each into ball. Set in greased muffin cup. Bake in 375°F (190°C) oven for 10 to 15 minutes until golden. Makes 16 marshmallow puffs.

1 puff: 92 Calories; 1 g Protein; 4 g Total Fat; 13 g Carbohydrate; 157 mg Sodium; trace Dietary Fiber

Pictured on page 73.

Maple-Flavored Syrup

This is always close by on the shelf to make at a moment's notice. Serve with Baked Pancake, above, regular pancakes, waffles or French toast.

Brown sugar, packed	2 cups	500 mL
Water	1 cup	250 mL
Maple flavoring	1 tsp.	5 mL

Combine brown sugar and water in small saucepan. Bring to a boil. Boil for 2 to 3 minutes. Remove from heat.

Add maple flavoring. Makes 2 cups (500 mL) syrup.

2 tbsp. (30 mL) syrup: 104 Calories; 0 g Protein; 0 g Total Fat; 27 g Carbohydrate; 8 mg Sodium; trace Dietary Fiber

Pictured on page 73.

"Real maple syrup in the 1950s was not considered an extravagant ingredient and was not expensive. Today, it's quite expensive and a real treat."

Jean Paré

Cakes

Cakes

Fruit cakes, pound cakes, sponge cakes and jelly rolls date way back. Angel food cake was quite popular in the 1880s and chocolate marble cakes became the rage after the American Civil War in 1865. The Great War created the necessity of making cakes with less butter, sugar and eggs; applesauce cake was the answer. Cake baking remained strong, even throughout the Great Depression of the 1930s, but then came the rationing of butter and sugar because of World War II. Fewer ingredients meant cakes were able to be made in one bowl, a preference which eventually led to the development of the commercial cake mix in 1947. The first cake mixes called only for the addition of water—a true cake mix! During the 1990s, when an appreciation of fitness and health became fashionable, non-fat and low-fat cake recipes that used applesauce or other puréed fruits as a substitute for fat, found their market. Likewise, using egg whites or egg substitute instead of the whole egg, also helped to reduce cholesterol and fat. Cakes have evolved and changed over time, but their popularity remains steadfast. We offer a variety of delicious recipes—both old and new—in this section.

Orange Cake, this page, with Chocolate Orange Icing, this page

Orange Cake

Orange both in appearance and in flavor. For the final touch, ice with Chocolate Orange Icing, below.

All-purpose flour	2¼ cups	560 mL
Baking powder	4 tsp.	20 mL
Salt	½ tsp.	2 mL
Hard margarine (or butter), softened	½ cup	125 mL
Granulated sugar	1½ cups	375 mL
Grated peel of 1 medium orange		
Large eggs	2	2
Frozen concentrated orange juice, thawed	⅓ cup	75 mL
Milk	1 cup	250 mL

Stir flour, baking powder and salt in medium bowl.

Cream margarine and sugar together in large bowl. Mix in orange peel. Beat in eggs, 1 at a time. Add concentrated orange juice. Mix.

Add flour mixture in 3 parts alternately with milk in 2 parts, beginning and ending with flour mixture. Turn into 2 greased 8 inch (20 cm) round cake pans. Bake in 350°F (175°C) oven for about 35 minutes until wooden pick inserted in center comes out clean. Let stand for 10 minutes before removing to rack to cool. Cuts into 16 pieces.

1 piece (without icing): 227 Calories; 3 g Protein; 7.1 g Total Fat; 38 g Carbohydrate; 177 mg Sodium; 1 g Dietary Fiber

Pictured on page 75 and on back cover.

Chocolate Orange Icing

Chocolate and orange flavors are meant to be together. Use to ice Orange Cake, above.

Hard margarine (or butter), softened	6 tbsp.	100 mL
Icing (confectioner's) sugar	2½ cups	625 mL
Cocoa	½ cup	125 mL
Frozen concentrated orange juice, thawed	2 tbsp.	30 mL

Combine all 4 ingredients in medium bowl. Beat on low to moisten. Beat on high to blend well. Add more icing sugar or liquid as needed to make proper spreading consistency. Makes about 2 cups (500 mL) icing.

2 tbsp. (30 mL) icing: 117 Calories; 1 g Protein; 4.5 g Total Fat; 21 g Carbohydrate; 50 mg Sodium; 1 g Dietary Fiber

Pictured on page 75 and on back cover.

Fruit Cake

(old recipe)

This recipe is from my Grandma Elford's cookbook. I wonder how this would turn out at today's prices?

Fruit Cake

1½ cups sugar
4 eggs, well beaten
½ cup coffee
½ cup chopped suet
1 teaspoon cinnamon
½ teaspoon allspice

1 cup butter
½ cup molasses
3 cups flour
1 teaspoon soda
½ teaspoon cloves
2 cups raisins

10 cents' worth of citron peel; 10 cents' worth of almond meats; 5 cents' worth of lemon and orange peel together; chop these very fine or put through a meat grinder.

Fruit Cake

Fruit Cake

(new recipe)

In the past, it was common to serve fruit cake at weddings. Guests would take their piece home and place it under their pillow for sweet dreams.

Raisins	2 cups	500 mL
Chopped citron	1 cup	250 mL
Slivered almonds, toasted in 350°F (175°C) oven for 5 to 8 minutes	1 cup	250 mL
Holiday fruit mix, with peel	1 cup	250 mL
Glazed cherries, chopped	¼ cup	60 mL
All-purpose flour	⅓ cup	75 mL
Hard margarine (or butter), softened	1 cup	250 mL
Granulated sugar	1½ cups	375 mL
Large eggs	4	4
Fancy molasses	½ cup	125 mL
Prepared coffee	½ cup	125 mL
All-purpose flour	3 cups	750 mL
Ground cinnamon	1 tsp.	5 mL
Ground allspice	½ tsp.	2 mL
Ground cloves	½ tsp.	2 mL
Baking soda	1 tsp.	5 mL

Measure first 6 ingredients into medium bowl. Toss well to coat with flour.

Cream margarine and sugar together in large bowl. Beat in eggs, 1 at a time. Mix in molasses and prepared coffee.

Stir remaining 5 ingredients together in separate medium bowl. Add to coffee mixture. Stir just to moisten. Add fruit mixture. Mix. Line 2 greased 9 x 5 x 3 inch (22 x 12.5 x 7.5 cm) loaf pans with greased brown paper. Divide dough between pans. Place separate pan, with about 1 inch (2.5 cm) water, on bottom rack in oven. Bake cakes on center rack in 275°F (140°C) oven for about 2 hours 50 minutes until wooden pick inserted in center comes out clean. Let stand for 10 minutes before removing to rack to cool. Makes 2 cakes. Each cake cuts into 20 pieces, for a total of 40 pieces.

1 piece: 422 Calories; 6 g Protein; 14.6 g Total Fat; 70 g Carbohydrate; 233 mg Sodium; 2 g Dietary Fiber

Pictured on this page.

Boiled Raisin Cake

Moist with raisins and spices. Caramel icing tops it off.

Raisins	1½ cups	375 mL
Water	2 cups	500 mL
All-purpose flour	1¾ cups	425 mL
Baking powder	1½ tsp.	7 mL
Baking soda	½ tsp.	2 mL
Ground cinnamon	¾ tsp.	4 mL
Ground nutmeg	½ tsp.	2 mL
Salt	½ tsp.	2 mL
Hard margarine (or butter), softened	½ cup	125 mL
Brown sugar, packed	1 cup	250 mL
Large egg, fork-beaten	1	1
Vanilla	1 tsp.	5 mL

Caramel Icing, page 172

Combine raisins and water in small saucepan. Boil gently for about 6 minutes. Drain and reserve ⅔ cup (150 mL) juice.

Stir next 6 ingredients in medium bowl.

Cream margarine, brown sugar, egg and vanilla together well in large bowl.

Add flour mixture in 3 parts and reserved juice in 2 parts, beginning and ending with flour mixture, stirring just to blend. Turn into greased 9 x 9 inch (22 x 22 cm) pan. Bake in 350°F (175°C) oven for about 40 minutes until wooden pick inserted in center comes out clean.

Ice with Caramel Icing. Cuts into 12 pieces.

1 piece with icing: 415 Calories; 3 g Protein; 13 g Total Fat; 74 g Carbohydrate; 335 mg Sodium; 1 g Dietary Fiber

Pictured below.

Boiled Raisin Cake

Piña Colada Cake

This PEEN-yah Koh-LAH-duh layer cake is nice and high with a light and fluffy icing.

White cake mix (2 layer size)	1	1
Instant vanilla pudding powder (4 serving size)	1	1
Water	⅔ cup	150 mL
White (or light) rum	⅓ cup	75 mL
Cooking oil	½ cup	125 mL
Large eggs	4	4
Coconut flavoring (optional)	1 tsp.	5 mL
Long thread coconut, toasted in 350°F (175°C) oven, stirring often, for 5 to 8 minutes	½ cup	125 mL
Pineapple Icing:		
Icing (confectioner's) sugar	½ cup	125 mL
Canned crushed pineapple, with juice	8 oz.	225 mL
Instant vanilla pudding powder (4 serving size)	1	1
White (or light) rum	1 tsp.	5 mL
Envelope dessert topping (not prepared)	1	1
Milk	⅓ cup	75 mL
Long thread coconut, toasted in 350°F (175°C) oven, stirring often, for 5 to 8 minutes, for garnish	2 tbsp.	30 mL

Combine first 7 ingredients in medium bowl. Beat on low until moistened. Beat on medium for about 2 minutes until smooth.

Stir in coconut. Turn into greased 9 x 13 inch (22 x 33 cm) pan. Bake in 350°F (175°C) oven for 35 to 45 minutes until wooden pick inserted in center comes out clean. Cool.

Pineapple Icing: Mix first 4 ingredients in small bowl. Let stand for 5 minutes.

Beat dessert topping with milk until stiff. Fold into pineapple mixture. Ice cake.

Sprinkle with coconut. Cuts into 18 pieces.

1 piece (with icing): 305 Calories; 3 g Protein; 13.6 g Total Fat; 41 g Carbohydrate; 160 mg Sodium; 1 g Dietary Fiber

Pictured on page 84.

Note: For a layer cake, turn into 2 greased 8 inch (20 cm) round cake pans. Bake for 30 to 35 minutes.

Pineapple Nut Coffee Cake

Rather a solid texture. Makes a nice coffee cake.
Garnish each slice with whipped cream.

All-purpose flour	2½ cups	625 mL
Baking powder	1½ tsp.	7 mL
Salt	½ tsp.	2 mL
Finely chopped walnuts (or pecans)	1 cup	250 mL
Finely chopped candied pineapple	¾ cup	175 mL
Hard margarine (or butter), softened	1 cup	250 mL
Granulated sugar	1 cup	250 mL
Large eggs	5	5
Crushed pineapple, with juice	¾ cup	175 mL
Brandy flavoring	2 tsp.	10 mL

Stir first 5 ingredients in large bowl. Make a well in center.

Cream margarine and sugar together in medium bowl. Beat in eggs, 1 at a time. Stir in pineapple with juice and brandy flavoring. Add to well. Stir just to moisten. Turn into greased 10 inch (25 cm) angel food tube pan. Bake in 275°F (140°C) oven for 2 hours until wooden pick inserted in center comes out clean. Let stand for 10 minutes before removing to rack to cool. Cuts into 24 pieces.

1 piece: 232 Calories; 4 g Protein; 12.8 g Total Fat; 27 g Carbohydrate; 168 mg Sodium; 1 g Dietary Fiber

Pictured on this page.

Lemon Rum Cake

A touch of the Caribbean.

Lemon cake mix (2 layer size)	1	1
Large eggs	4	4
Cooking oil	½ cup	125 mL
Milk	½ cup	125 mL
Grated peel of 1 medium lemon		
Dark rum	½ cup	125 mL
Glaze:		
Icing (confectioner's) sugar	1 cup	250 mL
Lemon juice	1 tbsp.	15 mL
Dark rum	1½ tsp.	7 mL

Combine first 6 ingredients in medium bowl. Beat on low to moisten. Beat on medium for about 2 minutes until smooth. Turn into greased 12 cup (2.7 L) bundt pan. Bake in 350°F (175°C) oven for about 1 hour until wooden pick inserted in center comes out clean. Let stand for 20 minutes. Invert onto plate or rack to cool.

Glaze: Mix icing sugar, lemon juice and rum in small bowl. Add a bit more icing sugar or lemon juice if needed to make a barely pourable consistency. Drizzle over cake. Cuts into 16 pieces.

1 piece: 273 Calories; 3 g Protein; 12.7 g Total Fat; 33 g Carbohydrate; 150 mg Sodium; trace Dietary Fiber

Pictured on this page.

Top: Lemon Rum Cake, this page
Center: Pineapple Nut Coffee Cake, this page
Bottom: Sour Cream Cake, below

Sour Cream Cake

This was one of the regulars on farms many years ago.
Cream was plentiful and easy to bake with. A light tasty cake.

Cake flour (sift before measuring)	1½ cups	375 mL
Baking powder	1½ tsp.	7 mL
Baking soda	¼ tsp.	1 mL
Salt	¼ tsp.	1 mL
Large eggs (room temperature)	2	2
Granulated sugar	¾ cup	175 mL
Vanilla	1 tsp.	5 mL
Sour cream (not light or low fat)	⅔ cup	150 mL

Sift cake flour, baking powder, baking soda and salt 2 times on large plate or waxed paper.

Beat eggs in medium bowl until light in color, very thick and increased in volume. This will take about 5 minutes. Gradually add sugar, 2 tbsp. (30 mL) at a time, beating well after each addition. Add vanilla. Stir.

Add flour mixture alternately in 3 parts with sour cream in 2 parts, beginning and ending with flour mixture. Turn into greased and floured 8 x 8 inch (20 x 20 cm) pan. Bake in 350°F (175°C) oven for 30 to 35 minutes until golden and wooden pick inserted in center comes out clean. Cuts into 12 pieces.

1 piece: 137 Calories; 3 g Protein; 2.8 g Total Fat; 25 g Carbohydrate; 104 mg Sodium; trace Dietary Fiber

Pictured above.

Chocolate Date Cake

A cook's choice—a cake you don't need to ice.

Boiling water	1¼ cups	300 mL
Chopped dates	2 cups	500 mL
Hard margarine (or butter), softened	¾ cup	175 mL
Granulated sugar	1 cup	250 mL
Large eggs	2	2
Vanilla	1 tsp.	5 mL
All-purpose flour	2 cups	500 mL
Cocoa	1 tbsp.	15 mL
Baking soda	1 tsp.	5 mL
Salt	½ tsp.	2 mL
Semisweet chocolate chips	½ cup	125 mL
Chopped walnuts (or pecans)	½ cup	125 mL

Pour boiling water over dates in small bowl. Let stand until cool.

Cream margarine and sugar together in large bowl. Beat in eggs, 1 at a time. Add vanilla. Add date mixture. Stir.

Add flour, cocoa, baking soda and salt. Mix. Turn into greased 9 x 13 inch (22 x 33 cm) pan.

Sprinkle with chocolate chips and walnuts. Bake in 350°F (175°C) oven for about 40 minutes. Cuts into 24 pieces.

1 piece: 208 Calories; 3 g Protein; 9.8 g Total Fat; 30 g Carbohydrate; 192 mg Sodium; 2 g Dietary Fiber

Pictured below.

Chocolate Date Cake

Dark Chocolate Cake

A very light texture to this delicious cake.
Ice with Chocolate Mocha Icing, below.

Cooking oil	½ cup	125 mL
Granulated sugar	¾ cup	175 mL
Brown sugar, packed	1 cup	250 mL
Large eggs	2	2
Vanilla	1 tsp.	5 mL
Buttermilk (or reconstituted from powder)	1 cup	250 mL
Strong prepared coffee	1 cup	250 mL
All-purpose flour	2 cups	500 mL
Cocoa (sifted if lumpy)	¾ cup	175 mL
Baking soda	2 tsp.	10 mL
Baking powder	1 tsp.	5 mL
Salt	1 tsp.	5 mL

Beat cooking oil and both sugars in large bowl. Beat in eggs, 1 at a time. Add vanilla. Mix.

Beat in buttermilk and prepared coffee.

Add remaining 5 ingredients. Beat until smooth. Batter will be thin. Pour into greased 9 x 13 inch (22 x 33 cm) pan. Bake in 350°F (175°C) oven for about 45 minutes until wooden pick inserted in center comes out clean. Cool. Cuts into 18 pieces.

1 piece (without icing): 214 Calories; 3 g Protein; 7.5 g Total Fat; 35 g Carbohydrate; 331 mg Sodium; 2 g Dietary Fiber

Pictured on page 84.

Variation: For a layer cake, turn into 2 greased, 8 inch (20 cm) round cake pans. Bake for 30 to 35 minutes.

Chocolate Mocha Icing

A wonderful blend of coffee and chocolate.
Use to ice Dark Chocolate Cake, above.

Icing (confectioner's) sugar	3 cups	750 mL
Hard margarine (or butter), softened	½ cup	125 mL
Cocoa	¼ cup	60 mL
Vanilla	2 tsp.	10 mL
Strong prepared coffee	¼ cup	60 mL

Measure all 5 ingredients into medium bowl. Beat on low to moisten. Beat on medium until smooth and creamy. Add more icing sugar or prepared coffee if needed to make proper spreading consistency. Makes 1½ cups (375 mL) icing.

2 tbsp. (30 mL) icing: 189 Calories; 1 g Protein; 8 g Total Fat; 31 g Carbohydrate; 92 mg Sodium; 1 g Dietary Fiber

Pictured on page 84.

Mock Angel Cake

(old recipe)

This is a recipe from my great-great-Aunt Frank (Francis). No temperature, no time given - but I bet it always turned out delicious!

Mock Angel Cake   FRM: Aunt Frank

1 cup   Flour   1 cup   Sugar
2 tsps   Baking Powder   Pinch of Salt

Put all into sifter, sift together 4 times; add 1 cup boiling milk; stir until smooth; lastly fold well beaten whites of 2 eggs; fold carefully until whites are evenly folded in batter; do not grease tin or flavor cake; ice to please

Mock Angel Cake

(new recipe)

This recipe has an extra half recipe added to take advantage of the larger modern angel food tube pan. If you have the smaller eight inch (20 cm) angel food tube pan, you can use the original recipe, this page.

All-purpose flour	1½ cups	375 mL
Granulated sugar	1½ cups	375 mL
Baking powder	1 tbsp.	15 mL
Salt	¼ tsp.	1 mL
Milk	1½ cups	375 mL
Egg whites (large), room temperature	3	3

Measure first 4 ingredients into flour sifter. Sift onto large plate or waxed paper. Sift 3 more times, sifting into large bowl for 4th sifting.

Heat milk in small saucepan until just boiling. Remove from heat immediately. Stir into flour mixture until smooth.

Beat egg whites in medium bowl until stiff. Fold into batter until no streaks remain. Turn into ungreased 10 inch (25 cm) angel food tube pan. Bake in 350°F (175°C) oven for about 45 minutes until golden. Invert pan onto rack to cool. Remove cake from pan when completely cooled. Cuts into 16 pieces.

1 piece: 135 Calories; 3 g Protein; 0.4 g Total Fat; 31 g Carbohydrate; 68 mg Sodium; trace Dietary Fiber

Pictured below.

Mock Angel Cake

Top: Coffee-Group Cake, this page
Bottom: Tomato Soup Cake, below

TIME-HONORED RECIPE

Tomato Soup Cake

An old family favorite without nuts or raisins. Cake is quite moist. Ice with your favorite chocolate icing or garnish with whipped topping and chopped walnuts.

Hard margarine (or butter)	1/2 cup	125 mL
Granulated sugar	1 cup	250 mL
Large egg	1	1
All-purpose flour	1 1/2 cups	375 mL
Ground cinnamon	1/2 tsp.	2 mL
Ground nutmeg	1/2 tsp.	2 mL
Ground cloves	1/2 tsp.	2 mL
Salt	1/2 tsp.	2 mL
Raisins (optional)	1 cup	250 mL
Chopped walnuts (optional)	3/4 cup	175 mL
Baking soda	1 tsp.	5 mL
Hot water	2 tsp.	10 mL
Condensed tomato soup	10 oz.	284 mL

Cream margarine and sugar together in large bowl. Add egg. Beat well.

Measure flour, cinnamon, nutmeg, cloves, salt, raisins and walnuts into small bowl. Mix thoroughly.

Combine baking soda and hot water in small cup. Mix well. Stir into tomato soup in small bowl. Add tomato soup mixture to sugar mixture in 2 parts alternately with flour mixture in 3 parts, beginning and ending with flour mixture. Turn into greased 9 x 13 inch (22 x 33 cm) pan. Bake in 325°F (160°C) oven for 35 to 45 minutes until wooden pick inserted in center comes out clean. Cool. Cuts into 18 pieces.

1 piece: 150 Calories; 2 g Protein; 6.1 g Total Fat; 22 g Carbohydrate; 336 mg Sodium;
   1 g Dietary Fiber

Pictured above.

Coffee-Group Cake

Serve this warm for rave reviews.
Orange-flavored with a crunchy topping. Scrumptious!

Boiling water	1 1/4 cups	300 mL
Quick-cooking rolled oats (not instant)	1 cup	250 mL
All-purpose flour	1 3/4 cups	425 mL
Baking powder	1 tsp.	5 mL
Baking soda	1 tsp.	5 mL
Salt	1/2 tsp.	2 mL
Ground cinnamon	1/2 tsp.	2 mL
Hard margarine (or butter), softened	1/2 cup	125 mL
Granulated sugar	1 cup	250 mL
Brown sugar, packed	1/2 cup	125 mL
Large eggs	2	2
Vanilla	1 tsp.	5 mL
Frozen concentrated orange juice, thawed	1/4 cup	60 mL
Coconut Topping:		
Hard margarine (or butter)	1/4 cup	60 mL
Brown sugar, packed	1/2 cup	125 mL
Frozen concentrated orange juice	2 tbsp.	30 mL
Flake coconut	1 cup	250 mL
Chopped walnuts	1/2 cup	125 mL

Pour boiling water over rolled oats in small bowl. Set aside.

Stir next 5 ingredients in separate small bowl.

Cream margarine and both sugars together in large bowl. Beat in eggs, 1 at a time. Add vanilla and concentrated orange juice. Mix.

Add rolled oat mixture in 2 parts alternately with flour mixture in 3 parts, beginning and ending with flour mixture. Turn into greased 9 x 13 inch (22 x 33 cm) pan. Bake in 350°F (175°C) oven for about 40 minutes until wooden pick inserted in center comes out clean.

Coconut Topping: Measure margarine, brown sugar and concentrated orange juice into small saucepan. Heat and stir until boiling. Boil for 1 minute.

Add coconut and walnuts. Stir. Spoon over hot cake. Return to oven. Broil until topping is golden. Cuts into 16 pieces.

1 piece: 348 Calories; 4 g Protein; 16.7 g Total Fat; 47 g Carbohydrate; 295 mg Sodium;
   2 g Dietary Fiber

Pictured on this page.

Queen Cakes

(old recipe)

A turn-of-the-century recipe from a good friend's aunt who emigrated from England to Canada. Note that everything is weighed—the British method of measurements.

Queen Cakes

½ lb. fine flour, ¼ lb. butter, ¼ lb. castor sugar, ¼ lb. currants, grated rind of ½ lemon, 3 eggs

Beat butter and sugar to a cream, sift in the flour and strain in the eggs by degrees, beating the mixture well. Add currants and flavoring. Beat for 10 minutes. Bake in small greased tins. ¼ hour.

Dainty Queen Cakes

Dainty Queen Cakes

(new recipe)

Margarine was unknown at the time of the original recipe. We've made the switch to the less expensive margarine. Cherries have been added for color.

Hard margarine (or butter), softened	½ cup	125 mL
Granulated sugar	½ cup	125 mL
Large eggs	3	3
Milk	¼ cup	60 mL
Grated lemon peel	1 tsp.	5 mL
Vanilla	1 tsp.	5 mL
All-purpose flour	1¾ cups	425 mL
Baking powder	1 tsp.	5 mL
Salt	½ tsp.	2 mL
Currants	⅓ cup	75 mL
Chopped glazed cherries	½ cup	125 mL

Cream margarine and sugar together in large bowl. Beat in eggs, 1 at a time. Add milk, lemon peel and vanilla. Mix.

Stir in flour, baking powder, salt, currants and cherries. Divide batter among 24 greased mini muffin cups. Bake in 375°F (190°C) oven for 12 to 15 minutes until wooden pick inserted in center comes out clean. Let stand for 5 minutes before turning out onto rack to cool. Makes 24 small cakes.

1 cake: 119 Calories; 2 g Protein; 4.8 g Total Fat; 17 g Carbohydrate; 115 mg Sodium; trace Dietary Fiber

Pictured on this page.

Red Velvet Cake

This red cake was all the rage at one time.
Tastes like a white cake. Three layers look impressive.

All-purpose flour	2½ cups	625 mL
Cocoa	1 tsp.	5 mL
Salt	1 tsp.	5 mL
Hard margarine (or butter), softened	½ cup	125 mL
Granulated sugar	1½ cups	375 mL
Large eggs	2	2
Red food coloring	2 oz.	56 mL
Vanilla	1 tsp.	5 mL
Buttermilk (or reconstituted from powder)	1 cup	250 mL
Baking soda	1 tsp.	5 mL
White vinegar	1 tsp.	5 mL
Icing:		
Milk	2 cups	500 mL
All-purpose flour	¼ cup	60 mL
Hard margarine (or butter), softened	2 cups	500 mL
Granulated sugar	2 cups	500 mL
Vanilla	2 tsp.	10 mL

Stir flour, cocoa and salt in medium bowl.

Cream margarine and sugar together in large bowl. Beat in eggs, 1 at a time. Add food coloring and vanilla. Add flour mixture alternately with buttermilk, beginning and ending with flour mixture.

Mix baking soda into vinegar in small cup. Add to batter. Stir to mix. Divide among 3 greased 9 inch (22 cm) round cake pans. Bake in 350°F (175°C) oven for 25 to 30 minutes until wooden pick inserted in center comes out clean. Let stand for 10 minutes before turning out onto racks to cool. Cut into 3 horizontal layers.

Icing: Gradually whisk milk into flour in small saucepan until smooth. Heat and stir until boiling and thickened.

Beat margarine on high. Gradually add sugar until completely dissolved. Add vanilla and milk mixture. Beat on high until light and fluffy. Fill and ice cake. Cuts into 16 pieces.

1 piece (with icing): 565 Calories; 5 g Protein; 32 g Total Fat; 66 g Carbohydrate; 655 mg Sodium; 1 g Dietary Fiber

Pictured on page 85.

Note: 2 x 1 oz. (2 x 28 g) bottles of red food coloring equals ¼ cup (60 mL). If you prefer to use only 1 bottle, it equals 2 tbsp. (30 mL).

1. Piña Colada Cake, page 78
2. Syrup Cake, page 88
3. Red Velvet Cake, above
4. Dark Chocolate Cake with Chocolate Mocha Icing, page 80

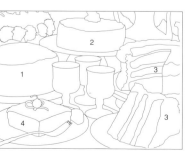

Top: Friendship Cake, this page   Bottom: Brown Sugar Pound Cake, below

TIME-HONORED RECIPE

Brown Sugar Pound Cake

This is it— that special cake from the past—before we started counting calories and fat grams! I found this in Great Grandma's cookbook. Absolutely incredible taste. A large nutty, moist cake. Garnish with whipped topping.

All-purpose flour	3 cups	750 mL
Baking powder	½ tsp.	2 mL
Salt	½ tsp.	2 mL
Butter (or hard margarine), softened (butter is best)	1½ cups	375 mL
Brown sugar, packed	4 cups	1 L
Large eggs	5	5
Vanilla	1 tsp.	5 mL
Maple flavoring	½ tsp.	2 mL
Milk	1 cup	250 mL
Finely chopped pecans (or walnuts)	1 cup	250 mL

Measure flour, baking powder and salt into medium bowl. Stir.

Cream butter in large bowl until fluffy. Gradually beat in brown sugar. Add eggs, 1 at a time, beating well after each addition. Mix in vanilla and maple flavoring.

Add flour mixture in 3 parts alternately with milk in 2 parts, beginning and ending with flour mixture. Fold in pecans. Turn into greased and floured 10 inch (25 cm) angel food tube pan. Bake in 325°F (160°C) oven for 1¼ to 1½ hours until wooden pick inserted in center comes out clean. Let stand for 10 minutes before turning out onto rack to cool. Cuts into 20 pieces.

1 piece: 443 Calories; 5 g Protein; 20.5 g Total Fat; 62 g Carbohydrate; 277 mg Sodium; 1 g Dietary Fiber

Pictured above.

Friendship Cake

Remember the one that took three weeks for the starter and 30 days to brandy the fruit? This is a much quicker and cheaper version.

Instant Starter:

Prepared orange (or pineapple or grapefruit) juice	¾ cup	175 mL
Granulated sugar	2 cups	500 mL
Canned sliced peaches, with juice, cut up	3 x 14 oz.	3 x 398 mL
Canned pineapple chunks, with juice, cut up	19 oz.	540 mL
Maraschino cherries, drained and halved (or quartered)	2 cups	500 mL

Instant Starter: Combine all 5 ingredients in large plastic ice cream pail or glass container. Stir. Let stand at room temperature overnight. Next day, drain fruit. Reserve juice to give to friends to use instead of orange juice in the starter. Use juice within a few days.

Cake:

Fruit from above, well drained		
Yellow (or white) cake mixes (2 layer size, each)	2	2
Large eggs, fork-beaten	16	16
Cooking oil	1½ cups	375 mL
Yellow (or white) cake mixes (2 layer size, each)	2	2
All-purpose flour	1 cup	250 mL
Chopped nuts	4 cups	1 L

Cake: Put drained fruit and first 2 cake mixes into large bowl. Toss to coat fruit. Set aside.

Combine eggs, cooking oil, remaining 2 cake mixes and flour in separate large bowl. Beat on high for about 2 minutes until smooth.

Add nuts and fruit mixture. Stir. Divide batter among 6 greased 9 x 5 x 3 inch (22 x 12.5 x 7.5 cm) loaf pans. Bake in 350°F (175°C) oven for 1 to 1¼ hours until wooden pick inserted in center comes out clean. Let stand for 10 minutes before turning out onto racks to cool completely. Makes 6 cakes. Each cake cuts into 16 pieces, for total of 96 pieces.

1 piece: 207 Calories; 3 g Protein; 10.6 g Total Fat; 26 g Carbohydrate; 98 mg Sodium; 1 g Dietary Fiber

Pictured on this page.

Sweet Cream Sponge Cake

(old recipe)

This recipe is from an old church cookbook. The amount of cream would probably vary according to the size of teacup used. That would mean the amount of flour would vary. No time or temperature given.

Sweet Cream Sponge Cake

2 eggs broken into tea cup; fill the cup with sweet cream and beat until light: 1 cup sugar, 1-1/2 cups flour, 2 teaspoons baking powder, any desired flavoring and a pinch of salt; beat the sugar with the eggs and cream, and have the batter so that it will run easily from the spoon. The better way is not to put in all the flour at once, as a stiff batter will never make a light sponge cake.

TIME-HONORED RECIPE

Old Hermit Cake

This is a huge cake and so good you will think it's full of hermit cookies. Recipe is over 100 years old so uses butter instead of margarine.

Butter (not margarine), softened	2 cups	500 mL
Brown sugar, packed	3 cups	750 mL
Large eggs	6	6
Juice of 1 lemon		
Vanilla	4 tsp.	20 mL
All-purpose flour	4½ cups	1.1 L
Baking powder	4 tsp.	20 mL
Ground cinnamon	2 tsp.	10 mL
Salt	¼ tsp.	1 mL
Chopped dates	3 cups	750 mL
Chopped walnuts	3 cups	750 mL

Cream butter and brown sugar together well in large bowl. Beat in eggs, 1 at a time. Mix in lemon juice and vanilla.

Add remaining 6 ingredients. Stir well. Turn into greased and floured 10 inch (25 cm) angel food tube pan. Bake in 275°F (140°C) oven for 2½ to 3 hours until wooden pick inserted in center comes out clean. Let stand for 10 minutes before turning out onto rack to cool. Cuts into 24 pieces.

1 piece: 525 Calories; 7 g Protein; 28 g Total Fat; 65 g Carbohydrate; 224 mg Sodium; 3 g Dietary Fiber

Pictured on this page.

Sweet Cream Sponge Cake

(new recipe)

In years gone by, whipping cream was practically a staple. Garnish with whipped topping.

Large eggs	2	2
Whipping cream	1 cup	250 mL
Granulated sugar	1 cup	250 mL
Vanilla	1 tsp.	5 mL
All-purpose flour	1½ cups	375 mL
Baking powder	2 tsp.	10 mL
Salt	½ tsp.	2 mL

Beat eggs in large bowl until light in color and thickened. Add whipping cream, sugar and vanilla. Beat well.

Add ½ of flour. Beat until smooth. Add second ½ of flour, baking powder and salt. Beat until smooth. Pour into greased 9 x 9 inch (22 x 22 cm) pan. Bake in 350°F (175°C) oven for about 30 minutes until wooden pick inserted in center comes out clean. Cuts into 24 pieces.

1 piece: 103 Calories; 2 g Protein; 3.9 g Total Fat; 16 g Carbohydrate; 67 mg Sodium; trace Dietary Fiber

Pictured below.

Top: Old Hermit Cake, this page
Bottom: Sweet Cream Sponge Cake, above

Lazy Daisy Cake

Good warm or cold. Without the topping it makes a good shortcake that doesn't crumble. A recipe this old and this good lasts through the years and stands the test of time.

Large eggs	2	2
Granulated sugar	1 cup	250 mL
Vanilla	1 tsp.	5 mL
All-purpose flour	1 cup	250 mL
Baking powder	1 tsp.	5 mL
Salt	½ tsp.	2 mL
Milk	½ cup	125 mL
Hard margarine (or butter)	1 tbsp.	15 mL
Topping:		
Hard margarine (or butter)	3 tbsp.	50 mL
Brown sugar, packed	½ cup	125 mL
Cream (or milk)	2 tbsp.	30 mL
Flake coconut	½ cup	125 mL

Beat eggs in medium bowl until frothy. Gradually add sugar while beating until thickened. Add vanilla. Mix.

Combine flour, baking powder and salt in small bowl. Stir into egg mixture.

Combine milk and margarine in small saucepan. Heat until hot and margarine is melted. Stir into batter. Turn into greased 9 x 9 inch (22x 22 cm) pan. Bake in 350°F (175°C) oven for 25 to 30 minutes until wooden pick inserted in center comes out clean.

Topping: Combine all 4 ingredients in small saucepan. Heat until margarine is melted and brown sugar is dissolved. Do not boil. Spread over cake. Return to oven for about 3 minutes until top is bubbling. Cuts into 12 pieces.

1 piece: 227 Calories; 3 g Protein; 7.9 g Total Fat; 37 g Carbohydrate; 182 mg Sodium; 1 g Dietary Fiber

Pictured below.

Lazy Daisy Cake

Syrup Cake

This has a taffy topping. For an extra special touch, sprinkle with finely chopped pecans or walnuts.

Cake flour (sift before measuring)	1¾ cups	425 mL
Baking powder	2 tsp.	10 mL
Salt	½ tsp.	2 mL
Hard margarine (or butter), softened	½ cup	125 mL
Granulated sugar	¼ cup	60 mL
Vanilla	1 tsp.	5 mL
Large eggs	2	2
White corn syrup	¾ cup	175 mL
Milk	½ cup	125 mL
Taffy Topping:		
Egg whites (large), room temperature	2	2
Golden corn syrup	¾ cup	175 mL
Granulated sugar	¼ cup	60 mL
Vanilla	1 tsp.	5 mL
Salt	⅛ tsp.	0.5 mL

Measure cake flour into medium bowl. Add baking powder and salt. Stir.

Cream margarine, sugar and vanilla together in large bowl. Beat in eggs, 1 at a time. Add corn syrup. Mix.

Add flour mixture in 3 parts alternately with milk in 2 parts, beginning and ending with flour mixture, stirring until just mixed. Turn into 2 greased and waxed paper-lined 8 inch (20 cm) round cake pans. Bake in 350°F (175°C) oven for about 30 minutes until wooden pick inserted in center comes out clean. Cool.

Taffy Topping: Measure all 5 ingredients in top of double boiler. Place over boiling water. Beat continuously with electric beater until peaks stand up when beater is lifted. This will take about 7 minutes. Fill and frost cake. Cuts into 16 pieces.

1 piece: 238 Calories; 3 g Protein; 6.9 g Total Fat; 42 g Carbohydrate; 222 mg Sodium; trace Dietary Fiber

Pictured on page 85.

Candy & Snacks

Before the twentieth century, fudges, fondants, caramels and mints were commonplace. These were very cumbersome to make as they required plenty of boiling, beating or pulling. The invention of candy thermometers has made judging the correct stage of sugar syrup much easier. Let Sponge Toffee and Brown Sugar Fudge bring back memories of childhood and the corner store as you enjoy these time-honored recipes. But don't forget to try Polynesian Popcorn for a burst of newer flavors.

Russian Toffee

Shiny deep brown. A delicious treat to be sure.

Hard margarine (or butter)	1 cup	250 mL
Corn syrup	1 cup	250 mL
Sweetened condensed milk	11 oz.	300 mL
Brown sugar, packed	2 cups	500 mL
Crushed pecans	1 cup	250 mL
Vanilla	1 tsp.	5 mL

Melt margarine, corn syrup and condensed milk in large saucepan. Add brown sugar. Bring mixture to a boil. Stir continually until mixture reaches firm ball stage on candy thermometer or until a small spoonful dropped into cold water forms a firm but pliable ball.

Stir in pecans and vanilla. Pour onto greased 11 x 17 inch (28 x 43 cm) baking sheet. Using a hot knife, cut into bite-size pieces while still warm. Cool. Wrap in waxed paper. Makes 3 lbs. (1.4 kg) toffee, about 70, 1 x 1 inch (2.5 x 2.5 cm) pieces.

1 piece: 94 Calories, 1 g Protein; 4.5 g Total Fat; 14 g Carbohydrate; 45 mg Sodium; trace Dietary Fiber

Pictured on this page.

Sponge Toffee

Looks just like a sea sponge. Melts in your mouth but be careful—it's chewy and sticky like toffee. Kids have been enjoying this for years and years.

Granulated sugar	1 cup	250 mL
Corn syrup	1 cup	250 mL
White vinegar	1 tbsp.	15 mL
Baking soda	1 tbsp.	15 mL

Grease 9 x 13 inch (22 x 33 cm) pan. Set aside. Put sugar, corn syrup and vinegar into heavy 3 quart (3 L) saucepan. Heat and stir over medium-low until sugar is dissolved and mixture is starting to boil. Boil, without stirring, until mixture reaches soft crack stage on candy thermometer or until a small spoonful dropped into cold water separates into hard strands that are still pliable. Remove from heat.

Put baking soda into small fine sieve. Quickly sieve over surface. Stir immediately and just enough to mix in baking soda. Bubbles disappear quickly if touched too much. While mixture is foaming, pour into pan. Allow candy to spread by itself. Do not spread or it will collapse. Cool. Break into pieces. Store in airtight container. Makes about 1 lb. (454 g) candy.

1 oz. (28 g) candy: 112 Calories; 0 g Protein; 0 g Total Fat; 29 g Carbohydrate; 235 mg Sodium; 0 g Dietary Fiber

Pictured below.

Top: Sponge Toffee
Bottom: Russian Toffee

Chocolate Crisps

Chocolate Crisps

This will remind you of a famous chocolate bar from the 1950s.

Semisweet chocolate chips	2 cups	500 mL
Butterscotch chips	2 cups	500 mL
Peanuts, chopped	½ cup	125 mL
Box of ripple potato chips, crushed (about 1⅓ cups, 325 mL, crushed)	½ × 6½ oz.	½ × 180 g

Melt chocolate chips and butterscotch chips together in medium saucepan, stirring often, over low.

Add peanuts and potato chips. Stir. Spoon 1 tbsp. (15 mL) into 1¼ inch (3 cm) double paper cups or foil candy cups. Makes about 32 chocolate crisps.

1 crisp: 134 Calories; 1 g Protein; 6 g Total Fat; 21 g Carbohydrate; 26 mg Sodium; 1 g Dietary Fiber

Pictured above.

PEANUT CRISPS: Omit potato chips. Add an extra ½ cup (125 mL) chopped peanuts. More like the real thing.

Honey Caramels

Mm-Mmm! Wonderful buttery flavor. A soft caramel.

Granulated sugar	2 cups	500 mL
Creamed honey	¼ cup	60 mL
Whipping cream	1 cup	250 mL
Butter (not margarine)	½ cup	125 mL
Vanilla	1 tsp.	5 mL

Measure all 5 ingredients into medium heavy saucepan. Boil over medium, stirring occasionally, until mixture reaches firm ball stage on candy thermometer or until a small spoonful dropped into cold water forms a firm but pliable ball. Remove from heat. Let stand for 10 minutes. Beat well, until signs of thickening appear. Quickly turn into greased 8 × 8 inch (20 × 20 cm) pan. Cool completely. Score into 64 squares. Makes 1¾ lbs. (790 g) candy, or 64 squares.

1 square: 55 Calories; trace Protein; 2.8 g Total Fat; 8 g Carbohydrate; 17 mg Sodium; 0 g Dietary Fiber

Pictured on page 91.

Date Loaf Candy

Tastes like a fudgy date-flavored candy.

Granulated sugar	3 cups	750 mL
Milk	1 cup	250 mL
Hard margarine (or butter)	1 tbsp.	15 mL
Chopped dates (1½ cups, 375 mL, lightly packed)	½ lb.	225 g
Chopped pecans (or walnuts)	1 cup	250 mL
Vanilla	½ tsp.	2 mL

Combine sugar, milk and margarine in 3 quart (3 L) heavy saucepan. Heat and stir over medium until boiling. Boil, without stirring, over medium-low until mixture reaches firm ball stage on candy thermometer or until a small spoonful dropped into cold water forms a firm but pliable ball. Remove from heat.

Add dates, pecans and vanilla. Mix well. Pour onto waxed paper. Cool enough to handle. Roll about ⅓ at a time into 5 inch (12 cm) roll. Wrap in plastic wrap. Chill. Cut each roll into about twenty ¼ inch (6 mm) slices, making about 60 slices in total. Makes 1¾ lbs. (790 g) candy.

1 slice: 68 Calories; trace Protein; 1.7 g Total Fat; 14 g Carbohydrate; 5 mg Sodium; trace Dietary Fiber

Pictured on page 91.

TIME-HONORED RECIPE

Ryley's Toffee

I used to make this after school on the wood stove—and without a candy thermometer! A yummy toffee.

Sweetened condensed milk	11 oz.	300 mL
Brown sugar, packed	1¼ cups	300 mL
Hard margarine (or butter)	¼ cup	60 mL
Corn syrup	¼ cup	60 mL

Stir all 4 ingredients together in medium heavy saucepan. Bring to a boil, stirring constantly over medium-low, until mixture reaches firm ball stage on candy thermometer or until a small spoonful dropped into cold water forms a hard ball that is firm but pliable. Pour into well greased 8 × 8 inch (20 × 20 cm) pan. Cool slightly. Score toffee into 1 inch (2.5 cm) squares with knife before too hard. When cold, remove from pan. Break over edge of counter or sink. Makes 64 pieces.

1 piece: 47 Calories; trace Protein; 1.3 g Total Fat; 9 g Carbohydrate; 19 mg Sodium; trace Dietary Fiber

Pictured on page 91.

1. Honey Caramels, page 90
2. Double-Decker Fudge, page 92
3. Date Loaf Candy, page 90
4. Dipped Truffles, page 92
5. Ryley's Toffee, page 90

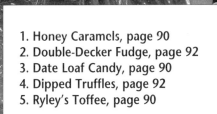

Truffles

For an elegant evening of entertaining. Also makes a nice gift.

Sweetened condensed milk (see Note)	11 oz.	300 mL
Vanilla	1 tsp.	5 mL
Salt	½ tsp.	2 mL
Bittersweet chocolate baking squares, cut up	9 × 1 oz.	9 × 28 g
Chocolate sprinkles, for rolling	2 tbsp.	30 mL
Cocoa, for rolling	2 tbsp.	30 mL
Ground pecans (or hazelnuts), for rolling	¼ cup	60 mL

Combine first 4 ingredients in medium heavy saucepan. Heat and stir over low until chocolate is melted and mixture is smooth. Cool.

With buttered fingers, shape into 1 inch (2.5 cm) balls. Roll ⅓ in chocolate sprinkles, ⅓ in cocoa and ⅓ in ground pecans. Keep chilled. Makes 4 dozen truffles.

1 coated truffle: 57 Calories; 1 g Protein; 3.2 g Total Fat; 7 g Carbohydrate; 39 mg Sodium; trace Dietary Fiber

Note: For 14 oz. (398 mL) can of sweetened condensed milk, use 12 × 1 oz. (12 x 28 g) chocolate baking squares.

Variation: Omit vanilla. Add 1 tbsp. (15 mL) of your favorite liqueur.

WHITE TRUFFLES: Use 9 × 1 oz. (9 x 28 g) squares of white chocolate instead of the bittersweet. Omit vanilla. Add 1 tbsp. (15 mL) of your favorite liqueur. Roll as for Truffles, above, or dip into chocolate as in Dipped Truffles, below.

DIPPED TRUFFLES: Melt 6 × 1 oz. (6 × 28 g) semisweet or white chocolate baking squares and 3 tbsp. (50 mL) paraffin wax in small saucepan over low, stirring often, until melted. Using fork, lower 1 truffle at a time into chocolate. Lift out, holding above saucepan to allow excess chocolate to drip, then transfer to waxed paper to set. Repeat with remaining truffles.

Pictured on page 91.

Vinegar Candy

Double-Decker Fudge

Creamy smooth with both dark and light layers in every piece. Very attractive on a dessert platter.

Peanut butter chips	1 cup	250 mL
Semisweet chocolate chips	1 cup	250 mL
Granulated sugar	2¼ cups	560 mL
Marshmallow cream (7 oz., 200 g, jar)	1½ cups	375 mL
Evaporated milk	¾ cup	175 mL
Hard margarine (or butter)	¼ cup	60 mL
Vanilla	1 tsp.	5 mL

Put peanut butter chips into medium bowl. Put chocolate chips into separate medium bowl.

Combine sugar, marshmallow cream, evaporated milk and margarine in 3 quart (3 L) heavy saucepan. Heat and stir until boiling. Boil slowly for 5 minutes, stirring constantly. Remove from heat.

Stir in vanilla. Measure 2 cups (500 mL) and pour over peanut butter chips. Stir vigorously until melted. Pour into greased 8 × 8 inch (20 × 20 cm) pan. Pour remaining marshmallow mixture over chocolate chips. Stir vigorously until melted. Pour over layer in pan. Cool. Makes 2¼ lbs. (1 kg) fudge. Cuts into 48 pieces.

1 piece: 107 Calories; 2 g Protein; 3.7 g Total Fat; 21 g Carbohydrate; 33 mg Sodium; trace Dietary Fiber

Pictured on page 91.

Vinegar Candy

A hard candy that lasts a long time and slowly disappears in the mouth. Shiny and looks like butterscotch.

Granulated sugar	2 cups	500 mL
White vinegar	½ cup	125 mL
Water	¼ cup	60 mL
Hard margarine (or butter)	2 tbsp.	30 mL
Salt, just a pinch		

Measure all 5 ingredients into large saucepan. Heat and stir until sugar is dissolved. Boil until mixture reaches hard ball stage on candy thermometer or until a small spoonful dropped into cold water forms a hard ball that is firm and barely pliable. Pour into greased 8 × 8 inch (20 × 20 cm) pan. Cool. Makes 1 lb. (454 g) candy. Break into pieces.

1 oz. (28 g) candy: 128 Calories; trace Protein; 3 g Total Fat; 26 g Carbohydrate; 36 mg Sodium; 0 g Dietary Fiber

Pictured on this page.

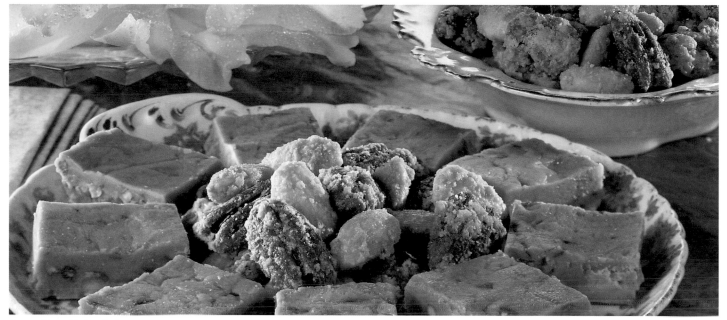

Brown Sugar Fudge, below

Sugar Nuts, below

Brown Sugar Fudge

This sets up firmly and melts in your mouth.

Brown sugar, packed	2 cups	500 mL
Granulated sugar	1 cup	250 mL
Corn syrup	2 tbsp.	30 mL
Hard margarine (or butter)	2 tbsp.	30 mL
Salt	1/8 tsp.	0.5 mL
Milk	2/3 cup	150 mL
Fine coconut (or finely ground nuts)	1/2 cup	125 mL

Measure first 6 ingredients into medium heavy saucepan. Heat over medium, stirring often, until boiling. Boil, without stirring, until mixture reaches soft ball stage on candy thermometer or until a small spoonful dropped into cold water forms a soft, very pliable ball. Remove from heat.

Cool until you can almost hold your hand against the bottom of saucepan. Beat until it has lost its gloss and begins to thicken. Stir in coconut. Pour into greased 8 x 8 inch (20 x 20 cm) pan. Cool. Cuts into 64 squares.

1 square: 51 Calories; trace Protein; 0.9 g Total Fat; 11 g Carbohydrate; 15 mg Sodium; trace Dietary Fiber

Pictured above.

Note: If you miss the crucial point of pouring fudge just before it sets, it can be shaped into rolls and coated with crushed or finely chopped nuts. Slice to serve.

Sugar Nuts

Addictive! Use whatever combination of nuts you prefer, for a total of 4 1/2 cups (1.1 L).

Egg whites (large), room temperature	2	2
Granulated sugar	1 cup	250 mL
Salt, just a pinch		
Pecans	1 1/2 cups	375 mL
Walnuts	1 1/2 cups	375 mL
Almonds	1 1/2 cups	375 mL
Hard margarine (or butter), melted	1/2 cup	125 mL

Beat egg whites in medium bowl until stiff. Beat in sugar and salt.

Fold in pecans, walnuts and almonds.

Pour margarine into 9 x 13 inch (22 x 33 cm) pan. Spread nut mixture over margarine. Bake in 325°F (160°C) oven for about 30 minutes, stirring every 10 minutes, until no margarine remains. Pour out onto waxed paper. Separate to cool. Makes 7 cups (1.75 L) nuts.

1/4 cup (60 mL) nuts: 180 Calories; 3 g Protein; 14.7 g Total Fat; 12 g Carbohydrate; 43 mg Sodium; 2 g Dietary Fiber

Pictured above.

Spicy Cheddar Popcorn

Polynesian Popcorn

Chili Popcorn

Spicy Cheddar Popcorn

Add more cayenne pepper if you like it real spicy!

Hard margarine (or butter), melted	¼ cup	60 mL
Popped corn (pop about ¼ cup, 60 mL)	8 cups	2 L
Dry grated Cheddar cheese powder	⅓ cup	75 mL
Seasoned salt	1 tsp.	5 mL
Onion powder	⅛ tsp.	0.5 mL
Garlic powder	⅛ tsp.	0.5 mL
Chili powder	¼ tsp.	1 mL
Cayenne pepper (optional)	⅛ tsp.	0.5 mL

Drizzle margarine over popped corn in large bowl. Toss well to coat.

Combine remaining 6 ingredients in small bowl. Sprinkle over popcorn. Toss well to coat each piece evenly. Makes 8 cups (2 L) flavored popcorn.

1 cup (250 mL) popcorn: 114 Calories; 3 g Protein; 7.8 g Total Fat; 9 g Carbohydrate; 268 mg Sodium; 1 g Dietary Fiber

Pictured on this page.

Polynesian Popcorn

A very unusual flavor. A good conversation appetizer.

Hard margarine (or butter), melted	¼ cup	60 mL
Soy sauce	2 tsp.	10 mL
Ground ginger	¾ tsp.	4 mL
Onion salt	½ tsp.	2 mL
Popped corn (pop about ¼ cup, 60 mL)	8 cups	2 L

Stir margarine, soy sauce, ginger and onion salt together in large bowl.

Add popped corn. Toss well to coat each piece evenly. Makes 8 cups (2 L) flavored popcorn.

1 cup (250 mL) popcorn: 95 Calories; 2 g Protein; 6.2 g Total Fat; 9 g Carbohydrate; 238 mg Sodium; 1 g Dietary Fiber

Pictured on this page.

Chili Popcorn

Easy to add more or less flavor to this. Reddish tinge.

Popped corn (pop about ¼ cup, 60 mL)	8 cups	2 L
Hard margarine, melted	¼ cup	60 mL
Salt	1 tsp.	5 mL
Chili powder	½ tsp.	2 mL
Paprika	⅛ tsp.	0.5 mL

Toss hot popped corn with margarine in large bowl.

Stir salt, chili powder and paprika together in small cup. Sprinkle over popcorn. Toss well to coat each piece evenly. Makes 8 cups (2 L) flavored popcorn.

1 cup (250 mL) popcorn: 96 Calories; 1 g Protein; 6.5 g Total Fat; 9 g Carbohydrate; 410 mg Sodium; 1 g Dietary Fiber

Pictured on this page.

Chicken

Many of us have special memories of Sunday roast chicken dinners. On homesteads, during the Depression years, unplanned guests were made welcome with a chicken dinner, as fresh chicken was readily accessible right outside the back door! Chicken cooked up fast either roasted, or fried in a lot of grease, and was always delicious. Today, almost everyone relies on the grocery store to supply us with our poultry. We have the luxury of choosing only selected parts, boned and skinned if we wish, to use in a wide variety of lighter, healthier recipes. Try Chicken Divan for a full-meal selection or Chicken And Chutney for a newer flavor over rice or noodles.

Chicken Divan

Chicken Divan

Delicate curry flavor. A divine dinner for six.

Boneless, skinless chicken breast halves (about 1½ lbs., 680 g)	6	6
Water	2 cups	500 mL
Vegetable bouillon powder	2 tsp.	10 mL
Long grain white rice	1¼ cups	300 mL
Water	2½ cups	625 mL
Condensed cream of chicken soup	10 oz.	284 mL
Light sour cream	½ cup	125 mL
Grated medium Cheddar cheese	½ cup	125 mL
Light salad dressing (or mayonnaise)	⅓ cup	75 mL
Curry powder	1 tsp.	5 mL
Water	½ cup	125 mL
Frozen cut broccoli, thawed and coarsely chopped	1 lb.	454 g

Cook chicken in first amount of water and vegetable stock in large uncovered saucepan for about 35 minutes until tender. Drain. Cool a bit. Cut chicken into cubes.

Cook rice in second amount of water in medium covered saucepan for about 20 minutes until water is absorbed and rice is tender.

Mix next 6 ingredients in medium bowl.

Spoon rice into ungreased 3 quart (3 L) casserole. Cover with broccoli. Lay chicken over broccoli. Pour soup mixture over all. Poke with fork here and there to allow some liquid to drizzle down to bottom. Bake, uncovered, in 350°F (175°C) oven for about 1 hour. Serves 6.

1 serving: 445 Calories; 37 g Protein; 13.2 g Total Fat; 43 g Carbohydrate; 767 mg Sodium; 3 g Dietary Fiber

Pictured above.

Chicken Casserole

A stew-like meal with the delicious flavor of roast chicken.

Chicken parts, with skin (see Note)	3 lbs.	1.4 kg
Elbow macaroni (about 8 oz., 225 g)	2 cups	500 mL
Boiling water	3 qts.	3 L
Cooking oil (optional)	1 tbsp.	15 mL
Salt	2 tsp.	10 mL
Large onion, sliced	1	1
Medium carrots, cut into thin strips, 3 inches (7.5 cm) long	4	4
Thinly sliced celery	1 cup	250 mL
Frozen green beans (or peas)	2 cups	500 mL
Condensed cream of mushroom soup	2 × 10 oz.	2 × 284 mL
Canned sliced mushrooms, with liquid	10 oz.	284 mL
Salt	½ tsp.	2 mL
Pepper	¼ tsp.	1 mL
Topping:		
Hard margarine (or butter)	2 tbsp.	30 mL
Dry bread crumbs	½ cup	125 mL
Grated medium Cheddar cheese	½ cup	125 mL

Arrange chicken in small roaster. Cover. Bake in 350°F (175°C) oven for 1 hour until tender. Remove chicken to large plate. Tilt roaster. Spoon off fat. Leave juices in roaster. Remove skin and bone from chicken. Chop chicken into bite-size pieces.

Cook macaroni in boiling water, cooking oil and first amount of salt in large uncovered pot or Dutch oven for 5 to 7 minutes until tender but firm. Drain. Turn into roaster. Add chicken.

Add onion, carrot, celery and green beans.

Mix soup, mushrooms with liquid, second amount of salt and pepper in medium bowl. Pour over all.

Topping: Melt margarine in small saucepan. Stir in bread crumbs and cheese. Sprinkle over top. Cover. Bake in 350°F (175°C) oven for 1¼ hours until carrot is tender. Remove cover. Bake for 10 minutes until topping dries a bit. Serves 8.

1 serving: 404 Calories; 27 g Protein; 14.5 g Total Fat; 41 g Carbohydrate; 1087 mg Sodium; 4 g Dietary Fiber

Pictured on this page.

Note: 4 cups (1 L) leftover chopped cooked chicken and ½ cup (125 mL) chicken broth may be substituted for the chicken parts.

Chicken Fried Rice

Serve as a side dish or main dish.

Cooking oil	1 tbsp.	15 mL
Garlic clove, minced (or ¼ tsp., 1 mL, powder)	1	1
Boneless, skinless chicken breast halves (about ½ lb., 225 g), cut into ¾ inch (2 cm) cubes	2	2
Cooking oil	1 tsp.	5 mL
Large eggs	3	3
Salt, sprinkle		
Pepper, sprinkle		
Cooking oil	2 tsp.	10 mL
Chopped onion	½ cup	125 mL
Thinly sliced celery	¾ cup	175 mL
Diced red or green pepper	¾ cup	175 mL
Chopped fresh mushrooms	1 cup	250 mL
Cold cooked rice, crumbled	4 cups	1 L
Soy sauce	2 tbsp.	30 mL
Frozen baby peas, thawed	1 cup	250 mL
Green onions, sliced	2	2

Heat first amount of cooking oil in large non-stick wok or frying pan. Add garlic and chicken. Sauté for about 4 minutes until chicken is no longer pink. Transfer to medium bowl.

Heat second amount of cooking oil in same wok. Break eggs into pan. Pierce each yolk. Sprinkle with salt and pepper. Cook for about 1 minute. Turn eggs over. When cooked, transfer to cutting board. Cut into shreds. Add to chicken.

Heat third amount of cooking oil. Add onion, celery, red pepper and mushrooms. Sauté until onion is soft and clear.

Add rice. Drizzle mixture with soy sauce. Stir. Add peas, green onion and chicken mixture. Stir until heated through. Makes 8 cups (2 L) fried rice.

1 cup (250 mL) fried rice: 262 Calories; 14 g Protein; 6.2 g Total Fat; 36 g Carbohydrate; 339 mg Sodium; 2 g Dietary Fiber

Pictured on page 97.

Chicken Casserole

Broccoli Rice Chicken, below   Chicken Fried Rice, page 96   Chicken Express, below

Broccoli Rice Chicken

A mild comfort food. A one-dish meal made in the frying pan.

Chicken thighs, skin removed (about 2 lbs., 900 g)	8	8
Garlic salt	½ tsp.	2 mL
Paprika	½ tsp.	2 mL
Pepper, sprinkle		
Cooking oil	1 tbsp.	15 mL
Large onion, sliced	1	1
Fresh broccoli, florets reserved and stems chopped	1 lb.	454 g
Condensed cream of mushroom (or celery) soup	10 oz.	284 mL
Water	1⅔ cups	400 mL
White (or alcohol-free white) wine	⅓ cup	75 mL
Uncooked converted rice	1½ cups	375 mL
Paprika, sprinkle		
Reserved broccoli florets		

Sprinkle chicken thighs with garlic salt, paprika and pepper. Brown both sides in cooking oil in non-stick frying pan. Transfer to medium bowl.

Sauté onion in same frying pan until soft.

Add broccoli stems, soup, water, wine and rice. Stir. Bring to a boil. Arrange chicken over top. Sprinkle generously with paprika. Cover. Cook over low for 30 minutes, stirring rice around chicken twice during cooking. Rice should be almost tender.

Stir in reserved broccoli florets. Cover. Cook for about 10 minutes until broccoli and rice are tender. Serves 4.

1 serving: 606 Calories; 37 g Protein; 15.5 g Total Fat; 75 g Carbohydrate; 935 mg Sodium; 5 g Dietary Fiber

Pictured above.

Chicken Express

This is served over a bed of rice. Sweet and sour flavor with lots of chicken and vegetables.

Boneless, skinless chicken breast halves (about 1½ lbs., 680 g), cut bite size	6	6
Cooking oil	2 tsp.	10 mL
Salt, sprinkle		
Pepper, sprinkle		
Sliced celery	2 cups	500 mL
Sliced fresh mushrooms	2 cups	500 mL
Chopped onion	½ cup	125 mL
Small green pepper, chopped	1	1
Canned crushed pineapple, with juice	14 oz.	398 mL
Water	2 tbsp.	30 mL
Cornstarch	2 tbsp.	30 mL
Soy sauce	¼ cup	60 mL
Brown sugar, packed	2 tbsp.	30 mL
White vinegar	2 tbsp.	30 mL
Garlic powder	¼-½ tsp.	1-2 mL
Ground ginger	¼-½ tsp.	1-2 mL

Cook chicken in cooking oil in non-stick frying pan. Sprinkle with salt and pepper. Transfer to medium bowl.

Add celery, mushrooms, onion and green pepper to same frying pan. Sauté until soft.

Add pineapple with juice. Heat and stir until boiling.

Mix water and cornstarch in small bowl. Add remaining 5 ingredients. Mix. Stir into vegetable mixture until boiling. Add chicken. Return to a boil. Serve immediately. Serves 6.

1 serving: 243 Calories; 30 g Protein; 3.3 g Total Fat; 24 g Carbohydrate; 849 mg Sodium; 2 g Dietary Fiber

Pictured above.

Chicken Chow Mein

A popular dish. To decrease the sodium, use
low-salt condensed soup and soy sauce.

Cooking oil	1 tbsp.	15 mL
Boneless, skinless chicken breast halves (about 1½ lbs., 680 g), cut into ¼ inch (6 mm) wide strips	6	6
Condensed cream of mushroom soup	10 oz.	284 mL
Condensed cream of chicken soup	10 oz.	284 mL
Water	1 cup	250 mL
Soy sauce	¼ cup	60 mL
Chicken bouillon powder	2 tsp.	10 mL
Chow mein noodles	2 cups	500 mL
Thinly sliced celery	2 cups	500 mL
Chopped onion	2 cups	500 mL
Chow mein noodles	2 cups	500 mL

Heat cooking oil in non-stick frying pan. Add chicken strips. Sauté quickly to brown.

Stir both soups, water, soy sauce and bouillon powder in large bowl. Add first amount of chow mein noodles. Add chicken. Stir. Add celery and onion. Mix in. Turn into ungreased 3 quart (3 L) casserole.

Sprinkle with second amount of chow mein noodles. Bake, uncovered, in 350°F (175°C) oven for 1½ to 2 hours until bubbly hot. Serves 6.

1 serving: 455 Calories; 34 g Protein; 20.6 g Total Fat; 33 g Carbohydrate; 2004 mg Sodium; 3 g Dietary Fiber

Pictured below.

Easy Chicken

Tender and tasty with a rich brown sauce. The addition of
thyme and rosemary enhances the flavor.

Chicken parts, skin removed	3 lbs.	1.4 kg
Medium onion, thinly sliced	1	1
Water	1 cup	250 mL
All-purpose flour	3 tbsp.	50 mL
Worcestershire sauce	1 tsp.	5 mL
Lemon juice	2 tbsp.	30 mL
Granulated sugar	2 tbsp.	30 mL
Parsley flakes	1 tsp.	5 mL
Ground thyme	1 tsp.	5 mL
Chicken bouillon powder	2 tsp.	10 mL
Dried rosemary, crushed	½ tsp.	2 mL
Salt	1 tsp.	5 mL
Pepper	½ tsp.	2 mL
Liquid gravy browner	1 tsp.	5 mL

Arrange chicken in ungreased 3 quart (3 L) casserole or small roaster. Scatter onion slices over chicken.

Measure remaining 12 ingredients into small bowl. Mix well. Pour over chicken. Cover. Bake in 350°F (175°C) oven for about 1½ hours until tender. Serves 4 to 6.

¼ recipe: 268 Calories; 38 g Protein; 5.3 g Total Fat; 15 g Carbohydrate; 1197 mg Sodium; 1 g Dietary Fiber

Pictured below.

Left: Easy Chicken, this page   Top Center: Chicken Chow Mein, above   Bottom Center: Chicken And Chutney, page 99   Right: Chicken In Gravy, page 99

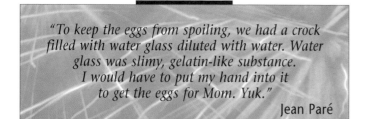

Chicken In Gravy

Rich, full-bodied flavor in a dark brown gravy.
Serve with broad noodles or mashed potato.

Hard margarine (or butter)	1 tbsp.	15 mL
Boneless, skinless chicken breast halves (about 1½ lbs., 680 g)	6	6
Sliced fresh mushrooms	2 cups	500 mL
Chili sauce	2 tbsp.	30 mL
Skim evaporated milk (or light cream)	½ cup	125 mL
Chicken bouillon powder	1 tbsp.	15 mL
Sherry (or alcohol-free sherry)	1 tbsp.	15 mL
Envelope onion gravy mix	1 × 1 oz.	1 × 28 g
Water	1¼ cups	300 mL

Melt margarine in non-stick frying pan. Add chicken. Brown well on both sides. Transfer to ungreased 2 quart (2 L) casserole.

Sauté mushrooms in same frying pan. Scatter over chicken.

Measure remaining 6 ingredients into frying pan. Heat and stir to remove any browned bits. Pour over all, making sure mushrooms are covered with sauce. Cover. Bake in 350°F (175°C) oven for about 1 hour until chicken is tender. Makes about 1½ cups (375 mL) gravy. Serves 6.

1 serving: 198 Calories; 30 g Protein; 4 g Total Fat; 9 g Carbohydrate; 724 mg Sodium; 1 g Dietary Fiber

Pictured on page 98.

Margo's Rosemary Chicken

This dish has such a wonderful flavor and aroma.

Boneless, skinless chicken breast halves (about 2½ lbs., 1.1 kg)	10	10
Cooking oil	2 tsp.	10 mL
Water	1 cup	250 mL
White (or alcohol-free white) wine	1 cup	250 mL
Red wine vinegar	⅓ cup	75 mL
Cornstarch	1 tbsp.	15 mL
Ketchup	¼ cup	60 mL
Grated onion	2 tbsp.	30 mL
Garlic clove, minced	1	1
Brown sugar, packed	2 tbsp.	30 mL
Dried rosemary	1 tsp.	5 mL
Dried whole oregano	1 tsp.	5 mL
Dill weed	1 tsp.	5 mL
Chicken bouillon powder	1 tsp.	5 mL
Salt	1 tsp.	5 mL
Soy sauce	1 tsp.	5 mL
Worcestershire sauce	1 tsp.	5 mL
Paprika	½ tsp.	2 mL

Sauté chicken quickly in cooking oil in non-stick frying pan to brown both sides. Transfer to ungreased 2½ quart (2.5 L) casserole.

Combine remaining 16 ingredients in medium saucepan. Heat and stir until boiling. Pour over chicken. Cover. Bake in 350°F (175°C) oven for about 1 hour until tender. Serves 10.

1 serving: 186 Calories; 28 g Protein; 2.5 g Total Fat; 6 g Carbohydrate; 543 mg Sodium; trace Dietary Fiber

Pictured on front cover.

Note: If desired, thicken sauce with a mixture of 1½ tbsp. (25 mL) cornstarch and 3 tbsp. (50 mL) water. Boil gently until thickened.

Chicken And Chutney

The chutney adds subtle sweetness. Ready in 30 minutes.

Boneless, skinless chicken breast halves (about 1½ lbs., 680 g), cut into ½ inch (12 mm) cubes	6	6
Hard margarine (or butter)	1 tbsp.	15 mL
Salt, sprinkle		
Pepper, sprinkle		
Skim evaporated milk	13½ oz.	385 mL
Mango chutney (or other), finely chopped	¼ cup	60 mL

Sauté chicken in margarine in non-stick frying pan until browned. Sprinkle with salt and pepper.

Add evaporated milk and chutney. Stir until boiling and slightly thickened. Serves 6.

1 serving: 213 Calories; 33 g Protein; 3.6 g Total Fat; 11 g Carbohydrate; 180 mg Sodium; trace Dietary Fiber

Pictured on page 98.

Brandied Chicken

Fried chicken with a saucy mushroom topping.

Cooking oil	2 tsp.	10 mL
Boneless, skinless chicken breast halves (about 1½ lbs., 680 g)	6	6
Salt, sprinkle		
Pepper, sprinkle		
Sliced fresh mushrooms	2 cups	500 mL
Skim evaporated milk	½ cup	125 mL
Brandy	1 tsp.	5 mL

Heat cooking oil in non-stick frying pan. Add chicken. Cook both sides until chicken is no longer pink. Sprinkle with salt and pepper. Remove chicken to warmed platter. Cover to keep warm.

Add mushrooms to same frying pan. Sauté quickly until golden and moisture is evaporated.

Add evaporated milk and brandy. Stir until hot, loosening any browned bits in pan. Spoon over chicken. Serves 6.

1 serving: 169 Calories; 29 g Protein; 3.2 g Total Fat; 4 g Carbohydrate; 104 mg Sodium; trace Dietary Fiber

Pictured below.

Whimsical Chicken

Chicken, covered with a piquant mustard sauce, bakes slowly to tender goodness.

Hard margarine (or butter), melted	⅓ cup	75 mL
Salad dressing (or mayonnaise)	⅓ cup	75 mL
Prepared mustard	1½ tbsp.	25 mL
Paprika	1 tsp.	5 mL
Parsley flakes	1 tsp.	5 mL
Salt	¾ tsp.	4 mL
Pepper	¼ tsp.	1 mL
Boneless, skinless chicken breast halves (about 2 lbs., 900 g), pounded flat	8	8
Fine dry bread crumbs	1 cup	250 mL

Mix margarine, salad dressing, prepared mustard, paprika, parsley, salt and pepper in small bowl.

Dip chicken into salad dressing mixture, then roll in bread crumbs being sure to coat well. Place in single layer on ungreased baking sheet. Bake in 325°F (160°C) oven for about 1½ hours until tender. Serves 8.

1 serving: 307 Calories; 29 g Protein; 14.8 g Total Fat; 12 g Carbohydrate; 626 mg Sodium; trace Dietary Fiber

Pictured below.

Left: Brandied Chicken, above   Top Center: Whimsical Chicken, above   Bottom Right: Mustard Chicken, page 101

Mustard Chicken

Coated then oven baked for very tender chicken.

Fine dry bread crumbs	3 tbsp.	50 mL
Grated Parmesan cheese	¼ cup	60 mL
Dry mustard	1 tsp.	5 mL
Ground rosemary	½ tsp.	2 mL
Salt (optional)	½ tsp.	2 mL
Pepper	¼ tsp.	1 mL
Boneless, skinless chicken breast halves (about 1½ lbs., 680 g)	6	6
Hot water	¼ cup	60 mL
Chicken bouillon powder	2 tsp.	10 mL
Light sour cream	¾ cup	175 mL

Paprika, sprinkle

Measure first 6 ingredients into small bowl. Mix well.

Dip chicken into Parmesan cheese mixture to coat. Place on greased baking sheet with sides.

Combine hot water and bouillon powder in separate small bowl. Stir well. Add sour cream. Mix until smooth. Spoon over chicken being sure to cover each piece.

Sprinkle with paprika. Bake in 350°F (175°C) oven for about 40 minutes until tender. Serves 6.

1 serving: 197 Calories; 31 g Protein; 5.4 g Total Fat; 5 g Carbohydrate; 415 mg Sodium; trace Dietary Fiber

Pictured on page 100/101.

Right: Reverse Cordon Bleu, this page

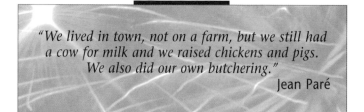
Reverse Cordon Bleu

You get the familiar flavor of the traditional cordon bleu, but with a lot less effort.

Hard margarine (or butter)	1 tbsp.	15 mL
Boneless, skinless chicken breast halves (about 1½ lbs., 680 g)	6	6
Apple juice	1 cup	250 mL
Large cooked ham slices (about 8 oz., 225 g)	6	6
Swiss cheese, thinly sliced	9 oz.	255 g
Sauce:		
Granulated sugar	4 tsp.	20 mL
All-purpose flour	1 tbsp.	15 mL
Dry mustard	½ tsp.	2 mL
Salt	¼ tsp.	1 mL
Reserved juice, plus water if needed to make	1 cup	250 mL
White vinegar	4 tsp.	20 mL
Skim evaporated milk (or light cream)	¼ cup	60 mL
Green onions, chopped	3	3

Melt margarine in non-stick frying pan. Add chicken. Quickly brown both sides.

Add apple juice. Cover. Simmer for about 15 minutes until chicken is no longer pink. Transfer chicken to large plate. Reserve juice.

Lay ham slices on working surface. Lay ½ of cheese on center of each piece of ham. Set 1 chicken breast half on each slice of cheese. Cover with second ½ of cheese. Fold ham edges over top. Lay folded side down in ungreased shallow 2 quart (2 L) casserole. Cover. Bake in 350°F (175°C) oven for about 8 minutes until cheese is melted.

Sauce: Stir sugar, flour, dry mustard and salt in small saucepan.

Mix in reserved juice until smooth. Add vinegar and evaporated milk. Heat and stir until boiling and thickened.

Stir in green onion. Pour over chicken. Serves 6.

1 serving: 423 Calories; 47 g Protein; 19.2 g Total Fat; 13 g Carbohydrate; 832 mg Sodium; trace Dietary Fiber

Pictured on this page.

Chicken With Ginger

Excellent served as-is or with a peanut or chili sauce for dipping.

Soy sauce	½ cup	125 mL
Liquid honey	⅓ cup	75 mL
White vinegar	3 tbsp.	50 mL
Garlic powder (or 2 cloves, minced)	½ tsp.	2 mL
Grated fresh gingerroot	1 tbsp.	15 mL
Boneless, skinless chicken breast halves (about 2 lbs., 900 g), cut bite size	8	8

Stir first 5 ingredients in small bowl.

Add chicken. Stir. Cover tightly. Marinate in refrigerator for about 3 hours, stirring occasionally.

Arrange chicken with marinade on greased baking sheet. Bake in 375°F (190°C) oven for about 25 minutes, stirring once or twice. Serves 8.

1 serving: 188 Calories; 29 g Protein; 1.5 g Total Fat; 14 g Carbohydrate; 1165 mg Sodium; trace Dietary Fiber

Pictured on page 103.

Variation: Soak 8, ten inch (25 cm) bamboo skewers in water for 10 minutes. Pound chicken flat. Cut into long strips. Marinate as above. Thread chicken strips onto skewers. Discard marinade. Arrange skewers on greased baking sheet. Bake in 375°F (190°C) oven for about 25 minutes. Makes 8 skewers.

Pictured on page 103.

Glazed Chicken

Great eye appeal! For easier cleanup line dish with foil.

Chicken parts, skin removed	3 lbs.	1.4 kg
Salad dressing (or mayonnaise)	⅔ cup	150 mL
Chili sauce	2 tbsp.	30 mL
Sweet pickle relish	1 tbsp.	15 mL
Lemon juice	1 tbsp.	15 mL
Worcestershire sauce	1 tsp.	5 mL
Envelope dry onion soup mix	1 × 1.4 oz.	1 × 38 g
Apricot jam	½ cup	125 mL
Brown sugar, packed	1 tbsp.	15 mL

Arrange chicken in greased 3 quart (3 L) casserole or small roaster.

Mix salad dressing, chili sauce, pickle relish, lemon juice and Worcestershire sauce in small bowl. Stir in soup mix, jam and brown sugar. Spoon over chicken being sure to get some on every piece. Bake, uncovered, in 350°F (175°C) oven for about 1 hour until tender. Baste chicken at half-time. Serves 4 to 6.

¼ recipe: 737 Calories; 57 g Protein; 35 g Total Fat; 47 g Carbohydrate; 1515 mg Sodium; 1 g Dietary Fiber

Pictured on page 103.

Chicken Breasts Supreme

Crispy golden-brown flavorful coating.

Boneless, skinless chicken breast halves (about 1½ lbs., 680 g)	6	6
Non-fat sour cream	1 cup	250 mL
Lemon juice	2 tbsp.	30 mL
Worcestershire sauce	1 tsp.	5 mL
Garlic powder (or 1 clove, minced)	¼ tsp.	1 mL
Celery salt	1 tsp.	5 mL
Paprika	1 tsp.	5 mL
Salt	1 tsp.	5 mL
Pepper	¼ tsp.	1 mL
Coarsely crushed corn flakes cereal (not crumbs)	1¾ cups	425 mL
Hard margarine (or butter), melted	3 tbsp.	50 mL

Put chicken into medium bowl or sealable plastic bag.

Stir next 8 ingredients in small bowl. Pour over chicken. Stir lightly to coat each piece. Cover or seal. Marinate in refrigerator for 6 hours or overnight.

Coat 1 piece of chicken at a time with crushed cereal. Arrange on greased baking sheet. Repeat. Refrigerate for 1 to 2 hours to make a crispier coating if desired.

Drizzle with margarine. Bake in 350°F (175°C) oven for about 1 hour until tender. Serves 6.

1 serving: 225 Calories; 29 g Protein; 6.9 g Total Fat; 10 g Carbohydrate; 931 mg Sodium; trace Dietary Fiber

Pictured on page 103.

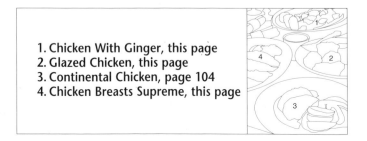

1. Chicken With Ginger, this page
2. Glazed Chicken, this page
3. Continental Chicken, page 104
4. Chicken Breasts Supreme, this page

Continental Chicken

This can be made in the slow cooker or oven.
Looks delicious with cranberries and a gravy-type sauce.

Boneless, skinless chicken breast halves (about 3 lbs., 1.4 kg)	12	12
Whole cranberry sauce	1¼ cups	300 mL
Envelope dry onion soup mix (stir before dividing)	½ × 1.4 oz.	½ × 38 g
French dressing	½ cup	125 mL
Granulated sugar	1 tbsp.	15 mL
Pepper	⅛ tsp.	0.5 mL

Arrange chicken in 5 quart (5 L) slow cooker.

Mix remaining 5 ingredients in small bowl. Spoon over chicken. Cover. Cook on Low for 8 to 10 hours or on High for 4 to 5 hours. Serves 12.

1 serving: 224 Calories; 27 g Protein; 5.9 g Total Fat; 15 g Carbohydrate; 415 mg Sodium; trace Dietary Fiber

Pictured on page 103.

Note: This may be baked, covered, in ungreased 4 quart (4 L) casserole in 325°F (160°C) oven for 1½ to 2 hours.

Elegant Chicken Phyllo

This recipe makes one pouch. Multiply by the number of servings. Very special indeed.

Phyllo pastry sheets	2	2
Hard margarine (or butter), melted	1 tbsp.	15 mL
Light spreadable cream cheese, mashed with fork to soften	1 tbsp.	15 mL
Chopped pimiento	1½ tsp.	7 mL
Boneless, skinless chicken breast half (about ¼ lb., 113 g), pounded flat and cut into thin strips	1	1
Salt, sprinkle		
Pepper, sprinkle		
Medium fresh mushroom, sliced	1	1

Lay 1 sheet of pastry on working surface. Brush with melted margarine. Fold in half crosswise. Repeat with second pastry sheet. Place second sheet on top of first sheet in opposite direction.

Spread cream cheese, 4 inches (10 cm) in diameter, in center of pastry. Sprinkle with pimiento. Lay strips of chicken over top. Sprinkle with salt and pepper. Arrange mushroom slices over chicken. Gather up pastry on top. Press together to seal. Frill edges outward. Place on greased baking sheet. Bake in 350°F (175°C) oven for about 30 minutes. Pastry should be browned and crisp. Serve immediately to prevent sogginess. Makes 1 pouch.

1 pouch: 409 Calories; 33 g Protein; 15.8 g Total Fat; 32 g Carbohydrate; 619 mg Sodium; 1 g Dietary Fiber

Pictured on this page.

Top: Ham And Chicken En Croûte, below
Bottom: Elegant Chicken Phyllo, this page

Ham And Chicken En Croûte

These neat little packets may also be cooked in puff pastry.
Brush with beaten egg before baking for a shiny finish.
Similar to, but easier than, Chicken Cordon Bleu.

Hard margarine (or butter)	1 tbsp.	15 mL
Dried thyme	¼ tsp.	1 mL
Boneless, skinless chicken breast halves (about 1½ lbs., 680 g)	6	6
Salt, sprinkle		
Pepper, sprinkle		
Pie crust pastry, enough for 2 crust pie		
Cooked ham slices	6	6
Slices of Gruyère (or Brie or Swiss) cheese	6	6

Combine margarine and thyme in non-stick frying pan.

Add chicken. Sauté until no longer pink. Sprinkle with salt and pepper. Cool.

Divide pastry into 2 portions. Roll out 1 portion into 8 × 18 inch (20 × 45 cm) rectangle. Cut rectangle into 3 equal 8 × 6 inch (20 × 15 cm) rectangles. Cut ham slices same size as chicken. Lay 1 ham slice near short edge of pastry. Place cheese and chicken on top of ham. Fold pastry over and roll up to cover. Dampen edges of side and top. Seal. Cut slits in top. Repeat with remaining pastry, ham, cheese and chicken. Arrange on ungreased baking sheet. Bake in 400°F (205°C) oven for 25 to 30 minutes until browned. Serves 6.

1 serving: 595 Calories; 43 g Protein; 33.7 g Total Fat; 28 g Carbohydrate; 1001 mg Sodium; 1 g Dietary Fiber

Pictured above.

Condiments

It wasn't until the 1906 edition of Fannie Farmer's cookbook that we saw a larger selection of butters and spreads. Today there are incredible choices of condiments available, including chutneys, compotes, salsas and relishes, to enhance our meals. The five recipes in this section are classics that you will be able to pass on to your families for generations to come. Give pork a boost with Curried Fruit Compote or serve an old family favorite, Chow Chow Maritime, with any meat.

TIME-HONORED RECIPE

Spiced Plums

An old family recipe. Especially good with baked ham or cold beef. Also good served over cream cheese, cottage cheese or just to eat a spoonful.

Prune plums	3¹/₂ lbs.	1.6 kg
Granulated sugar	6 cups	1.5 L
Ground cinnamon	1 tbsp.	15 mL
Ground cloves	1¹/₂ tsp.	7 mL
Salt	¹/₂ tsp.	2 mL
White vinegar	1¹/₂ cups	375 mL

Cut plums in half. Remove stones. If you don't have a food processor, cut each plum half into at least 8 pieces. If you do have a food processor or blender, cut each half into 3 or 4 pieces. You will need to process later. Place in large pot or Dutch oven.

Add remaining 5 ingredients. Stir over medium-high until sugar is dissolved. Bring to a boil. Boil, stirring occasionally, for about 5 minutes until plums are mushy. Cool. Pour into food processor or blender in batches. Process. Some bits of skin should show. Return to pot. Bring to a boil. Boil, stirring often, until desired thickness. Pour into hot sterilized jars to within ¹/₄ inch (6 mm) of top. Place sterilized metal lids on jars and screw metal bands on securely. For added assurance against spoilage, you may choose to process in a boiling water bath for 10 minutes. Makes 5¹/₂ pints (11 cups, 2.75 L) plums.

¹/₂ cup (125 mL) plums: 261 Calories; 1 g Protein; 0.5 g Total Fat; 67 g Carbohydrate; 63 mg Sodium; 1 g Dietary Fiber

Pictured on this page.

Curried Fruit Compote

This can be made in the slow cooker or oven. A beautiful sight. Mild curry flavor. Serve hot or cold. Delicious over ice cream or served as a side dish with beef, chicken or pork.

Canned sliced peaches, juice reserved	14 oz.	398 mL
Canned pears, cut each ¹/₂ pear into 3 pieces, juice reserved	14 oz.	398 mL
Canned pineapple tidbits, juice reserved	14 oz.	398 mL
Canned mandarin orange segments, discard juice	12 oz.	341 mL
Maraschino cherries	20	20
Brown sugar, packed	³/₄ cup	175 mL
Cornstarch	3 tbsp.	50 mL
Curry powder	1¹/₂ tsp.	7 mL
All reserved juice, approximately	2 cups	500 mL

Place peaches, pears, pineapple, orange segments and cherries in 3¹/₂ quart (3.5 L) slow cooker.

Mix brown sugar, cornstarch and curry powder in small saucepan. Add reserved juice. Heat and stir until boiling and thickened. Pour over fruit. Cover. Cook on Low for 3 hours. Makes 6¹/₄ cups (1.55 L) fruit.

¹/₂ cup (125 mL) fruit: 32 Calories; trace Protein; trace Total Fat; 8 g Carbohydrate; 2 mg Sodium; trace Dietary Fiber

Pictured below.

Note: This may be baked, covered, in ungreased 2 quart (2 L) casserole in 350°F (175°C) oven for 30 to 40 minutes until hot.

Spiced Plums

Curried Fruit Compote

Top: Old-Time Butter, below
Center: Chow Chow Maritime, this page
Bottom: Pickled Peaches, this page

Old-Time Butter

*Butter making is almost a lost art. Have kids and
adults gather 'round while you make some from
sweet pasteurized cream. In days gone by,
unpasteurized soured cream was used.*

Whipping cream, chilled	2 cups	500 mL
Lots of cold water		
Salt	1/8 tsp.	0.5 mL

Beat whipping cream on high in large bowl until
thickened. Notice you now have whipped cream.
Continue to beat until the smooth shiny appearance
changes to a grainy look. Keep beating until cream starts to
separate into little goblets and liquid. Stop beating
occasionally to see if little particles can be pushed together
with spoon or collected by gathering with spoon. When it
becomes lumpy, use slotted spoon to remove lumps to
small bowl, or strain liquid through sieve. The liquid is
buttermilk. The lumps are butter.

Work butter lumps into 1 lump. Pour cold water over
butter. Work with spoon until water is milky looking. Drain.
Repeat until water runs clear. This will take at least 4 rinses.
Work more to release all water from butter.

Sprinkle with salt. Work in. Press in, or pipe butter into,
small dish. Makes 3/4 cup (175 mL) butter.

2 tsp. (10 mL) butter: 46 Calories; trace Protein; 5.2 g Total Fat; 0 g Carbohydrate;
  53 mg Sodium; 0 g Dietary Fiber

Pictured above.

Pickled Peaches

Serve hot or cold with baked ham, beef or pork.

Granulated sugar	1 1/3 cups	325 mL
White vinegar	1/2 cup	125 mL
Cinnamon sticks (3 inches, 7.5 cm, each), broken up (see Note)	3	3
Whole cloves	10	10
Fresh (or frozen) peaches, sliced (about 2 1/2 cups, 625 mL)	1 1/2 lbs.	680 g

Measure sugar and vinegar into medium saucepan. Tie
cinnamon and cloves in small cheesecloth bag. Add to
saucepan. Stir.

Add peaches. Heat, stirring occasionally, until peaches are
tender. Discard cheesecloth bag. Cool. Refrigerate. When
ready to serve, drain, reserving juice to store leftover
peaches. Makes 2 1/2 cups (625 mL) peaches.

1/2 cup (125 mL) peaches: 153 Calories; 1 g Protein; 0.1 g Total Fat; 40 g Carbohydrate;
  trace Sodium; 2 g Dietary Fiber

Pictured on this page.

Note: Put cinnamon sticks into plastic bag. Break up with
bottom of glass.

TIME-HONORED RECIPE

Chow Chow Maritime

*Triple this good old recipe so you have some to give to
family and friends. Especially good with meats served
with gravy—beef, pork, chicken or turkey.*

Medium green tomatoes, stem ends and cores removed, sliced	5 1/3 lbs.	2.5 kg
Onions, cut up	1 1/2 lbs.	680 g
Coarse (pickling) salt	1/3 cup	75 mL
Granulated sugar	3 1/3 cups	825 mL
Mixed pickling spice, tied in double layer of cheesecloth	4 1/2 tbsp.	67 mL
Turmeric	2 tsp.	10 mL
White vinegar	2 cups	500 mL

Layer tomato, onion and salt in large saucepan. Cover and
let stand on counter overnight. Drain.

Add remaining 4 ingredients. Vinegar should just be a bit
visible. Too much will make excessive juice. Heat and
stir until sugar is dissolved. Bring to a boil. Simmer,
uncovered, stirring occasionally, for 2 hours. More turmeric
can be added for color and more sugar can be added for
taste. In order to obtain an accurate taste, cool a spoonful
and then sample. Discard cheesecloth bag. Pour into hot
sterilized pint jars to within 1/2 inch (12 mm) of top. Place
sterilized metal lids on jars and screw metal bands on
securely. For added assurance against spoilage, you may
choose to process in a boiling water bath for 5 minutes.
Makes 4 pints (8 cups, 2 L) preserves.

1/2 cup (125 mL) preserves: 232 Calories; 2 g Protein; 0.4 g Total Fat; 58 g Carbohydrate;
  1183 mg Sodium; 3 g Dietary Fiber

Pictured on this page.

Cookies

Cookies

In the days when ovens could not be relied

on for regular, even heat, many batches of cookies

burned or were unevenly browned. In 1920, gas ranges

started to phase out coal, wood and petroleum stoves. The

evolution of the oven had a great deal to do with the kinds

of cookies that were baked. Hermits, macaroons,

sugar cookies, molasses cookies, and gingersnaps

were just a few of the cookie recipes that

appeared repeatedly in late nineteenth century

cookbooks and are still made today. When electric

ranges were popular in homes in the 1930s, baking

cookies became common practice until butter and sugar

rationing during World War II. After the war, many people

turned to baking a wider variety of cookies. And with

convenience cooking and baking the preference of the busy

latter half of the century, cookie mixes and refrigerated,

slice-and-bake cookie dough emerged. Serve a plateful

of memories with Soft Molasses Drops,

War-Time Cookies and Hermits.

1. Oatmeal Macaroons,
   this page
2. Chocolate Oatmeal
   Cookies, this page
3. Circus Cookies,
   page 109

Chocolate Oatmeal Cookies

Soft on the inside and crunchy on the outside.
Balanced flavors of chocolate and oatmeal.

Hard margarine (or butter), softened	½ cup	125 mL
Granulated sugar	1 cup	250 mL
Large egg	1	1
Milk	¼ cup	60 mL
Vanilla	1 tsp.	5 mL
Unsweetened chocolate baking squares, cut up	2 × 1 oz.	2 × 28 g
Quick-cooking rolled oats (not instant)	1½ cups	375 mL
All-purpose flour	1 cup	250 mL
Baking powder	2 tsp.	10 mL
Salt	⅛ tsp.	0.5 mL

Cream margarine and sugar together in large bowl. Beat in egg. Add milk and vanilla. Beat.

Place chocolate in small saucepan over low. Heat, stirring often, until melted. Add to batter. Stir.

Add rolled oats, flour, baking powder and salt. Mix well. Drop by tablespoonfuls onto greased cookie sheet. Bake in 350°F (175°C) oven for 12 to 15 minutes. Makes about 3 dozen cookies.

1 cookie: 85 Calories; 1 g Protein; 4 g Total Fat; 12 g Carbohydrate; 46 mg Sodium; 1 g Dietary Fiber

Pictured on page 107.

Oatmeal Macaroons

Crunchy oatmeal but with the distinctive coconut taste.
Look more like macaroons than oatmeal cookies.

Hard margarine (or butter), softened	2 tbsp.	30 mL
Granulated sugar	½ cup	125 mL
Large eggs	2	2
Corn flakes cereal	2 cups	500 mL
Quick-cooking rolled oats (not instant)	¾ cup	175 mL
Medium (or flake) coconut	⅔ cup	150 mL
Baking powder	½ tsp.	2 mL
Salt	½ tsp.	2 mL

Beat margarine, sugar and eggs in medium bowl until smooth and increased in volume.

Mix in remaining 5 ingredients. Drop by tablespoonfuls onto greased cookie sheet. Bake in 350°F (175°C) oven for 13 to 15 minutes. Makes 2 dozen cookies.

1 cookie: 69 Calories; 1 g Protein; 3.3 g Total Fat; 9 g Carbohydrate; 99 mg Sodium; trace Dietary Fiber

Pictured on page 107.

Circus Cookies

*Crispy outside and soft inside. Colorful
candies add the circus touch.*

Hard margarine (or butter), softened	1 cup	250 mL
Brown sugar, packed	2 cups	500 mL
Large eggs	2	2
Vanilla	1 tsp.	5 mL
All-purpose flour	2 cups	500 mL
Baking powder	1 tsp.	5 mL
Baking soda	1/2 tsp.	2 mL
Salt	1/2 tsp.	2 mL
Quick-cooking rolled oats (not instant)	2 cups	500 mL
Chopped walnuts (or pecans)	1/2 cup	125 mL
Candy-coated chocolate bits (about 3 oz., 85 g)	1/3 cup	75 mL

Cream margarine and brown sugar together in large bowl.
Beat in eggs, 1 at a time. Add vanilla. Mix.

Stir next 6 ingredients together in medium bowl. Add to
batter. Mix in. Drop by tablespoonfuls onto greased cookie
sheet.

Press candy pieces into dough. Bake in 400°F (205°C) oven
for 10 to 12 minutes. Makes about 4 1/2 dozen cookies.

1 cookie: 113 Calories; 2 g Protein; 5.1 g Total Fat; 16 g Carbohydrate; 87 mg Sodium;
1 g Dietary Fiber

Pictured on page 107.

Oatmeal Crisps

Chewy while warm; crispy when cooled.

Hard margarine (or butter), softened	1 cup	250 mL
Brown sugar, packed	1 1/2 cups	375 mL
Large egg	1	1
Corn syrup	1/2 cup	125 mL
Fancy molasses	1/4 cup	60 mL
Vanilla	1 tsp.	5 mL
Quick-cooking rolled oats (not instant)	2 1/2 cups	625 mL
All-purpose flour	2 1/2 cups	625 mL
Baking soda	2 tsp.	10 mL
Ground cinnamon	1 tsp.	5 mL
Ground nutmeg	1 tsp.	5 mL
Ground allspice	1 tsp.	5 mL

Cream margarine, brown sugar and egg together in large
bowl. Mix in corn syrup, molasses and vanilla.

Add remaining 6 ingredients. Mix well. Shape into 1 inch
(2.5 cm) balls. Arrange on greased cookie sheet. Flatten
with floured fork. Bake in 375°F (190°C) oven for 8 to
10 minutes until lightly browned. Makes about 5 dozen
cookies.

1 cookie: 98 Calories; 1 g Protein; 3.6 g Total Fat; 15 g Carbohydrate; 89 mg Sodium;
1 g Dietary Fiber

Pictured on this page.

Oatmeal Cookies

*Cinnamon, walnuts and raisins combine
to make this a nutritious and delicious cookie.*

Hard margarine (or butter), softened	1 cup	250 mL
Brown sugar, packed	1 cup	250 mL
Granulated sugar	1/2 cup	125 mL
Large eggs	2	2
Vanilla	1 tsp.	5 mL
Quick-cooking rolled oats (not instant)	2 cups	500 mL
All-purpose flour	2 1/2 cups	625 mL
Baking soda	1 tsp.	5 mL
Ground cinnamon	1 tsp.	5 mL
Chopped walnuts	1 cup	250 mL
Dark raisins	2 cups	500 mL
Golden raisins	1 cup	250 mL

Cream margarine and both sugars together in large bowl.
Beat in eggs, 1 at a time. Add vanilla. Mix.

Stir in rolled oats.

Add flour, baking soda and cinnamon. Mix well.

Add walnuts and both raisins. Mix well. Drop by
rounded tablespoonfuls onto greased cookie sheet about
1 inch (2.5 cm) apart. Bake in 375°F (190°C) oven for 12 to
15 minutes. Makes about 4 1/2 dozen cookies.

1 cookie: 133 Calories; 2 g Protein; 5.5 g Total Fat; 20 g Carbohydrate; 71 mg Sodium;
1 g Dietary Fiber

Pictured below.

Oatmeal Crisps

Oatmeal Cookies

TIME-HONORED RECIPE

Soft Molasses Drops

An old-time recipe that Mom used to bake. Moist and spicy.

All-purpose flour	3½ cups	875 mL
Granulated sugar	¾ cup	175 mL
Ground ginger	1 tsp.	5 mL
Ground cinnamon	1 tsp.	5 mL
Salt	½ tsp.	2 mL
Fancy molasses	¾ cup	175 mL
Hard margarine (or butter), softened	¾ cup	175 mL
Large egg	1	1
Baking soda	1½ tsp.	7 mL
Hot prepared coffee (or hot milk)	½ cup	125 mL

Measure first 8 ingredients into large bowl. Mix well.

Stir baking soda into hot prepared coffee in small cup. Add to dough. Beat well until blended. Drop by tablespoonfuls onto greased cookie sheet. Bake in 375°F (190°C) oven for 10 to 12 minutes. Makes 5 dozen cookies.

1 cookie: 72 Calories; 1 g Protein; 2.5 g Total Fat; 11 g Carbohydrate; 86 mg Sodium; trace Dietary Fiber

Pictured on page 111.

Snappy Gingersnaps

Great with tea, and even better for dunking in a glass of milk.

All-purpose flour	3 cups	750 mL
Baking powder	1 tsp.	5 mL
Baking soda	½ tsp.	2 mL
Ground ginger	1 tsp.	5 mL
Ground cinnamon	½ tsp.	2 mL
Salt	½ tsp.	2 mL
Cayenne pepper, just a pinch		
Hard margarine (or butter), softened	½ cup	125 mL
Granulated sugar	½ cup	125 mL
Fancy molasses	½ cup	125 mL
Cold prepared tea	2 tbsp.	30 mL

Measure first 7 ingredients into medium bowl. Stir well.

Cream margarine and sugar together in large bowl. Add molasses and prepared tea. Mix well. Add flour mixture. Mix well. Cover. Refrigerate for several hours or overnight. Roll out on lightly floured surface about ⅛ inch (3 mm) thick. Cut into 2½ inch (6.4 cm) circles. Place on greased cookie sheet. Bake in 375°F (190°C) oven for 10 to 12 minutes. Makes 4½ dozen cookies.

1 cookie: 59 Calories; 1 g Protein; 1.9 g Total Fat; 10 g Carbohydrate; 60 mg Sodium; trace Dietary Fiber

Pictured on this page.

Snappy Gingersnaps, this page   War-Time Cookies, below

TIME-HONORED RECIPE

War-Time Cookies

During World War II when sugar was scarce, people were in luck if pudding powders were available. Today, this is still a favorite.

Butterscotch (or caramel) pudding powder (not instant), 6 serving size	1	1
Hard margarine (or butter), softened	¾ cup	175 mL
Granulated sugar	1 tbsp.	15 mL
All-purpose flour	1 cup	250 mL
Quick-cooking rolled oats (not instant)	1½ cups	375 mL
Baking powder	¼ tsp.	1 mL
Baking soda	¼ tsp.	1 mL
Salt	⅛ tsp.	0.5 mL
Vanilla	1 tsp.	5 mL
Large egg	1	1

Measure all 10 ingredients into large bowl. Mix well. Roll into balls, 1 to 1¼ inches (2.5 to 3 cm) in diameter. Place on greased cookie sheet. Press with fork. Bake in 375°F (190°C) oven for 10 to 15 minutes. Makes about 3 dozen cookies.

1 cookie: 79 Calories; 1 g Protein; 4.5 g Total Fat; 9 g Carbohydrate; 79 mg Sodium; trace Dietary Fiber

Pictured above.

Top: Soft Molasses Drops, page 110   Bottom Center: Nutri Cookies, below   Right: Hermits, below

Nutri Cookies

Tell the kids they can have cookies for breakfast. They'll love it.

Hard margarine (or butter), softened	½ cup	125 mL
Smooth peanut butter	½ cup	125 mL
Liquid honey	1 cup	250 ml
Large eggs	2	2
Vanilla	1 tsp.	5 mL
All-purpose flour	1½ cups	375 mL
Quick-cooking rolled oats (not instant)	3 cups	750 mL
Medium coconut	1 cup	250 mL
Natural bran	¾ cup	175 mL
Sunflower seeds	½ cup	125 mL
Baking soda	1 tsp.	5 mL
Salt	1 tsp.	5 mL
Raisins	1 cup	250 mL
Chopped walnuts (or your choice of nuts)	½ cup	125 mL

Beat margarine and peanut butter in large bowl until blended. Add honey, eggs and vanilla. Beat slowly until blended.

Add remaining 9 ingredients. Mix well. Shape into balls using 1 tbsp. (15 mL) each. Flatten between your palms. Arrange on ungreased cookie sheet. Bake in 375°F (190°C) oven for about 12 minutes. Makes 8 dozen small cookies.

1 cookie: 69 Calories; 2 g Protein; 3.5 g Total Fat; 9 g Carbohydrate; 64 mg Sodium; 1 g Dietary Fiber

Plctured above.

Variation: Omit sunflower seeds. Add ¼ cup (60 mL) wheat germ.

TIME-HONORED RECIPE

Hermits

One of the best known drop cookies. Mom kept our cookie jar filled with these.

Hard margarine (or butter), softened	1 cup	250 mL
Brown sugar, packed	1½ cups	375 mL
Large eggs	3	3
Vanilla	1 tsp.	5 mL
All-purpose flour	3 cups	750 mL
Baking powder	1 tsp.	5 mL
Baking soda	1 tsp.	5 mL
Salt	½ tsp.	2 mL
Ground cinnamon	1 tsp.	5 mL
Ground nutmeg	½ tsp.	2 mL
Ground allspice	¼ tsp.	1 mL
Raisins	1 cup	250 mL
Chopped dates	1 cup	250 mL
Chopped nuts	⅔ cup	150 mL

Cream margarine and brown sugar together in large bowl. Beat in eggs, 1 at a time. Add vanilla.

Add remaining 10 ingredients. Mix well. Drop by tablespoonfuls onto greased cookie sheet. Bake in 375°F (190°C) oven for 6 to 8 minutes. Makes 4½ dozen cookies.

1 cookie: 115 Calories; 2 g Protein; 5 g Total Fat; 17 g Carbohydrate; 99 mg Sodium; 1 g Dietary Fiber

Pictured above.

Brown Sugar Cookies

An old-fashioned cookie taste. Not too sweet with little bits of almond crunch.

Hard margarine (or butter), softened	1 cup	250 mL
Brown sugar, packed	1⅓ cups	325 mL
Large eggs	2	2
Vanilla	½ tsp.	2 mL
All-purpose flour	3¼ cups	810 mL
Baking soda	1¼ tsp.	6 mL
Ground cinnamon	¾ tsp.	4 mL
Salt	¼ tsp.	1 mL
Chopped almonds	⅓ cup	75 mL

Cream margarine and brown sugar together in large bowl. Beat in eggs, 1 at a time. Add vanilla. Mix.

Stir in remaining 5 ingredients. Form into 2 rolls, 2 inches (5 cm) in diameter. Cover. Refrigerate overnight. Slice ¼ inch (6 mm) thick. Arrange on ungreased cookie sheet. Bake in 375°F (190°C) oven for 10 to 12 minutes until browned. Makes 3½ dozen cookies.

1 cookie: 117 Calories; 2 g Protein; 5.6 g Total Fat; 15 g Carbohydrate; 117 mg Sodium; 1 g Dietary Fiber

Pictured below.

TIME-HONORED RECIPE

Pan Shortbread

This recipe came from one of Mom's friends. A favorite recipe for shortbread that always turns out.

Butter (not margarine)	1 cup	250 mL
Icing (confectioner's) sugar	½ cup	125 mL
All-purpose flour	2 cups	500 mL

Combine all 3 ingredients in large bowl. Cut in butter until mixture is mealy. Using your hands, mix until you get a smooth ball. Press flat in ungreased 9 × 9 inch (22 × 22 cm) pan. Poke all over with fork right through to the bottom. Bake in 300°F (150°C) oven for 50 to 60 minutes until set and very lightly golden. Cut into 36 squares while warm.

1 square: 81 Calories; 1 g Protein; 5.5 g Total Fat; 7 g Carbohydrate; 55 mg Sodium; trace Dietary Fiber

Pictured below.

Brown Sugar Cookies, above

Pan Shortbread, above

Desserts

Our obsession with the sweet taste of dessert dates back to the 1820s. Puddings, pies, ice cream and sauces were enjoyed throughout the nineteenth century. Custards, steamed puddings and whips were often served, along with ice cream desserts such as Baked Alaska, and a variety of desserts using fresh fruits and berries. Chocolate desserts did not make an appearance until the twentieth century when chocolate became more widely available and reasonably priced. As our kitchens were modernized with gas and electric ranges, electric mixers, blenders and food processors, the variety and complexity of desserts changed. With the introduction of flavored jelly powders, packaged puddings and toppings, frozen puff pastry and phyllo after World War II, desserts now can be as simple as Fruit In Jelly or as elaborate as Turtle Cheesecake.

Chocolate Raspberry Dessert

A rich creamy dessert. Garnish with whipped topping.

Crust:

Hard margarine (or butter)	½ cup	125 mL
Graham cracker crumbs	1½ cups	375 mL
Finely chopped pecans	⅓ cup	75 mL

Filling:

Hard margarine (or butter), softened	½ cup	125 mL
Icing (confectioner's) sugar	1½ cups	375 mL
Light cream cheese, softened	4 oz.	125 g
Unsweetened chocolate baking squares, cut up	2 × 1 oz.	2 × 28 g
Raspberry jam	½ cup	125 mL
Envelope unflavored gelatin	1 × ¼ oz.	1 × 7 g
Water	¼ cup	60 mL
Envelope dessert topping (prepared according to package directions), or 1 cup (250 mL) whipping cream, whipped	1	1
Frozen raspberries in syrup, thawed, drained and syrup reserved	15 oz.	425 g

Raspberry Sauce:

Cornstarch	1½ tbsp.	25 mL
Reserved raspberry syrup, plus water to make	1¼ cups	300 mL

Crust: Melt margarine in small saucepan. Stir in graham crumbs and pecans. Press in ungreased 9 inch (22 cm) springform pan. Bake in 350°F (175°C) oven for 10 minutes. Cool.

Filling: Cream margarine, icing sugar and cream cheese together in medium bowl.

Combine chocolate and jam in small saucepan. Heat and stir over low until chocolate is melted.

Sprinkle gelatin over water in small bowl. Let stand for 1 minute. Add to chocolate mixture in saucepan. Stir until gelatin is dissolved. Chill until syrupy. Beat into cream cheese mixture.

Fold in dessert topping and raspberries. Pour over crust. Chill.

Raspberry Sauce: Stir cornstarch into reserved raspberry syrup in small saucepan. Heat and stir until boiling and thickened. Cool thoroughly. Spoon over each piece. Cuts into 12 wedges.

1 wedge: 438 Calories; 5 g Protein; 26.1 g Total Fat; 51 g Carbohydrate; 399 mg Sodium; 3 g Dietary Fiber

Pictured on page 115.

Turtle Cheesecake

*A bit more costly than most but it serves a large crowd.
Can be made ahead and frozen.*

Crust:

All-purpose flour	1½ cups	375 mL
Granulated sugar	3 tbsp.	50 mL
Hard margarine (or butter), softened	¾ cup	175 mL
Finely chopped pecans	¾ cup	175 mL

Caramel Layer:

Evaporated milk (or light cream)	3 tbsp.	50 mL
Caramels	32	32
Chopped pecans, toasted in 350°F (175°C) oven for 5 to 8 minutes	1 cup	250 mL

Cheese Layer:

Cream cheese, softened	3 × 8 oz.	3 × 250 g
Brown sugar, packed	1 cup	250 mL
All-purpose flour	2 tbsp.	30 mL
Large eggs	3	3
Creamed cottage cheese, run through blender (or sieved)	1 cup	250 mL
Vanilla	1½ tsp.	7 mL

Topping:

Whipping cream	1 cup	250 mL
Semisweet chocolate baking squares, cut up	7 × 1 oz.	7 × 28 g

Chopped pecans, toasted in 350°F (175°C) oven for 5 to 8 minutes, for garnish (optional)

Crust: Mix flour, sugar and margarine in medium bowl until crumbly. Add pecans. Stir. Press in bottom and 1 inch (2.5 cm) up sides of greased 10 inch (25 cm) springform pan. Bake in 350°F (175°C) oven for 15 to 20 minutes until edges are browning a bit. Cool slightly.

Caramel Layer: Heat evaporated milk and caramels in small saucepan, stirring often until smooth. Pour over crust.

Sprinkle with pecans.

Cheese Layer: Beat cream cheese and brown sugar in medium bowl until smooth. Beat in flour. Beat in eggs, 1 at a time just to mix. Add cottage cheese and vanilla. Beat on low just to mix. Pour over pecans. Bake in 350°F (175°C) oven for 1 hour. Turn off heat. Leave cheesecake in oven for 45 minutes. Set pan on rack. Run sharp knife around edge of cheesecake so top will settle evenly. Cool. Remove sides of pan. Place waxed paper under rack.

Topping: Heat whipping cream in small saucepan until barely simmering. Add chocolate. Stir until melted and smooth. Cool until barely warm. Pour over cheesecake, allowing topping to drip down sides in smooth even coating.

Sprinkle with pecans. Serves 16 lucky friends.

1 serving: 655 Calories; 12 g Protein; 48.4 g Total Fat; 50 g Carbohydrate; 388 mg Sodium; 3 g Dietary Fiber

Pictured on page 115.

Berry Spectacular

Dark chocolate cake covered with strawberries that are hidden from view with a pink strawberry mousse.

Dark chocolate cake mix (2 layer size)	1	1
Granulated sugar	⅔ cup	150 mL
Cornstarch	3 tbsp.	50 mL
Water	1½ cups	375 mL
Strawberry-flavored gelatin (jelly powder)	1 × 3 oz.	1 × 85 g
Frozen whipped topping (in a tub), thawed (or 1 envelope dessert topping, prepared according to package directions)	2 cups	500 mL
Whole medium fresh strawberries, to cover cake	30-35	30-35

Chocolate curls, for garnish

Prepare cake mix according to package directions. Pour into greased 10 inch (25 cm) springform pan. Bake in 350°F (175°C) oven for 55 to 60 minutes until wooden pick inserted in center comes out clean. While cake is still warm, press down lightly on center to make top level. Cool in pan.

Combine sugar, cornstarch and water in small saucepan. Heat and stir until boiling and thickened.

Stir in gelatin until dissolved. Chill, stirring and scraping down sides often, until syrupy.

Fold in whipped topping.

Trim strawberries to make same size if necessary. Arrange strawberries, pointed ends up, over surface of cake in pan about 1 inch (2.5 cm) in from edge.

Pour creamy mixture over top, filling in all spaces around berries. Chill until firm. Run knife around edge of cake. Remove sides of pan. Garnish with chocolate curls. Cuts into 12 wedges.

1 wedge: 309 Calories; 3 g Protein; 8.1 g Total Fat; 59 g Carbohydrate; 261 mg Sodium; 1 g Dietary Fiber

Pictured on front cover.

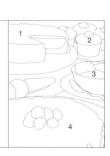

Cool Lime Soufflé

Present this in a soufflé dish for a lasting impression.
Garnish with whipped topping and lime peel.

Envelope unflavored gelatin	1 × ¼ oz.	1 × 7 g
Cold water	⅓ cup	75 mL
Granulated sugar	½ cup	125 mL
Lime juice	½ cup	125 mL
Egg yolks (large)	4	4
Salt, sprinkle		
Finely grated lime peel	1½ tsp.	7 mL
Drops of green food coloring	4	4
Egg whites (large), room temperature	4	4
Granulated sugar	½ cup	125 mL
Envelope dessert topping (not prepared)	1	1
Milk	½ cup	125 mL

Sprinkle gelatin over cold water in small bowl. Let stand while making custard.

Combine next 4 ingredients in top of double boiler. Cook over slowly boiling water, stirring constantly, until thickened enough to coat back of spoon. Add gelatin mixture. Stir until dissolved.

Add lime peel and food coloring. Chill, stirring and scraping down sides occasionally, until cool and beginning to gel.

Beat egg whites in medium bowl until soft peaks form. Gradually add second amount of sugar while beating until stiff and glossy.

Using same beaters, beat dessert topping and milk on low in small bowl. Beat on medium until stiff. Fold egg whites into thickened mixture. Add whipped topping. Gently fold in until no white streaks remain. Tie waxed paper collar, about 3 inches (7.5 cm) high, around top of ungreased 4 cup (1 L) soufflé dish or 6 individual ramekins. Turn mixture into soufflé dish or divide evenly among ramekins. Chill well. Remove collar before serving. Serves 6.

1 serving: 244 Calories; 6 g Protein; 6.4 g Total Fat; 42 g Carbohydrate; 63 mg Sodium; trace Dietary Fiber

Pictured on page 115.

Rhubarb Cobbler

A cobbler with a pinwheel design topping—a different look!
Scrumptious any time of the year.

Cut up fresh (or frozen) rhubarb (½ inch, 12 mm, lengths)	6 cups	1.5 L
Minute tapioca	3 tbsp.	50 mL
Granulated sugar	1½ cups	375 mL
Water	⅓ cup	75 mL
Lemon juice	1 tbsp.	15 mL
Topping:		
All-purpose flour	2 cups	500 mL
Granulated sugar	1½ tbsp.	25 mL
Baking powder	4 tsp.	20 mL
Salt	½ tsp.	2 mL
Milk	⅔ cup	150 mL
Cooking oil	3 tbsp.	50 mL
Hard margarine (or butter), softened	½ tbsp.	7 mL
Grated peel of ½ large lemon		
Granulated sugar	2 tbsp.	30 mL
Grated peel of ½ large lemon		
Granulated sugar	2 tbsp.	30 mL

Stir rhubarb, tapioca, sugar, water and lemon juice in large saucepan. Heat, stirring occasionally, until boiling. Turn into ungreased 3 quart (3 L) casserole. Bake, uncovered, in 450°F (230°C) oven for about 20 minutes.

Topping: Measure first 4 ingredients into medium bowl. Stir.

Add milk and cooking oil. Stir to make soft ball. Turn out onto lightly floured surface. Knead 8 times. Roll out ½ inch (12 mm) thick into rectangle 10 inches (25 cm) long.

Brush margarine over surface.

Stir first amounts of lemon peel and sugar in small cup. Sprinkle over top. Roll up like jelly roll from 10 inch (25 cm) side. Cut into 14 slices. Arrange over rhubarb, cut side down.

Stir second amounts of lemon peel and sugar in small cup. Sprinkle over pinwheels. Return to oven. Bake for about 25 minutes. Serves 8.

1 serving: 404 Calories; 5 g Protein; 6.6 g Total Fat; 83 g Carbohydrate; 202 mg Sodium; 3 g Dietary Fiber

Pictured on page 115.

Quick Date Pudding

Serve with a scoop of ice cream for the ultimate finish.

All-purpose flour	1 cup	250 mL
Granulated sugar	⅔ cup	150 mL
Baking powder	2 tsp.	10 mL
Salt	¼ tsp.	1 mL
Milk	½ cup	125 mL
Hard margarine (or butter), melted	2 tbsp.	30 mL
Chopped dates	1 cup	250 mL
Chopped walnuts	½ cup	125 mL
Brown sugar, packed	1 cup	250 mL
Hard margarine (or butter), softened	1 tbsp.	15 mL
Vanilla	1 tsp.	5 mL
Boiling water	2 cups	500 mL

Measure first 8 ingredients into medium bowl. Mix well. Turn into greased 8 inch (20 cm) round casserole.

Stir remaining 4 ingredients in separate medium bowl. Pour carefully over batter. Do not stir. Bake, uncovered, in 350°F (175°C) oven for 30 to 35 minutes until top crust is firm to touch. Serves 6.

1 serving: 522 Calories; 5 g Protein; 13.2 g Total Fat; 100 g Carbohydrate; 212 mg Sodium; 4 g Dietary Fiber

Pictured on this page.

Tapioca Pudding

A creamy blend of orange and pineapple.
Quite a refreshing dessert.

Water	1⅔ cups	400 mL
Tapioca pudding powder (not instant), 6 serving size (see Note)	1	1
Orange-flavored gelatin (jelly powder)	1 × 3 oz.	1 × 85 g
Envelope dessert topping (prepared according to package directions)	1	1
Canned crushed pineapple, drained	8 oz.	227 mL
Canned mandarin orange segments, drained	12 oz.	341 mL

Gradually mix water into pudding powder in medium saucepan. Heat and stir until boiling and thickened.

Add gelatin. Stir until dissolved. Chill, stirring and scraping down sides occasionally, until thickened.

Fold in dessert topping. Fold in pineapple and orange segments. Chill for several hours. Makes 4 cups (1 L) pudding.

⅔ cup (150 mL) pudding: 208 Calories; 2 g Protein; 3.3 g Total Fat; 44 g Carbohydrate; 122 mg Sodium; 1 g Dietary Fiber

Pictured on this page.

Note: If you can't find tapioca pudding powder, substitute coconut or vanilla pudding powder.

Hazelnut Dip

Tastes like European chocolate spread. Serve separately as a fruit dip or arrange mixture of fruit on each plate with large dollops of dip in center.

Sliced hazelnuts (filberts), toasted in 350°F (175°C) oven for 5 to 8 minutes	3½ oz.	100 g
Vanilla	1 tsp.	5 mL
Water	½ cup	125 mL
Envelope dessert topping (not prepared)	1	1
Milk	⅓ cup	75 mL
Brown sugar, packed	2 tbsp.	30 mL
Amaretto (or Frangelico) liqueur	4 tsp.	20 mL
Chocolate syrup (optional)	2 tsp.	10 mL

Combine first 3 ingredients in blender. Process until smooth.

Stir dessert topping and milk in medium bowl. Beat until stiff.

Beat in remaining 3 ingredients. Fold in hazelnut mixture. Makes 2½ cups (625 mL) dip.

2 tbsp. (30 mL) dip: 53 Calories; 1 g Protein; 3.9 g Total Fat; 4 g Carbohydrate; 51 mg Sodium; trace Dietary Fiber

Pictured below.

Top: Hazelnut Dip, above   Center: Tapioca Pudding, this page
Bottom: Quick Date Pudding, this page

Top Left: Strawberries And Cream, below
Top Right and Center: Choco Peanut Dessert Topping, this page
Bottom: Creamy Blueberry Dessert, this page

Strawberries And Cream

Rich and wonderful without being too sweet.

Sweetened condensed milk	11 oz.	300 mL
Water	1½ cups	375 mL
Instant vanilla pudding powder (4 serving size)	1	1
Frozen whipped topping, (in a tub), thawed	4 cups	1 L
Frozen pound cake, cut into ½ inch (12 mm) cubes (about 5 cups, 1.25 L)	10½ oz.	298 g
Sliced fresh strawberries	4 cups	1 L
Slivered almonds, toasted in 350°F (175°C) oven for 5 to 8 minutes	¼ cup	60 mL

Beat condensed milk and water in medium bowl until blended. Add pudding powder. Beat until smooth. Chill until set.

Stir pudding mixture. Fold in whipped topping.

Pour 2 cups pudding mixture into bottom of glass bowl. Spread with ½ of cake cubes and ½ of strawberries. Spoon ½ of remaining pudding mixture over strawberries. Cover with second ½ of cake cubes and second ½ of strawberries. Spoon remaining pudding mixture over top.

Sprinkle with almonds. Serves 12.

1 serving: 355 Calories; 5 g Protein; 15.7 g Total Fat; 50 g Carbohydrate; 120 mg Sodium; 1 g Dietary Fiber

Pictured above.

Creamy Blueberry Dessert

This is a great dessert to make ahead. Tastes even better the second day.

Crust:		
Hard margarine (or butter), softened	½ cup	125 mL
Brown sugar, packed	¼ cup	60 mL
All-purpose flour	1 cup	250 mL
Filling:		
Hard margarine (or butter), softened	½ cup	125 mL
Non-fat spreadable cream cheese	4 oz.	125 g
Icing (confectioner's) sugar	1 cup	250 mL
Canned blueberry pie filling	19 oz.	540 mL
Chopped pecans	½ cup	125 mL
Frozen whipped topping (in a tub), thawed	2 cups	500 mL

Crust: Mix margarine, brown sugar and flour in small bowl until crumbly. Pack in ungreased 9 x 9 inch (22 x 22 cm) pan. Bake in 350°F (175°C) oven for 10 minutes. Cool.

Filling: Cream margarine, cream cheese and icing sugar together well in small bowl. Spread over crust.

Spread pie filling over top. Sprinkle with pecans.

Put dabs of whipped topping here and there over top of pie filling. Spread to cover. Chill. Cuts into 12 pieces.

1 piece: 386 Calories; 3 g Protein; 23.4 g Total Fat; 43 g Carbohydrate; 196 mg Sodium; 1 g Dietary Fiber

Pictured on this page.

Choco Peanut Dessert Topping

Spoon this warm topping over vanilla ice cream. Not too sweet. Garnish with crushed peanuts.

Chocolate pudding powder (not instant), 6 serving size	1	1
Water	1⅓ cups	325 mL
Corn syrup	1 cup	250 mL
Smooth peanut butter	¾ cup	175 mL

Stir pudding powder and water in medium saucepan. Heat and stir until boiling and thickened. Remove from heat.

Add corn syrup and peanut butter. Stir until smooth. Makes 2 cups (500 mL) topping.

¼ cup (60 mL) topping: 352 Calories; 7 g Protein; 13.1 g Total Fat; 57 g Carbohydrate; 246 mg Sodium; 2 g Dietary Fiber

Pictured on this page.

Steamed Ginger Pudding

This recipe was passed down from Gram to Mom and then to me. Mom would serve this with applesauce or whipped cream. Or serve with Brown Sugar Sauce, this page.

All-purpose flour	2 cups	500 mL
Granulated sugar	2 tbsp.	30 mL
Ground ginger	1 tsp.	5 mL
Hard margarine (or butter), softened	¼ cup	60 mL
Raisins	½ cup	125 mL
Fancy molasses	2 tbsp.	30 mL
Baking soda	1 tsp.	5 mL
Milk	1 cup	250 mL

Measure flour, sugar and ginger into medium bowl. Add margarine. Mix until crumbly. Stir in raisins to coat with flour mixture.

Add molasses.

Mix baking soda and milk in small bowl. Add to flour mixture. Stir to mix. Turn into greased 1½ quart (1.5 L) pudding pan. Cover with double square greased foil, tying sides down with string. Place in steamer with boiling water ⅔ up sides of pan. Steam for 2 hours, adding more boiling water as needed to keep level up. Serves 6.

1 serving (without sauce): 325 Calories; 6 g Protein; 9.2 g Total Fat; 55 g Carbohydrate; 350 mg Sodium; 2 g Dietary Fiber

Pictured below.

Brown Sugar Sauce

The finishing touch for all steamed and cottage fruit puddings.

Brown sugar, packed	1 cup	250 mL
All-purpose flour	¼ cup	60 mL
Salt	½ tsp.	2 mL
Water	2 cups	500 mL
Vanilla	1 tsp.	5 mL

Mix brown sugar, flour and salt well in medium saucepan. This allows water to be mixed in with no lumps.

Stir in water and vanilla. Heat over medium, stirring constantly, until boiling and thickened. Makes about 2½ cups (625 mL) sauce.

2 tbsp. (30 mL) sauce: 48 Calories; trace Protein; trace Total Fat; 12 g Carbohydrate; 69 mg Sodium; trace Dietary Fiber

Pictured below and on page 120.

Steamed Ginger Pudding with Brown Sugar Sauce

TIME-HONORED RECIPE

Brown Betty

Good hot or cold. Serve with cream or ice cream.

Cooking apples, peeled and sliced	6 cups	1.5 L
Granulated sugar	¾ cup	175 mL
Topping:		
All-purpose flour	1¼ cups	300 mL
Brown sugar, packed	¾ cup	175 mL
Hard margarine (or butter)	½ cup	125 mL
Salt	½ tsp.	2 mL

Fill greased 10 inch (25 cm) round casserole with apples about 2 to 3 inches (5 to 7.5 cm) deep. Sprinkle sugar over top.

Topping: Mix flour, brown sugar, margarine and salt until crumbly. Scatter over apples. Pat down lightly with hand. Bake, uncovered, in 375°F (190°C) oven for about 40 minutes until apples are tender. Serves 8 generously.

1 serving: 392 Calories; 2 g Protein; 12.7 g Total Fat; 70 g Carbohydrate; 320 mg Sodium; 2 g Dietary Fiber

Pictured on this page.

TIME-HONORED RECIPE

Carrot Pudding

Fruity, dark and moist. Ice cream makes a good addition. Serve with Brown Sugar Sauce, page 119.

Grated carrot	1 cup	250 mL
Grated potato	1 cup	250 mL
Ground suet	1 cup	250 mL
Granulated sugar	1 cup	250 mL
Raisins	1 cup	250 mL
Currants	¼ cup	60 mL
All-purpose flour	1½ cups	375 mL
Baking powder	1 tsp.	5 mL
Baking soda	1 tsp.	5 mL
Ground cinnamon	1 tsp.	5 mL
Ground allspice	½ tsp.	2 mL

Measure all 11 ingredients into large bowl. Stir together well. Pack in greased 10 cup (2.5 L) pudding pan. If you don't have a pudding pan, you can use sealer jars, vegetable or juice cans or even a bowl, filling ⅔ full. Cover with double square greased foil, tying sides down with string. Place in steamer with boiling water ⅔ up sides of pan. Steam for at least 3 hours, adding more boiling water as needed to keep level up. Serves 15.

1 serving: 282 Calories; 2 g Protein; 14.7 g Total Fat; 37 g Carbohydrate; 98 mg Sodium; 1 g Dietary Fiber

Pictured on this page.

Fruit Cobbler

A pretty cobbler that makes and bakes quickly.

Frozen raspberries in syrup, thawed, drained and syrup reserved	15 oz.	425 g
Canned pears, drained and juice reserved, cut up	14 oz.	398 mL
Granulated sugar	⅓ cup	75 mL
All-purpose flour	1½ tbsp.	25 mL
Ground cinnamon	¼ tsp.	1 mL
Reserved raspberry syrup, plus pear juice to make	¾ cup	175 mL
Topping:		
Large egg	1	1
Hard margarine (or butter), melted	¼ cup	60 mL
Milk	⅓ cup	75 mL
All-purpose flour	1 cup	250 mL
Granulated sugar	¼ cup	60 mL
Baking powder	1½ tsp.	7 mL
Salt	¼ tsp.	1 mL

Layer raspberries and pears in ungreased 2 quart (2 L) casserole.

Combine sugar, flour and cinnamon in small saucepan. Add reserved juices. Mix well. Heat and stir until boiling and thickened. Pour over fruit. Stir. Place in 425°F (220°C) oven to heat while preparing topping.

Topping: Beat egg in medium bowl. Stir in margarine. Add milk. Stir.

Add flour, sugar, baking powder and salt. Stir just to moisten. Drop by tablespoonfuls over juice mixture. Return to oven. Bake, uncovered, for about 20 minutes until risen and browned. Serves 6.

1 serving: 340 Calories; 5 g Protein; 8.9 g Total Fat; 62 g Carbohydrate; 227 mg Sodium; 4 g Dietary Fiber

Pictured on page 121.

Top Left: Carrot Pudding, this page
Top Right: Brown Sugar Sauce, page 119
Bottom: Brown Betty, this page

Nothing Dessert, below   Fruit Cobbler, page 120   Fruit In Jelly, below

Nothing Dessert

So light, it's like eating nothing.

Large marshmallows (8 oz., 250 g)	32	32
Milk	⅓ cup	75 mL
Envelopes dessert topping (not prepared)	2	2
Milk	1 cup	250 mL
Vanilla	1 tsp.	5 mL
Fresh blueberries (or frozen, thawed and dried with paper towel)	2 cups	500 mL
Graham cracker crumbs	1-2 tbsp.	15-30 mL

Combine marshmallows and first amount of milk in large saucepan. Heat, stirring often, until marshmallows are melted. Transfer to large bowl. Cool, stirring often, until thickened.

Combine dessert topping, second amount of milk and vanilla in medium bowl. Beat until stiff. Fold into marshmallow mixture.

Reserve about ¼ cup (60 mL) blueberries for garnish. Add remaining blueberries to marshmallow mixture. Fold in lightly. Turn into serving bowl.

Sprinkle with graham crumbs and reserved blueberries. Chill. Makes 6 cups (1.5 L) dessert.

½ cup (125 mL) dessert: 137 Calories; 2 g Protein; 3.3 g Total Fat; 26 g Carbohydrate; 47 mg Sodium; 1 g Dietary Fiber

Pictured above.

Fruit In Jelly

A fast and easy favorite dessert for longer than can be remembered. It was served in a wide shallow bowl so that everyone got fruit and cream.

Raspberry-flavored gelatin (jelly powder), see Note	2 × 3 oz.	2 × 85 g
Boiling water	2 cups	500 mL
Cold water	2 cups	500 mL
Medium banana, sliced to cover	1	1
Frozen whipped topping (in a tub), thawed	2 cups	500 mL

Stir gelatin into boiling water in medium bowl. Stir well until dissolved. Stir in cold water. Cool to room temperature on counter or put into refrigerator. When jelly gets syrupy but before it begins to set, lay banana slices on top. Push down into jelly to coat. Chill.

Spread with whipped topping. Serves 8.

1 serving: 155 Calories; 2 g Protein; 5.1 g Total Fat; 27 g Carbohydrate; 66 mg Sodium; trace Dietary Fiber

Pictured above.

Note: Other flavors of jelly powder can be used. Other fruits and food to use (the ones that float) are fresh diced apple, fresh pear and peach slices, raspberries, strawberry slices, marshmallows and chopped nuts.

Fish & Seafood

In the 1940s we were told that every homemaker should replace meat courses with fish at least twice a week. Today, the benefits of including more fish in our diets are well documented. Fish and seafood are also more popular now because of the availability of recipes for varied preparation. You will have every member of the family enjoying the dishes in this section. Fish Sticks remain a classic favorite among children and Lobster Newburg is an elegant dish to serve for a special adult occasion.

Fish Sticks

Serve with tartar sauce or ketchup.
Every member of the family will love these!

All-purpose flour	⅓ cup	75 mL
Large eggs	2	2
Water	4 tsp.	20 mL
Fine dry bread crumbs	1 cup	250 mL
Salt	1 tsp.	5 mL
Pepper	¼ tsp.	1 mL
Paprika	1 tsp.	5 mL
Cod fish fillets, skin removed, cut 3½ × 1 inch (9 × 2.5 cm)	1 lb.	454 g
Hard margarine (or butter)	2 tbsp.	30 mL

Put flour into small bowl.

Beat eggs and water in separate small bowl.

Stir bread crumbs, salt, pepper and paprika in separate small bowl.

Dip each fish piece into flour to coat, then dip into egg mixture, then into bread crumb mixture. Set on large plate.

Melt margarine in non-stick frying pan. Add fish sticks. Brown both sides until medium to medium-dark and fish flakes easily when tested with fork. Makes about 20 fish sticks.

3 fish sticks: 202 Calories; 17 g Protein; 6.4 g Total Fat; 18 g Carbohydrate; 631 mg Sodium; 1 g Dietary Fiber

Pictured below.

Fish Sticks, above

Finnan Haddie, page 123

Finnan Haddie

This smoked and salted haddock is a member of the cod family. It's very popular in Scotland and in Atlantic Canada.

Finnan haddie, cut into serving size pieces	2 lbs.	900 g
Water, to cover		
Hard margarine (or butter)	3 tbsp.	50 mL
All-purpose flour	3 tbsp.	50 mL
Salt	1/2 tsp.	2 mL
Pepper	1/8 tsp.	0.5 mL
Milk	1 1/2 cups	375 mL
Parsley flakes (optional)	1/2 tsp.	2 mL

Put fish into medium saucepan. Cover with water. Bring to a boil. Simmer slowly for 5 to 8 minutes to poach until fish flakes easily when tested with fork. Drain. Keep warm.

Melt margarine in small saucepan. Mix in flour, salt and pepper. Stir in milk and parsley until boiling and thickened. Cover fish with sauce in serving bowl. Serves 5 to 6.

1/5 recipe: 322 Calories; 49 g Protein; 9.6 g Total Fat; 7 g Carbohydrate; 1766 mg Sodium; trace Dietary Fiber

Pictured on page 122.

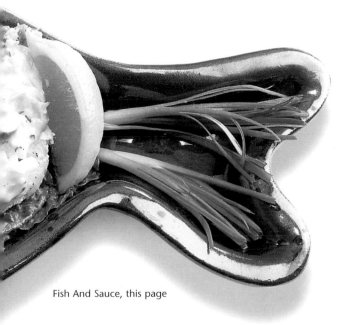

Fish And Sauce, this page

Fish And Sauce

Sauce complements fish well. A good mushroom flavor. If making sauce ahead, add a bit of milk when reheating to thin.

Mushroom Sauce:		
Hard margarine (or butter)	2 tsp.	10 mL
Chopped onion	1/2 cup	125 mL
Sliced fresh mushrooms	2 cups	500 mL
All-purpose flour	1 tbsp.	15 mL
Salt	1/4 tsp.	1 mL
Pepper	1/16 tsp.	0.5 mL
Parsley flakes	1/2 tsp.	2 mL
Milk	1/2 cup	125 mL
Fish:		
Hard margarine (or butter)	2 tsp.	10 mL
Fish fillets (such as cod, perch, jack fish or haddock)	1 1/4 lbs.	568 g
Lemon juice	1 tsp.	5 mL
Salt	1/4 tsp.	1 mL
Pepper, sprinkle		

Mushroom Sauce: Melt margarine in non-stick frying. Add onion and mushrooms. Sauté until onion is soft and mushrooms are golden.

Mix in flour, salt, pepper and parsley. Stir in milk until boiling and thickened. Makes 1 1/4 cups (300 mL) sauce.

Fish: Melt margarine in non-stick frying pan. Add fish fillets. Brown both sides. Drizzle with lemon juice. Sprinkle with salt and pepper. Cook for about 8 minutes until fish flakes when tested with fork. Place on platter or individual plates. Spoon sauce over top. Serves 4.

1 serving: 188 Calories; 27 g Protein; 5.4 g Total Fat; 7 g Carbohydrate; 479 mg Sodium; 1 g Dietary Fiber

Pictured page 122/123.

"It was difficult to get fresh fish. During the War, Fridays (and eventually Tuesdays) were designated as 'fish only' days. The stores weren't allowed to sell meat on those days, even if they had it."

Jean Paré

Salmon Pasta Dish, below   Baked Fish Fillets, below   Salmon Casserole, page 125

Salmon Pasta Dish

Visual appearance is best when using red salmon. A homey dish. Peas, carrots and corn show their colors.

Elbow macaroni (about 4 oz.,113 g)	1 cup	250 mL
Diced (or chopped) carrot	½ cup	125 mL
Chopped onion	½ cup	125 mL
Boiling water	2 qts.	2 L
Cooking oil (optional)	2 tsp.	10 mL
Salt	2 tsp.	10 mL
Condensed cream of celery soup	10 oz.	284 mL
Reserved liquid from salmon	⅓ cup	75 mL
Worcestershire sauce	½ tsp.	2 mL
Canned salmon, drained, liquid reserved, skin and round bones removed	7½ oz.	213 g
Frozen peas	½ cup	125 mL
Frozen kernel corn	⅓ cup	75 mL
Salt	½ tsp.	2 mL
Pepper	⅛ tsp.	0.5 mL

Combine first 6 ingredients in large pot or Dutch oven. Cook, uncovered, for 5 to 7 minutes, stirring occasionally, until macaroni is tender but firm. Drain. Return to pot.

Stir soup, reserved salmon liquid and Worcestershire sauce together well in large bowl. Add macaroni mixture. Stir.

Break up salmon. Add to macaroni mixture. Add remaining 4 ingredients. Stir lightly. Turn into ungreased 2 quart (2 L) casserole. Bake, uncovered, in 350°F (175°C) oven for about 30 minutes. Serves 4.

1 serving: 272 Calories; 15 g Protein; 8 g Total Fat; 35 g Carbohydrate; 1194 mg Sodium; 3 g Dietary Fiber

Pictured above.

Baked Fish Fillets

This recipe will turn hesitant fish eaters into fish lovers. Delicious. Serve with lemon wedges.

Thick fish fillets, (your favorite), cut bite size	1½ lbs.	680 g
Milk	1¼ cups	300 mL
All-purpose flour	3 tbsp.	50 mL
Dill weed	½ tsp.	2 mL
Salt	½ tsp.	2 mL
Pepper	⅛ tsp.	0.5 mL
Topping:		
Hard margarine (or butter)	2 tbsp.	30 mL
Dry bread crumbs	½ cup	125 mL
Poultry seasoning	¼ tsp.	1 mL
Parsley flakes	1 tsp.	5 mL
Onion powder	½ tsp.	2 mL
Pepper	⅛ tsp.	0.5 mL

Place fish pieces in ungreased shallow 2 quart (2 L) casserole.

Whisk milk into flour in small saucepan until no lumps remain. Add dill weed, salt and pepper. Heat and stir until boiling and thickened. Pour over fish.

Topping: Melt margarine in small saucepan. Mix in remaining 5 ingredients. Sprinkle over sauce. Bake, uncovered, in 400°F (205°C) oven for about 40 minutes until fish flakes when tested with fork. Serves 6.

1 serving: 204 Calories; 24 g Protein; 5.7 g Total Fat; 13 g Carbohydrate; 431 mg Sodium; trace Dietary Fiber

Pictured above.

Salmon Casserole

Nothing could be easier and quicker to prepare.

Canned salmon, drained, skin and round bones removed	7½ oz.	213 g
Dry bread crumbs	½ cup	125 mL
Sauce:		
Hard margarine (or butter)	6 tbsp.	100 mL
All-purpose flour	6 tbsp.	100 mL
Salt	¾ tsp.	4 mL
Pepper	¼ tsp.	1 mL
Milk	3⅓ cups	825 mL
Canned salmon, drained, skin and round bones removed	7½ oz.	213 g
Dry bread crumbs	½ cup	125 mL

Crumble first amount of salmon into ungreased 1½ quart (1.5 L) casserole. Sprinkle first amount of bread crumbs over top.

Sauce: Melt margarine in medium saucepan. Mix in flour, salt and pepper. Stir in milk. Heat, stirring constantly, until boiling and thickened. A whisk works really well to prevent lumps. Pour ⅓ of sauce over bread crumbs in casserole.

Crumble second amount of salmon over top. Sprinkle second amount of bread crumbs over salmon. Pour remaining sauce over top layer of crumbs. Use a knife to poke holes here and there to allow a bit of sauce to sink to bottom. Bake, uncovered, in 350°F (175°C) oven for 30 minutes until hot and bubbly. Serves 6.

1 serving: 359 Calories; 19 g Protein; 19.1 g Total Fat; 27 g Carbohydrate; 1001 mg Sodium; 1 g Dietary Fiber

Pictured on page 124.

Salmon Loaf

When few households had refrigerators, canned goods came in handy. An old standby. Serve with or without sauce.

Canned salmon (red is best for color), drained, skin and round bones removed	2 × 7½ oz.	2 × 213 g
Large eggs, fork-beaten	2	2
Dry bread crumbs	2 cups	500 mL
Finely chopped onion	½ cup	125 mL
Lemon juice	2 tbsp.	30 mL
Milk	½ cup	125 mL
Salt	¼ tsp.	1 mL
Dill weed	¼ tsp.	1 mL
Dill Sauce:		
Salad dressing (or mayonnaise)	½ cup	125 mL
Sour cream	¼ cup	60 mL
Lemon juice	2 tsp.	10 mL
Dill weed	1 tsp.	5 mL

Mix first 8 ingredients in medium bowl. Round bones of salmon may be added if mashed well. Pack in greased 8 × 4 × 3 inch (20 × 10 × 7.5 cm) loaf pan. Bake in 350°F (175°C) oven for 30 to 40 minutes.

Dill Sauce: Mix all 4 ingredients in small bowl. Put a dollop on each slice of loaf. Serves 6.

1 serving (with sauce): 400 Calories; 19 g Protein; 20.2 g Total Fat; 34 g Carbohydrate; 874 mg Sodium; 1 g Dietary Fiber

Pictured below.

Salmon Loaf

Lobster Newburg

Serve this chunky rich sauce in pastry cups or patty shells for a special evening. Elegant in a chafing dish.

Hard margarine (or butter)	3 tbsp.	50 mL
Frozen canned lobster meat	11.3 oz.	320 g
All-purpose flour	2 tbsp.	30 mL
Salt	½ tsp.	2 mL
Cayenne pepper	⅛ tsp.	0.5 mL
Half-and-half	1½ cups	375 mL
Sherry (or alcohol-free sherry)	2 tbsp.	30 mL
Egg yolks (large)	4	4

Melt margarine in medium saucepan. Add lobster meat. Stir well to coat.

Sprinkle with flour, salt and cayenne pepper. Mix.

Stir in half-and-half and sherry until beginning to boil.

Put egg yolks into small bowl. Stir about ¼ cup (60 mL) lobster mixture into egg yolks. Mix well. Stir back into lobster mixture. Stir constantly until boiling and thickened. Keep warm to serve. Makes 3¼ cups (810 mL) sauce, enough for 4 servings.

1 serving: 343 Calories; 21 g Protein; 24.3 g Total Fat; 8 g Carbohydrate; 726 mg Sodium; trace Dietary Fiber

Pictured above.

Pasta

In 1900, U.S. President Thomas Jefferson imported pasta from Italy, but very few cooks in North America knew how to prepare it. Italian pasta recipes were not commonly found in cookbooks until the early twentieth century. At that time, the most recognizable dishes were Macaroni and Cheese, and Spaghetti and Meatballs. In today's supermarkets the varieties of pasta are endless. You'll enjoy exploring the diversity of dishes in this section. Many can be served as an entrée such as Cheesy Manicotti, or as a side dish such as One-Pot Noodles.

Parsley Pesto Pasta

Rich with fresh parsley and pine nuts. An attractive accompaniment to chicken, beef, fish or pork.

Linguine pasta	12 oz.	340 g
Boiling water	3 qts.	3 L
Cooking oil (optional)	1 tbsp.	15 mL
Salt	2 tsp.	10 mL
Chopped fresh parsley	1 cup	250 mL
Pine nuts (or walnuts)	1/2 cup	125 mL
Garlic cloves, quartered	2	2
Olive (or cooking) oil	1/3 cup	75 mL
Water	2 tbsp.	30 mL
Salt	1/2 tsp.	2 mL
Pepper	1/8 tsp.	0.5 mL
Grated Parmesan cheese	1/2 cup	125 mL

Grated Parmesan cheese,
   sprinkle

Cook pasta in boiling water, cooking oil and first amount of salt in large uncovered pot or Dutch oven for 7 to 8 minutes until tender but firm. Drain. Return pasta to pot.

Put next 8 ingredients into blender. Process until smooth. Add to pasta.

Sprinkle with Parmesan cheese. Makes 7 1/2 cups (1.8 L).

1 cup (250 mL): 352 Calories; 12 g Protein; 18.8 g Total Fat; 37 g Carbohydrate;
   319 mg Sodium; 3 g Dietary Fiber

Pictured on front cover.

Pasta And Mushrooms

The sour cream adds the perfect zip to this sauced dish.

Medium egg noodles	8 oz.	225 g
Boiling water	2 qts.	2 L
Cooking oil (optional)	1 tbsp.	15 mL
Salt	2 tsp.	10 mL
Hard margarine (or butter)	1 tbsp.	15 mL
Sliced fresh mushrooms	4 cups	1 L
Garlic clove, minced (or 1/4 tsp., 1 mL, powder)	1	1
Chopped fresh parsley	1 cup	250 mL
Light sour cream	2 cups	500 mL
Grated Parmesan cheese	1/2 cup	125 mL
Salt	1 tsp.	5 mL

Grated Parmesan cheese,
   generous sprinkle
Chopped fresh parsley,
   for garnish

Cook noodles in boiling water, cooking oil and first amount of salt in large uncovered pot or Dutch oven for 5 to 7 minutes until tender but firm. Drain. Return noodles to pot.

Melt margarine in non-stick frying pan. Add mushrooms. Sauté until soft. Add to noodles.

Sauté garlic and parsley in frying pan, adding more margarine if needed. Add to noodle mixture.

Add sour cream, Parmesan cheese and second amount of salt. Stir over medium until hot.

Turn into serving bowl or platter. Sprinkle with Parmesan cheese and parsley. Makes 5 1/3 cups (1.25 L).

1 cup (250 mL): 344 Calories; 15 g Protein; 13.8 g Total Fat; 41 g Carbohydrate;
   775 mg Sodium; 3 g Dietary Fiber

Pictured on page 128.

Top: Peanut-Sauced Pasta, below
Center Left: Pasta And Mushrooms, page 127
Center Right and Bottom: Four Cheese Lasagne, this page

Four Cheese Lasagne

Layers of four varieties of white cheese keep this light colored. Reminds you of Swiss fondue! Very rich so serve small portions with a nice green salad.

Lasagne noodles (about 12 oz., 340 g)	16	16
Boiling water	3 qts.	3 L
Cooking oil (optional)	1 tbsp.	15 mL
Salt	2 tsp.	10 mL
Sauce:		
Hard margarine (or butter)	1/3 cup	75 mL
All-purpose flour	1/3 cup	75 mL
Salt	1 tsp.	5 mL
Pepper	1/4 tsp.	1 mL
Milk	3 cups	750 mL
Sherry (or alcohol-free sherry)	3 tbsp.	50 mL
Ground nutmeg	1/4 tsp.	1 mL
Garlic powder	1/16 tsp.	0.5 mL
Cayenne pepper	1/16 tsp.	0.5 mL
Grated Gruyére cheese	3/4 cup	175 mL
Grated white Cheddar (or Havarti) cheese	1 cup	250 mL
Freshly grated Parmesan cheese	1/2 cup	125 mL
Grated mozzarella cheese	1 cup	250 mL

Cook noodles in boiling water, cooking oil and salt in large uncovered pot or Dutch oven for 14 to 16 minutes until tender but firm. Drain. Rinse with cold water. Drain.

Sauce: Melt margarine in medium saucepan. Mix in flour, salt and pepper. Stir in milk, sherry, nutmeg, garlic powder and cayenne pepper until boiling and thickened.

Assemble in greased 9 x 13 inch (22 x 33 cm) pan in layers as follows:

1. 4 lasagne noodles
2. All Gruyére cheese
3. 3/4 cup (175 mL) sauce
4. 4 lasagne noodles
5. All white Cheddar cheese
6. 3/4 cup (175 mL) sauce
7. 4 lasagne noodles
8. All Parmesan cheese
9. 3/4 cup (175 mL) sauce
10. 4 lasagne noodles
11. Remaining sauce
12. All mozzarella cheese

Bake, uncovered, in 325°F (160°C) oven for 30 to 40 minutes until hot and cheese is melted. Let stand for 10 minutes before cutting. Serve immediately. Cuts into 12 pieces.

1 piece: 318 Calories; 11 g Protein; 13.3 g Total Fat; 28 g Carbohydrate; 524 mg Sodium; 1 g Dietary Fiber

Pictured on this page.

Peanut-Sauced Pasta

Peanut butter flavor is mild enough to allow the soy sauce flavor to come through. Serve as an accompaniment to spicy chicken or skewered beef.

Peanut Sauce:		
Smooth (or chunky) peanut butter	1/3 cup	75 mL
Cooking oil	1 tbsp.	15 mL
Soy sauce	2 tbsp.	30 mL
White vinegar	1 tbsp.	15 mL
Garlic powder	1/4 tsp.	1 mL
Granulated sugar	1/2 tsp.	2 mL
Water	1/4 cup	60 mL
Hot pepper sauce	1/4 tsp.	1 mL
Linguine pasta	8 oz.	225 g
Boiling water	2 qts.	2 L
Cooking oil (optional)	1 tbsp.	15 mL
Salt	2 tsp.	10 mL
Chopped green onion	1 tbsp.	15 mL

Peanut Sauce: Mix first 8 ingredients in small bowl.

Cook pasta in boiling water, cooking oil and salt in large uncovered pot or Dutch oven until tender but firm. Drain. Return pasta to pot. Add sauce. Toss. Turn into serving bowl.

Sprinkle with green onion. Makes 4 cups (1 L).

1 cup (250 mL): 403 Calories; 14 g Protein; 15.7 g Total Fat; 53 g Carbohydrate; 634 mg Sodium; 3 g Dietary Fiber

Pictured above.

Garden Pasta

Crispy vegetables with pasta. Serve this colorful dish warm.

Radiatore pasta	8 oz.	225 g
Boiling water	3 qts.	3 L
Cooking oil (optional)	1 tbsp.	15 mL
Salt	1 tbsp.	15 mL
Fresh pea pods (small handful)		
Fresh (or frozen) peas	½ cup	125 mL
Broccoli florets	1 cup	250 mL
Sliced small zucchini, with peel	1 cup	250 mL
White (or alcohol-free white) wine	¾ cup	175 mL
Dried sweet basil	1 tsp.	5 mL
Pepper	1/16 tsp.	0.5 mL
Garlic clove, minced (or ¼ tsp., 1 mL, powder)	1	1
Sliced fresh mushrooms	¾ cup	175 mL
Grated carrot	¼ cup	60 mL
Light cream cheese, cut up	4 oz.	125 g
Cherry tomatoes, halved	8	8
Chopped fresh parsley	¼ cup	60 mL
Grated Parmesan cheese	2 tbsp.	30 mL

Cook pasta in boiling water, cooking oil and salt in large uncovered pot or Dutch oven for 6 minutes. Pasta will be undercooked.

Add next 4 ingredients. Stir. Return to a boil. Boil for 2 minutes. Drain. Return pasta and vegetables to pot. Cover to keep warm.

Combine next 6 ingredients in small saucepan. Bring to a simmer. Simmer until vegetables are tender.

Add cream cheese. Stir until melted. Add to pasta mixture.

Add tomatoes, parsley and Parmesan cheese. Toss. Serve immediately. Makes 8 cups (2 L).

1 cup (250 mL): 184 Calories; 8 g Protein; 3.5 g Total Fat; 27 g Carbohydrate; 188 mg Sodium; 3 g Dietary Fiber

Pictured on page 131.

> *"Pasta was fairly common when I was growing up. But it was just things like macaroni and cheese or spaghetti and meatballs. Nothing like the variety we have today."*
>
> Jean Paré

One-Pot Noodles

These brownish noodles are easy to prepare. A perfect accompaniment to any meal.

Hard margarine (or butter)	1 tbsp.	15 mL
Chopped onion	½ cup	125 mL
Canned sliced mushrooms, drained	10 oz.	284 mL
Beef bouillon cubes	5 × 1/5 oz.	5 × 6 g
Boiling water	2½ cups	625 mL
Fusilli pasta	8 oz.	250 g
Pine nuts (or almonds), toasted in 350°F (175°C) oven for 5 to 8 minutes (optional)	½ cup	125 mL

Melt margarine in large pot or Dutch oven. Add onion and mushrooms. Sauté until onion is soft.

Dissolve bouillon cubes in boiling water in small bowl. Add to mushroom mixture.

Add pasta. Bring to a boil. Cover. Simmer slowly for about 10 minutes until pasta is tender and liquid is absorbed. Add a bit more boiling water if needed during cooking. If mixture boils too fast pasta won't have time to cook before liquid is absorbed.

Serve with nuts stirred in, or sprinkled over, pasta. Makes 6 cups (1.5 L).

1 cup (250 mL): 195 Calories; 7 g Protein; 3.1 g Total Fat; 35 g Carbohydrate; 668 mg Sodium; 2 g Dietary Fiber

Pictured on page 130.

Noodles With Herbs

A tasty combination of herbs.

Broad noodles	8 oz.	225 g
Boiling water	2 qts.	2 L
Cooking oil (optional)	1 tbsp.	15 mL
Salt	2 tsp.	10 mL
Olive (or cooking) oil	1 tbsp.	15 mL
Hard margarine (or butter)	1 tbsp.	15 mL
Garlic cloves, minced	2	2
Chopped fresh parsley	½ cup	125 mL
Dried sweet basil	1 tsp.	5 mL
Salt	½ tsp.	2 mL
Dried crushed chilies	¼ tsp.	1 mL
Grated Parmesan cheese, sprinkle		

Cook noodles in boiling water, cooking oil and first amount of salt in large uncovered pot or Dutch oven for 5 to 7 minutes until tender but firm. Drain. Return noodles to pot.

Heat olive oil and margarine in non-stick frying pan. Add garlic, parsley, basil, second amount of salt and crushed chilies. Sauté until garlic is soft. Add to pasta. Mix.

Sprinkle with Parmesan cheese. Makes about 3½ cups (875 mL).

1 cup (250 mL): 337 Calories; 10 g Protein; 8.5 g Total Fat; 55 g Carbohydrate; 438 mg Sodium; 2 g Dietary Fiber

Pictured on page 131.

Casserole Lasagne

A jumbled lasagne with a cheesy top.

Lean ground beef	1 lb.	454 g
Canned stewed tomatoes, with juice	14 oz.	398 mL
Envelope spaghetti sauce mix	1 × 1½ oz.	1 × 43 g
Frozen peas	2 cups	500 mL
Creamed cottage cheese	1 cup	250 mL
Large egg, fork-beaten	1	1
Medium egg noodles (about 3⅓ cups, 825 mL)	8 oz.	225 g
Boiling water	2½ qts.	2.5 L
Cooking oil (optional)	1 tbsp.	15 mL
Salt	2 tsp.	10 mL
Grated Parmesan cheese	¼ cup	60 mL
Grated part-skim mozzarella cheese	¾ cup	175 mL

Scramble-fry ground beef in non-stick frying pan until no longer pink. Drain.

Add tomatoes with juice and spaghetti sauce mix. Stir well. Add peas, cottage cheese and egg. Stir. Turn into ungreased 3 quart (3 L) casserole.

Cook noodles in boiling water, cooking oil and salt in large uncovered pot or Dutch oven for 5 to 7 minutes until tender but firm. Drain. Add to casserole. Stir lightly.

Sprinkle with both cheeses. Bake, uncovered, in 350°F (175°C) oven for about 45 minutes. Serves 8.

1 serving: 325 Calories; 25 g Protein; 9.9 g Total Fat; 33 g Carbohydrate; 903 mg Sodium; 3 g Dietary Fiber

Pictured on page 131.

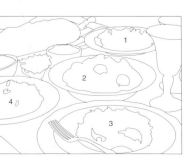
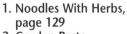

Perogies

When you have some extra time, make these savory potato cheese filled perogies. Serve with sour cream, diced cooked bacon and fried onion.

Dough:

All-purpose flour	2¹⁄₃ cups	575 mL
Cooking oil	2 tbsp.	30 mL
Water (or more if needed)	³⁄₄ cup	175 mL
Salt	¹⁄₂ tsp.	2 mL

Filling:

Warm cooked mashed potato	2 cups	500 mL
Grated medium Cheddar cheese	1 cup	250 mL
Hard margarine (or butter)	2 tbsp.	30 mL
Onion flakes, crushed	2 tsp.	10 mL
Salt	¹⁄₂ tsp.	2 mL
Pepper	¹⁄₈ tsp.	0.5 mL
Boiling water	4 qts.	4 L

Hard margarine (or butter), melted (optional)

Dough: Mix all 4 ingredients well in medium bowl. Knead on lightly floured surface until smooth. Return to bowl. Let rest for 20 minutes.

Filling: Mix first 6 ingredients well in separate medium bowl. Turn out dough onto lightly floured surface. Roll out about ¹⁄₁₆ inch (1.5 mm) thin. Cut into 2¹⁄₂ inch (6.4 cm) circles. Place rounded teaspoonful of filling in center of each. Fold dough over, pressing edges together to seal. Transfer to lightly floured baking sheet. Cover to prevent drying out until all are made.

Drop by batches into boiling water. Stir with wooden spoon to keep from sticking to bottom. Boil for 3 to 4 minutes. They will float to top and be puffed up when cooked.

Remove with slotted spoon to large bowl. Add melted margarine. Toss gently so they won't stick together. Cover. Keep hot while rest are cooking. Makes about 7 dozen perogies.

4 perogies: 121 Calories; 3 g Protein; 4.5 g Total Fat; 17 g Carbohydrate; 179 mg Sodium; 1 g Dietary Fiber

Pictured on page 133.

Note: These may be frozen uncooked individually on trays, then bagged, before cooking. Cook from frozen state.

Red Pepper Sauce

Citric acid enhances the flavor and adds zip! Makes a fairly thin sauce. Best with a shaped pasta such as radiatore or fusilli.

Chopped red pepper	2 cups	500 mL
Water	¹⁄₂ cup	125 mL
Chicken bouillon powder	1 tbsp.	15 mL
Skim evaporated milk	1 cup	250 mL
Salt	¹⁄₄ tsp.	1 mL
Pepper, light sprinkle		
Onion powder	¹⁄₄ tsp.	1 mL
Citric acid (available at drug stores), optional	¹⁄₈ tsp.	0.5 mL

Put red pepper, water and bouillon powder into medium saucepan. Cover. Simmer until tender. Do not drain. Cool slightly. Turn into blender. Process until smooth.

Combine evaporated milk, salt, pepper, onion powder and citric acid in small saucepan. Bring to a boil. Add red pepper mixture. Return to a boil. Makes about 2 cups (500 mL) sauce.

¹⁄₂ cup (125 mL) sauce: 76 Calories; 6 g Protein; 0.6 g Total Fat; 12 g Carbohydrate; 736 mg Sodium; 1 g Dietary Fiber

Pictured below.

Note: For a thicker sauce, mix 2 tsp. (10 mL) cornstarch and 2 tsp. (10 mL) water. Stir into boiling sauce until thickened.

Red Pepper Sauce

Top Left: Perogies, page 132   Bottom Left: Cheesy Manicotti, this page   Right: Armenian Pilaf, below

Cheesy Manicotti

An attractive dish. Very filling.

Meat Sauce:

Lean ground beef	½ lb.	225 g
Chopped onion	½ cup	125 mL
Chopped fresh mushrooms	1 cup	250 mL
Garlic clove, minced (or ¼ tsp., 1 mL, powder)	1	1
Tomato paste	5½ oz.	156 mL
Water	1½ cups	375 mL
Salt	½ tsp.	2 mL
Pepper	⅛ tsp.	0.5 mL
Manicotti shells	8	8
Boiling water	3 qts.	3 L
Cooking oil (optional)	1 tbsp.	15 mL
Salt	2 tsp.	10 mL

Cheese Filling:

Large egg	1	1
Creamed cottage cheese	¾ cup	175 mL
Grated part-skim mozzarella cheese	¾ cup	175 mL
Grated Parmesan cheese	¼ cup	60 mL
Parsley flakes	1½ tsp.	7 mL

Meat Sauce: Scramble-fry ground beef, onion, mushrooms and garlic in non-stick frying pan until beef is no longer pink. Drain.

Add next 4 ingredients. Stir. Spoon enough sauce into ungreased 9 x 9 inch (22 x 22) pan or shallow casserole to rest manicotti on.

Cook manicotti shells in boiling water, cooking oil and salt in large uncovered pot or Dutch oven for 6 to 7 minutes until tender but firm. Drain. Rinse with cold water. Drain.

Cheese Filling: Stir all 5 ingredients together in small bowl. Spoon filling into each shell. Lay all shells in single layer over sauce in pan. Spoon remaining sauce over top. Cover. Bake in 350°F (175°C) oven for about 40 minutes. Serves 4.

1 serving: 351 Calories; 31 g Protein; 12.9 g Total Fat; 28 g Carbohydrate; 827 mg Sodium; 3 g Dietary Fiber

Pictured above.

Armenian Pilaf

Both a pasta and rice dish. The perfect accompaniment to beef, chicken, fish or pork.

Hard margarine (or butter)	2 tbsp.	30 mL
Uncooked vermicelli (or angel hair) pasta, broken up	½ cup	125 mL
Long grain white rice	1½ cups	375 mL
Water	3 cups	750 mL
Chicken bouillon powder	2 tbsp.	30 mL
Salt	½ tsp.	2 mL
Pepper	¼ tsp.	1 mL

Melt margarine in large saucepan. Add vermicelli. Stir occasionally as pasta browns.

Add remaining 5 ingredients. Stir. Cover. Simmer for 15 to 20 minutes until rice and pasta are tender. Makes 5 cups (1.25 L).

¾ cup (175 mL): 223 Calories; 4 g Protein; 4.4 g Total Fat; 40 g Carbohydrate; 835 mg Sodium; 1 g Dietary Fiber

Pictured above.

Pies

Pie are the great North American dessert,

and people have been making them for

centuries. We love to indulge in a slice of pie

after any meal, whether it's dinner, lunch or even

breakfast. Over the years we have tried to master

the art of making pastry. Today, it has become so

easy and convenient to buy a frozen pie shell

or packaged pre-mixed dough. Simply pick

up a can of your favorite pie filling, and voilà—

a homemade pie! Try the old-fashioned taste of

Oatmeal Pie or a more modern Frozen Peanut

Butter Pie for your next gathering.

Top: Toffee Pie, this page
Bottom: Cherry Cream Pie, page 136

Toffee Pie

Smooth and crunchy. A great make-ahead.

Graham Cracker Crust:		
Hard margarine (or butter)	⅓ cup	75 mL
Graham cracker crumbs	1¼ cups	300 mL
Filling:		
Envelope unflavored gelatin	1 × ¼ oz.	1 × 7 g
Water	¼ cup	60 mL
Caramels	30	30
Milk	1¾ cups	425 mL
Vanilla	½ tsp.	2 mL
Envelope dessert topping (prepared according to package directions)	1	1
Chocolate-covered crisp butter toffee bars (such as Skor or Heath), finely processed in blender	2 × 1½ oz.	2 × 39 g

Graham Cracker Crust: Melt margarine in small saucepan. Stir in graham crumbs. Press in ungreased 9 inch (22 cm) pie plate. Bake in 350°F (175°C) oven for 10 minutes. Cool.

Filling: Sprinkle gelatin over water in small bowl.

Heat caramels, milk and vanilla in medium saucepan, stirring often, until caramels are melted. Add gelatin mixture. Stir until dissolved. Chill, stirring and scraping down sides often, until thickening.

Fold dessert topping into caramel mixture. Turn into crust.

Sprinkle with crushed toffee bars. Cuts into 8 wedges.

1 wedge: 397 Calories; 7 g Protein; 17.9 g Total Fat; 56 g Carbohydrate; 383 mg Sodium; trace Dietary Fiber

Pictured on page 134.

"I started making pies when we only had the wood stove. The fire was hot enough for cake if it felt real hot on your arm, but it would singe the hairs on your arm when it was hot enough for pies!"
Jean Paré

Blue Banana Pie, this page

Blue Banana Pie

Actually with blueberries, not blue bananas. A natural combination. Very showy. Garnish with whipped topping.

Small bananas, sliced	2	2
Baked 10 inch (25 cm) pie shell (or deep 9 inch, 22 cm, pie shell)	1	1
Cream cheese, softened	8 oz.	250 g
Granulated sugar	¾ cup	175 mL
Envelope dessert topping (prepared according to package directions)	1	1
Canned blueberry pie filling	19 oz.	540 mL

Lay banana slices over bottom of pie shell to cover.

Beat cream cheese and sugar in medium bowl until smooth.

Fold in dessert topping. Spoon over banana.

Place dabs of pie filling here and there over top. Spread as best you can. Chill well. Cuts into 8 wedges.

1 wedge: 442 Calories; 5 g Protein; 22 g Total Fat; 59 g Carbohydrate; 258 mg Sodium; 1 g Dietary Fiber

Pictured on this page.

Cherry Cream Pie

A creamy cheesecake layer tops a red cherry layer. Lovely contrast.

Pastry for 10 inch, 25 cm (or deep 9 inch, 22 cm) pie shell (your own or a mix)		
Canned cherry pie filling	19 oz.	540 mL
Topping:		
Light cream cheese	8 oz.	250 g
Large eggs	2	2
Granulated sugar	⅔ cup	150 mL
All-purpose flour	3 tbsp.	50 mL
Vanilla	1 tsp.	5 mL
Frozen whipped topping (in a tub), thawed	1 cup	250 mL

Roll out pastry on lightly floured surface. Fit into ungreased pie plate. Crimp and trim edge.

Spread pie filling in pie shell. Bake on bottom rack in 425°F (220°C) oven for 15 minutes.

Topping: Beat cream cheese, eggs, sugar, flour and vanilla in medium bowl until smooth. Spoon dabs over cherry filling. Smooth. Reduce heat to 350°F (175°C). Bake for about 30 minutes. Chill.

Garnish with dabs of dessert topping. Cuts into 8 wedges.

1 wedge: 392 Calories; 7 g Protein; 16.7 g Total Fat; 55 g Carbohydrate; 454 mg Sodium; 1 g Dietary Fiber

Pictured on page 134.

Working Man's Pie

Anyone would work all day for this. The pie forms a natural nest to accommodate whipped topping.

Brown sugar, packed	¾ cup	175 mL
Maple syrup	¾ cup	175 mL
Evaporated milk (or light cream)	⅓ cup	75 mL
Hard margarine (or butter)	3 tbsp.	50 mL
Egg yolks (large)	3	3
Egg whites (large), room temperature	3	3
Ground nutmeg, sprinkle		
Unbaked deep 9 inch (22 cm) pie shell	1	1
Envelope dessert topping (prepared according to package directions), or 1 cup (250 mL) whipping cream, whipped	1	1

Whisk first 5 ingredients together in small saucepan. Heat, stirring constantly, until hot and slightly thickened. Remove from heat.

Beat egg whites in medium bowl until stiff. Sprinkle with nutmeg. Gradually fold in hot mixture.

Pour into pie shell. Bake on bottom rack in 350°F (175°C) oven for 40 to 50 minutes until browned. Cool. Filling will collapse in center.

Fill center of pie with dessert topping. Cuts into 8 wedges.

1 wedge: 387 Calories; 5 g Protein; 16.4 g Total Fat; 56 g Carbohydrate; 249 mg Sodium; trace Dietary Fiber

Pictured on page 137.

Oatmeal Pie

Rich like pecan pie. You would never know oatmeal is in the pie. Scrumptious!

Hard margarine (or butter), softened	6 tbsp.	100 mL
Granulated sugar	1 cup	250 mL
Large eggs	2	2
Golden corn syrup	3/4 cup	175 mL
Vanilla	1 tsp.	5 mL
Quick-cooking rolled oats (not instant)	1 cup	250 mL
Unbaked 9 inch (22 cm) pie shell	1	1

Cream margarine and sugar together in medium bowl. Beat in eggs, 1 at a time. Add corn syrup and vanilla. Mix.

Stir in rolled oats.

Pour into pie shell. Bake on bottom rack in 350°F (175°C) oven for 40 to 50 minutes until set. Lay a piece of foil over pie if crust browns too much. Cuts into 8 wedges.

1 wedge: 449 Calories; 5 g Protein; 18.2 g Total Fat; 68 g Carbohydrate; 280 mg Sodium; 1 g Dietary Fiber

Pictured below.

Glazed Fresh Raspberry Pie

Garnish with whipped cream for the final touch.

Water	1 1/2 cups	375 mL
Granulated sugar	3/4 cup	175 mL
Cornstarch	2 tbsp.	30 mL
Raspberry-flavored gelatin (jelly powder)	1 × 3 oz.	1 × 85 g
Fresh raspberries	4 cups	1 L
Baked 9 inch (22 cm) pie shell	1	1

Mix water, sugar and cornstarch in small saucepan over medium. Stir until boiling and thickened.

Add gelatin. Stir until dissolved. Cool for 30 minutes.

Pile raspberries evenly in pie shell. Pour gelatin mixture over berries. Chill until set. Cuts into 8 wedges.

1 wedge: 267 Calories; 3 g Protein; 7.9 g Total Fat; 48 g Carbohydrate; 168 mg Sodium; 3 g Dietary Fiber

Pictured below.

Top Left: Oatmeal Pie, above   Top Right and Bottom Left: Working Man's Pie, page 136   Bottom Right: Glazed Fresh Raspberry Pie, above

Top: Butter Date Pie, this page   Bottom: Frozen Peanut Butter Pie, below

Frozen Peanut Butter Pie

What could be more convenient and more tempting than a frozen pie waiting in the freezer. Serve with whipped topping or chocolate syrup, or both!

Chocolate Crumb Crust:		
Hard margarine (or butter)	⅓ cup	75 mL
Chocolate wafer crumbs	1⅓ cups	325 mL
Granulated sugar	¼ cup	60 mL
Vanilla ice cream	3 cups	750 mL
Smooth (or chunky) peanut butter	½ cup	125 mL
Unsalted peanuts, crushed or ground	¼ cup	60 mL
Envelope dessert topping (not prepared)	1	1
Milk	½ cup	125 mL
Unsalted peanuts, crushed or ground	2 tbsp.	30 mL

Chocolate Crumb Crust: Melt margarine in small saucepan. Stir in wafer crumbs and sugar. Press in ungreased 9 inch (22 cm) pie plate. Bake in 350°F (175°C) oven for 10 minutes. Cool well.

Stir ice cream, peanut butter and first amount of peanuts in medium bowl until well mixed.

Beat dessert topping and milk in small bowl until stiff. Fold into ice cream mixture. Pour into pie shell.

Sprinkle with second amount of peanuts. Freeze. Remove from freezer about 10 minutes before cutting. Cuts into 8 wedges.

1 wedge: 468 Calories; 10 g Protein; 31.1 g Total Fat; 42 g Carbohydrate; 263 mg Sodium; 2 g Dietary Fiber

Pictured above.

Butter Date Pie

Delicious and incredibly good. Garnish with whipped topping.

Pastry for 9 inch (22 cm) pie shell (your own or a mix)		
Filling:		
Hard margarine (or butter)	½ cup	125 mL
Brown sugar, packed	½ cup	125 mL
Granulated sugar	½ cup	125 mL
Egg yolks (large)	2	2
Vanilla	½ tsp.	2 mL
White vinegar	1 tbsp.	15 mL
Chopped pecans (or walnuts)	¾ cup	175 mL
Chopped dates	1 cup	250 mL
Egg whites (large), room temperature	2	2

Roll out pastry on lightly floured surface. Fit into ungreased pie plate. Crimp and trim edge.

Filling: Cream margarine, both sugars, egg yolks and vanilla together in medium bowl until smooth.

Stir in vinegar, pecans and dates.

Beat egg whites in small bowl until stiff. Fold into date mixture. Turn into pie shell. Bake in 350°F (175°C) oven for 45 to 55 minutes. Cuts into 8 wedges.

1 wedge: 477 Calories; 4 g Protein; 29 g Total Fat; 54 g Carbohydrate; 302 mg Sodium; 3 g Dietary Fiber

Pictured on this page.

Lemon Cheese Pie

Delicate lemon flavor with a smooth texture.

Granulated sugar	1¼ cups	300 mL
Cornstarch	¼ cup	60 mL
Hot water	1 cup	250 mL
Lemon juice	⅓ cup	75 mL
Finely grated lemon peel	1 tsp.	5 mL
Large egg, fork-beaten	1	1
Cream cheese, cut up	8 oz.	250 g
Envelope dessert topping (prepared according to package directions)	1	1
Baked 9 inch (22 cm) pie shell	1	1

Stir sugar and cornstarch together in medium saucepan. Add hot water and mix. Add lemon juice, lemon peel and egg. Heat and stir over medium until boiling and thickened.

Add cream cheese. Stir until melted and mixture is smooth. Cool completely.

Fold dessert topping into lemon filling.

Pour into pie shell. Chill. Cuts into 8 wedges.

1 wedge: 406 Calories; 5 g Protein; 20.6 g Total Fat; 52 g Carbohydrate; 243 mg Sodium; trace Dietary Fiber

Pictured on page 139.

Lemon Cheese Pie, page 138

Mock Mince Pie, this page

Mock Mince Pie

*During the Depression, this was an economical
way to still have a mince-flavored pie.*

Granulated sugar	1 cup	250 mL
Ground cinnamon	½ tsp.	2 mL
Ground nutmeg	¼ tsp.	1 mL
Ground cloves	¼ tsp.	1 mL
Salt	¼ tsp.	1 mL
Raisins	1 cup	250 mL
Sour cream	1 cup	250 mL
Egg yolks (large)	3	3
Unbaked 9 inch (22 cm) pie shell	1	1
Meringue: (see Note)		
Egg whites (large), room temperature	3	3
Cream of tartar	¼ tsp.	1 mL
Granulated sugar	6 tbsp.	100 mL

Measure first 5 ingredients into medium bowl. Stir well.

Mix in raisins, sour cream and egg yolks.

Pour into pie shell. Bake on bottom rack in 425°F (220°C) oven for 10 minutes. Reduce heat to 350°F (175°C). Bake for about 50 minutes until set.

Meringue: Beat egg whites and cream of tartar in medium bowl until almost stiff. Gradually beat in sugar until stiff and sugar is dissolved. Spread over hot pie. Return to oven for about 15 minutes until browned. Cuts into 8 wedges.

1 wedge: 383 Calories; 5 g Protein; 13.8 g Total Fat; 62 g Carbohydrate; 273 mg Sodium; 1 g Dietary Fiber

Pictured above.

Note: To make pie without meringue, use 2 whole eggs in filling instead of 3 egg yolks.

Strawberry Pie

A delicious double crust red pie that Mom made. Glazed pies had not been "invented" yet. Serve with whipped cream.

Pastry, enough for 2 crust pie (your own or a mix)		
Fresh strawberries, halved (quartered if large)	4 cups	1 L
Granulated sugar	1 cup	250 mL
Minute tapioca	3 tbsp.	50 mL
Granulated sugar	¼-½ tsp.	1-2 mL

Roll out pastry on lightly floured surface. Fit into ungreased 9 inch (22 cm) pie plate. Roll out top crust.

Place strawberries, first amount of sugar and tapioca in large bowl. Mix. Let stand for 15 minutes. Stir. Pour into pie shell. Dampen edge of pastry. Cover with top crust. Trim and crimp to seal. Cut vents in top.

Sprinkle with second amount of sugar. Bake on bottom rack in 350°F (175°C) oven for about 45 minutes until cooked. Cuts into 8 wedges.

1 wedge: 361 Calories; 3 g Protein; 15.3 g Total Fat; 54 g Carbohydrate; 277 mg Sodium; 2 g Dietary Fiber

Pictured below.

Marmalade Tarts, page 141

"The whole family watched Bonanza on TV every Sunday evening and had hot chocolate and cinnamon toast."

Jean Paré

Strawberry Pie

Marmalade Tarts

Even though this is such an odd mixture, you will be pleasantly surprised by the tasty results.

Pastry, enough for 2 crust pie
(your own or a mix)

Orange marmalade	³/₄ cup	175 mL
Grated sharp Cheddar cheese	³/₄ cup	175 mL
Granulated sugar	¹/₄-¹/₂ tsp.	1-2 mL

Roll out pastry on lightly floured surface. Cut out 24 circles, 3 inches (7.5 cm) in diameter. Fit into 24 greased muffin cups. Roll remaining dough to cut out 24 decorative tops.

Combine marmalade and cheese in small bowl. Divide among tart shells. Cover with pastry cut out.

Sprinkle each with a pinch of sugar. Bake in 450°F (230°C) oven for 12 to 15 minutes until golden. Makes 24 tarts.

1 tart: 117 Calories; 2 g Protein; 6.3 g Total Fat; 14 g Carbohydrate; 117 mg Sodium; 1 g Dietary Fiber

Pictured on this page and on page 140.

Kahlua Pie

Kahlua Pie

Incredibly good! Garnish with chocolate curls and/or whipped topping.

Chocolate Graham Crumb Crust:		
Hard margarine (or butter)	6 tbsp.	100 mL
Graham cracker crumbs	1¹/₄ cups	300 mL
Cocoa	1 tbsp.	15 mL
Granulated sugar	2 tbsp.	30 mL
Filling:		
Large marshmallows	30	30
Milk	¹/₄ cup	60 mL
Prepared coffee	¹/₄ cup	60 mL
Kahlua liqueur	¹/₂ cup	125 mL
Envelope dessert topping (prepared according to package directions)	1	1

Chocolate Graham Crumb Crust: Melt margarine in small saucepan. Stir in graham crumbs, cocoa and sugar. Press in ungreased 9 inch (22 cm) pie plate. Bake in 350°F (175°C) oven for 10 minutes. Cool completely.

Filling: Heat marshmallows, milk and prepared coffee in large saucepan, stirring often, until marshmallows are melted.

Stir in Kahlua. Chill, stirring occasionally, until starting to thicken.

Fold in dessert topping. Turn into pie crust. Chill. Cuts into 8 wedges.

1 wedge: 347 Calories; 3 g Protein; 13.3 g Total Fat; 48 g Carbohydrate; 267 mg Sodium; 1 g Dietary Fiber

Pictured above.

Carrot Pie, below

Vinegar Pie, below

 TIME-HONORED RECIPE

Carrot Pie

From the period of the Depression. Tastes like pumpkin pie.

Large eggs	2	2
Granulated sugar	½ cup	125 mL
Ground cinnamon	¾ tsp.	4 mL
Ground nutmeg	½ tsp.	2 mL
Ground ginger	½ tsp.	2 mL
Ground cloves	⅛ tsp.	0.5 mL
Cooked mashed carrot	1 cup	250 mL
Milk	1½ cups	375 mL
Fancy molasses (optional but good)	1 tbsp.	15 mL
Unbaked 10 inch (25 cm) pie shell	1	1
Envelope dessert topping (prepared according to package directions)	1	1

Beat eggs lightly in medium bowl. Add and mix in next 8 ingredients in order given.

Pour into pie shell. Bake on bottom rack in 450°F (230°C) oven for 10 minutes. Reduce heat to 350°C (175°C). Bake for about 45 minutes until knife inserted in center comes out clean. Cool.

Smooth dessert topping over pie. Cuts into 8 wedges.

1 wedge: 269 Calories; 6 g Protein; 12.8 g Total Fat; 33 g Carbohydrate; 226 mg Sodium; 1 g Dietary Fiber

Pictured above.

Note: An unbaked 9 inch (22 cm) pie shell may be used. There will be about ⅔ cup (150 mL) filling left over that will need to be baked in a separate container.

 TIME-HONORED RECIPE

Vinegar Pie

When grocery stores were far away and fresh lemons were scarce, this pie was a good substitute. Tastes like lemon pie.

White vinegar	⅓ cup	75 mL
Granulated sugar	½ cup	125 mL
Water	1¾ cups	425 mL
Granulated sugar	½ cup	125 mL
All-purpose flour	6 tbsp.	100 mL
Egg yolks (large)	3	3
Water	¼ cup	60 mL
Lemon flavoring	1 tsp.	5 mL
Baked 9 inch (22 cm) pie shell	1	1
Meringue:		
Egg whites (large), room temperature	3	3
White vinegar	½ tsp.	2 mL
Granulated sugar	6 tbsp.	100 mL

Measure vinegar and first amounts of sugar and water into medium saucepan. Stir. Bring to a boil over medium.

Mix next 5 ingredients in small bowl. Stir into boiling mixture until boiling and thickened.

Pour into pie shell.

Meringue: Beat egg whites and vinegar in small bowl until a stiff froth. Gradually add sugar, beating until stiff and sugar is dissolved. Spread over pie, sealing well to crust. Bake in 350°F (175°C) oven for about 10 minutes until browned. Cuts into 8 wedges.

1 wedge: 301 Calories; 4 g Protein; 9.5 g Total Fat; 51 g Carbohydrate; 162 mg Sodium; trace Dietary Fiber

Pictured above.

Custard Pie Without Crust

(old recipe)

This recipe is from an 1886 cookbook lent to me by a friend. An interesting way to make a crustless pie. The amount of milk will vary depending on the cook's interpretation of "fill the pie pan."

Custard Pie Without Crust

Three eggs, 3 tablespoons sugar, ½ cup Graham flour, Salt and flavour. The flour settles to the bottom and forms a good crust. Fill the pie-pan with milk, mixing a part of it with the other ingredients first.

Impossible Pie

(new recipe)

This has evolved from a plain custard pie to one with coconut added for flavor. A bit larger recipe also suits today's pie plate better. Serve with a dab of jam on each slice.

Large eggs	3	3
Milk	2 cups	500 mL
Granulated sugar	3 tbsp.	50 mL
All-purpose flour	½ cup	125 mL
Vanilla	1 tsp.	5 mL
Salt	¼ tsp.	1 mL
Medium coconut	1 cup	250 mL

Measure first 6 ingredients into blender. Process until smooth. If you don't have a blender, simply beat together in medium bowl.

Sprinkle coconut in bottom of greased 9 inch (22 cm) pie plate. Pour blender contents over coconut. Bake on bottom rack in 350°F (175°C) oven for 45 to 55 minutes until knife inserted in center comes out clean. Cuts into 8 wedges.

1 wedge: 184 Calories; 6 g Protein; 10.3 g Total Fat; 17 g Carbohydrate; 145 mg Sodium; 1 g Dietary Fiber

Pictured below.

Impossible Pie

Pork

Pork roasts, pork chops, pork tenderloin and bacon have been served at the table for centuries. With the luxury of refrigeration and freezers in today's modern society we have the opportunity to stock up on pork and plan a few weeks of meals in advance. As far back as can be remembered, applesauce has been a favorite to serve with pork and this is still the trend today. However, once you try the distinctive flavors of Blackberry Ribs and our Ham And Chicken Loaf, we know they'll become favorites.

Blackberry Ribs

Tangy sweet when glazed. Broil or barbecue.

Pork spareribs, cut into 2 or 3 rib sections	3½ lbs.	1.6 kg
Water, to cover		
Salt	1 tsp.	5 mL
Blackberry Glaze:		
Blackberry jam (or jelly)	½ cup	125 mL
Ketchup	⅓ cup	75 mL
Steak sauce	1 tbsp.	15 mL
Dry mustard	½ tsp.	2 mL
Garlic powder	⅛ tsp.	0.5 mL

Boil spareribs in water and salt in large saucepan for about 1 hour until very tender. Drain. Arrange on greased baking sheet with sides. Line with greased foil for easy cleanup.

Blackberry Glaze: Mix all 5 ingredients in small saucepan. Heat, stirring often, until boiling. Simmer for 5 to 10 minutes. Makes 1 cup (250 mL) glaze. Brush hot ribs with glaze. Broil or barbecue for about 5 minutes per side. Serves 4.

1 serving: 611 Calories; 37 g Protein; 35.8 g Total Fat; 35 g Carbohydrate; 761 mg Sodium; 1 g Dietary Fiber

Pictured on page 145.

BLACKBERRY CHICKEN: Cook about 3 lbs. (1.4 kg) chicken parts in water and salt for about 40 minutes. Brush with glaze and broil or barbecue.

Sweet And Sour Ribs

Sweet, sour, spicy and tender. All this in one roaster.

Pork spareribs, cut into 2 or 3 rib sections	5 lbs.	2.3 kg
Water, to cover		
Smoky Sweet And Sour Sauce:		
Brown sugar, packed	¾ cup	175 mL
Chili powder	½ tsp.	2 mL
Apple cider vinegar	¾ cup	175 mL
Ketchup	½ cup	125 mL
Small onion, chopped	1	1
Worcestershire sauce	2 tbsp.	30 mL
Water	½ cup	125 mL
Salt	½ tsp.	2 mL
Cornstarch	1 tbsp.	15 mL
Dry mustard	1 tsp.	5 mL
Liquid smoke	⅛ tsp.	0.5 mL
Liquid gravy browner	⅛ tsp.	0.5 mL

Boil ribs in water in large uncovered pot or Dutch oven for 15 minutes. Drain. Arrange ribs in small roaster.

Smoky Sweet And Sour Sauce: Mix all 12 ingredients in medium bowl. Pour over ribs. Cover. Bake in 350°F (175°C) oven for 1 to 1½ hours until pork is falling-off-the-bone tender. Serves 6.

1 serving: 607 Calories; 35 g Protein; 34.3 g Total Fat; 39 g Carbohydrate; 714 mg Sodium; 1 g Dietary Fiber

Pictured on page 145.

1. Sweet And Sour Ribs, above
2. Blackberry Ribs, this page
3. Sweet And Sour Pork, page 145

Sweet And Sour Pork

This is all meat which makes it so easy to serve over rice.

Lean boneless pork steaks, trimmed of fat, cut into 1½ inch (3.8 cm) cubes	3 lbs.	1.4 kg
Water, to cover		
Sweet And Sour Sauce:		
Reserved stock	1 cup	250 mL
Brown sugar, packed	⅔ cup	150 mL
White vinegar	½ cup	125 mL
Ketchup	½ cup	125 mL

Cook pork cubes in water in large uncovered pot or Dutch oven for 1 to 1½ hours. Drain stock, reserving 1 cup (250 mL).

Sweet And Sour Sauce: Stir all 4 ingredients in small bowl. Pour over pork. Simmer slowly, stirring occasionally, for 30 minutes. Serves 8.

1 serving: 259 Calories; 25 g Protein; 6.6 g Total Fat; 24 g Carbohydrate; 315 mg Sodium; trace Dietary Fiber

Pictured on this page.

Ham Cauliflower Bake

Ham Cauliflower Bake

This is a dish the whole family will enjoy.
Cheesy and delicious.

Cauliflower pieces	5 cups	1.25 L
Water, to cover		
Condensed cream of chicken soup	10 oz.	284 mL
Light sour cream	1/3 cup	75 mL
Canned whole mushrooms, drained	10 oz.	284 mL
Chopped green onion	1/4 cup	60 mL
Grated medium Cheddar cheese	1/2 cup	125 mL
Cubed cooked ham (3/4 inch, 2 cm)	2 cups	500 mL
Grated medium Cheddar cheese	3/4 cup	175 mL

Cook cauliflower in water in large saucepan until tender-crisp. Drain.

Mix next 6 ingredients in medium bowl. Stir in cauliflower. Turn into ungreased 2 quart (2 L) casserole.

Sprinkle with second amount of cheese. Bake, uncovered, in 350°F (175°C) oven for 30 to 40 minutes. Makes 4 generous servings.

1 serving: 432 Calories; 30 g Protein; 26.9 g Total Fat; 20 g Carbohydrate; 2024 mg Sodium; 6 g Dietary Fiber

Pictured above.

Quick Ham Bake

Once the tiny onions are peeled, this is in the oven in a flash.

Tiny white pearl onions, peeled (see Note)	24	24
Water, to cover		
Milk	1 cup	250 mL
All-purpose flour	2 tbsp.	30 mL
Salt	1/2 tsp.	2 mL
Pepper	1/8 tsp.	0.5 mL
Boneless ham steak	1 lb.	454 g
Thin process cheese slices, to cover	6	6

Cook onions in water in large uncovered saucepan until tender. Drain.

Gradually whisk milk into flour in medium saucepan until smooth. Add salt and pepper. Heat and stir until boiling and thickened. Add onions. Stir.

Brown ham quickly in non-stick frying pan. Lay ham slice in ungreased shallow 2 quart (2 L) casserole. Cover with cheese. Spoon creamed onions over top. Bake, uncovered, in 350°F (175°C) oven for 25 to 30 minutes until bubbly hot. Serves 4.

1 serving: 343 Calories; 33 g Protein; 15.5 g Total Fat; 17 g Carbohydrate; 2262 mg Sodium; 2 g Dietary Fiber

Pictured on page 147.

Note: To peel onions easily, blanch in boiling water for about 2 minutes before peeling.

Super Sauerkraut Supper

The perfect Oktoberfest meal.

Hard margarine (or butter)	2 tsp.	10 mL
Large onion, thinly sliced	1	1
Jar of sauerkraut, drained	17 1/2 oz.	500 mL
Water	3/4 cup	175 mL
Brown sugar, packed	2 tsp.	10 mL
Chicken bouillon powder	1 tsp.	5 mL
Bay leaf	1	1
Dijon mustard	1 tbsp.	15 mL
New baby potatoes, with peel, halved	1 lb.	454 g
Salt	1/4 tsp.	1 mL
Pepper	1/16 tsp.	0.5 mL
Lean ham garlic sausage (kielbasa), sliced	12 oz.	340 g

Heat margarine in non-stick frying pan. Add onion. Sauté until soft.

Add next 5 ingredients. Stir. Bring to a boil. Cover. Simmer for 10 minutes.

Stir in remaining 5 ingredients. Cover. Cook for about 30 minutes until potato is tender. Discard bay leaf. Serves 4.

1 serving: 430 Calories; 16 g Protein; 27.7 g Total Fat; 31 g Carbohydrate; 2014 mg Sodium; 5 g Dietary Fiber

Pictured on page 147.

Ham Loaf

A layer of browned pineapple rings adds lots of flavor.
Topped with a sweet and sour glaze.

Large eggs	2	2
Milk	½ cup	125 mL
Pepper	¼ tsp.	1 mL
Prepared horseradish	1 tsp.	5 mL
Sweet pickle relish	1 tbsp.	15 mL
Dry bread crumbs	1 cup	250 mL
Brown sugar, packed	2 tbsp.	30 mL
White vinegar	1 tbsp.	15 mL
Cooked ham, ground	2 lbs.	900 g
Hard margarine (or butter)	2 tsp.	10 mL
Granulated sugar	2 tbsp.	30 mL
Canned pineapple slices, drained, juice reserved	14 oz.	398 mL
Topping:		
Brown sugar, packed	⅓ cup	75 mL
Prepared mustard	2 tsp.	10 mL
Reserved pineapple juice	1 tbsp.	15 mL

Beat eggs in large bowl until smooth. Add next 7 ingredients. Stir.

Add ground ham. Mix well. Press ½ of ham mixture in greased 9 x 5 x 3 inch (22 x 12.5 x 7.5 cm) loaf pan. It is easy to remove loaf if you line pan with foil.

Melt margarine in non-stick frying pan. Sprinkle with sugar. Lay pineapple slices over top. Brown both sides. Arrange over ham mixture in loaf pan. Cover with second ½ of ham mixture.

Topping: Stir brown sugar, prepared mustard and pineapple juice in small bowl. Spread over top of loaf. Bake in 350°F (175°C) oven for 1½ hours. Cuts into 8 slices.

1 slice: 391 Calories; 24 g Protein; 15.1 g Total Fat; 40 g Carbohydrate; 1655 mg Sodium; 1 g Dietary Fiber

Pictured below.

Ham And Chicken Loaf

Flavors of both ham and chicken come through in this loaf.
Gravy browner may be used for color.

Large eggs, fork-beaten	2	2
Milk	⅔ cup	150 mL
Prepared mustard	1 tbsp.	15 mL
Finely chopped onion	⅓ cup	75 mL
Salt	¼ tsp.	1 mL
Pepper	¼ tsp.	1 mL
Ground thyme	⅛ tsp.	0.5 mL
Coarsely crushed corn flakes cereal (not crumbs)	1 cup	250 mL
Liquid gravy browner, as needed for color (optional)		
Ground chicken	1 lb.	454 g
Ground ham (see Note)	2 cups	500 mL

Combine first 9 ingredients in large bowl. Mix well.

Add ground chicken and ground ham. Mix well. Pack in greased 9 x 5 x 3 inch (22 x 12.5 x 7.5 cm) loaf pan. Cover. Bake in 350°F (175°C) oven for 1 hour. Cuts into 8 slices.

1 slice: 180 Calories; 20 g Protein; 4.7 g Total Fat; 13 g Carbohydrate; 822 mg Sodium; 1 g Dietary Fiber

Pictured below.

Note: A food processor works well for grinding.

Top Left: Ham Loaf, above
Bottom Left: Ham And Chicken Loaf, this page

Top Right: Super Sauerkraut Supper, page 146
Bottom Right: Quick Ham Bake, page 146

Apple Pork Chops

Dark brown rich looking dish.

Cooking oil	2 tsp.	10 mL
Pork chops, trimmed of fat (about 2¼ lbs.,1 kg)	6	6
Medium cooking apples, peeled and sliced (McIntosh is good)	3	3
Brown sugar, packed	¼ cup	60 mL
Ground cinnamon	½ tsp.	2 mL

Heat cooking oil in non-stick frying pan. Add pork chops. Brown both sides. Transfer to ungreased 2 quart (2 L) casserole or small roaster.

Layer apple over each chop.

Mix brown sugar and cinnamon in small cup. Sprinkle over apple. Cover. Bake in 350°F (175°C) oven for 1 to 1¼ hours. Serves 6.

1 serving: 243 Calories; 24 g Protein; 8 g Total Fat; 19 g Carbohydrate; 70 mg Sodium; 1 g Dietary Fiber

Pictured below.

Top: Breaded Pork Cutlets, this page
Center: Apple Pork Chops, above
Bottom: Baked Chops And Stuffing, this page

Breaded Pork Cutlets

A slight taste of wine clings to these moist tender cutlets.

Large egg, fork-beaten	1	1
Fine dry bread crumbs	½ cup	125 mL
Pork cutlets (about 1¼ lbs., 568 g)	4	4
Cooking oil	1 tbsp.	15 mL
Salt, sprinkle		
Pepper, sprinkle		
Chicken bouillon powder	2 tsp.	10 mL
Hot water	½ cup	125 mL
Red (or alcohol-free red) wine	½ cup	125 mL

Place egg and bread crumbs in separate small dishes. Dip pork cutlets into egg, then into bread crumbs to coat.

Brown pork in cooking oil in non-stick frying pan. Sprinkle with salt and pepper.

Stir bouillon powder into hot water in small cup. Add wine. Stir. Pour over pork cutlets. Cover. Simmer for 50 to 60 minutes until tender and most of liquid is evaporated. Serves 4.

1 serving: 339 Calories; 35 g Protein; 13.8 g Total Fat; 12 g Carbohydrate; 537 mg Sodium; trace Dietary Fiber

Pictured on this page.

Baked Chops And Stuffing

Pre-browning is not required. Just lay chops in pan, cover with stuffing mixture and bake. Very easy.

Pork chops, trimmed of fat (about 2¼ lbs.,1 kg)	6	6
Salt, sprinkle		
Pepper, sprinkle		
Condensed cream of mushroom soup	10 oz.	284 mL
Seasoned stuffing mix	1 cup	250 mL
Canned cream-style corn	14 oz.	398 mL
Chopped celery	½ cup	125 mL
Chopped onion	½ cup	125 mL

Lay pork chops in ungreased baking pan large enough to hold in single layer. Sprinkle with salt and pepper.

Mix remaining 5 ingredients in medium bowl. Spoon over pork chops. Bake, uncovered, in 325°F (160°C) oven for about 1½ hours until tender. Serves 6.

1 serving: 314 Calories; 28 g Protein; 10.9 g Total Fat; 27 g Carbohydrate; 853 mg Sodium; 2 g Dietary Fiber

Pictured on this page.

Salads

Pesto-Sauced Salad, page 150

Salads

Prior to the twentieth century, a wedge of iceberg lettuce with seasoned cream poured over top, or some leftover meat with lettuce or fruit, was about the extent of a "served salad." Molded salads were first made with calfs' foot jelly, later with sheet gelatin, and then finally with the new granulated gelatin. The advent of flavored jelly powders made molded salads appealing as desserts as well. After World War II, North Americans travelling abroad began to discover other varieties of lettuce. Herb gardens and flavored oils became fashionable, and new exotic vegetables added a delicious touch. Now, our own imaginations are the only limits on the kinds of salads we're able to create. Try the Sweet Wheat Salad or the Pesto-Sauced Salad for two unique options.

Pesto-Sauced Salad

Pesto (PEH-stoh) is a rich sauce made from fresh sweet basil. It is available in supermarkets and Italian stores. A real Italian salad.

Fusilli pasta	1 lb.	454 g
Boiling water	4 qts.	4 L
Cooking oil (optional)	1 tbsp.	15 mL
Salt	4 tsp.	20 mL
Broccoli, cut up and cooked tender-crisp	2 cups	500 mL
Cauliflower, cut up and cooked tender-crisp	2 cups	500 mL
Pea pods, cooked tender-crisp	2 cups	500 mL
Sliced carrot, cooked tender-crisp	1½ cups	375 mL
Sliced fresh mushrooms	1 cup	250 mL
Pesto Dressing:		
Commercial basil pesto	¾ cup	175 mL
White vinegar	⅓ cup	75 mL
Olive oil	⅔ cup	150 mL
Grated Parmesan cheese	½ cup	125 mL
Salt	1 tsp.	5 mL

Cook pasta in boiling water, cooking oil and salt in large uncovered pot or Dutch oven for 8 to 10 minutes until tender but firm. Drain. Rinse with cold water. Drain. Return to pot.

Add broccoli, cauliflower, pea pods, carrot and mushrooms.

Pesto Dressing: Mix all 5 ingredients in small bowl. Pour over pasta mixture. Toss to coat. Serves 8.

1 serving: 529 Calories; 14 g Protein; 29.5 g Total Fat; 54 g Carbohydrate; 501 mg Sodium; 5 g Dietary Fiber

Pictured on page 149 and on back cover.

Pasta Salad Oriental

Add some crusty dinner rolls and you have a complete meal. Refreshing and delicious.

Vermicelli (or angel hair) pasta	12 oz.	340 g
Boiling water	2½ qts.	2.5 L
Cooking oil	1 tbsp.	15 mL
Salt	1 tbsp.	15 mL
Sesame (or cooking) oil	1 tbsp.	15 mL
Julienned English cucumber	2 cups	500 mL
Julienned carrot	1½ cups	375 mL
Diced cooked chicken (or 2 cans, 6½ oz., 184 g, each, chicken flakes, drained)	2 cups	500 mL
Sliced green onion	½ cup	125 mL
Dressing:		
Boiling water	½ cup	125 mL
Chicken bouillon powder	1 tsp.	5 mL
Cooking oil	2 tbsp.	30 mL
Soy sauce	¼ cup	60 mL
White vinegar	2 tbsp.	30 mL
Granulated sugar	1 tbsp.	15 mL
Pepper	⅛ tsp.	0.5 mL
Toasted sesame seeds	¼ cup	60 mL

Cook pasta in boiling water, cooking oil and salt in large uncovered pot or Dutch oven for 4 to 6 minutes until tender but firm. Drain. Rinse with cold water. Drain well. Transfer to large bowl.

Add sesame oil. Toss well to coat.

Add cucumber, carrot, chicken and green onion. Toss.

Dressing: Stir boiling water and bouillon powder in small bowl.

Add remaining 6 ingredients. Stir. Pour over pasta mixture. Toss together well. Makes about 10 cups (2.5 L) salad.

1 cup (250 mL) salad: 258 Calories; 15 g Protein; 7.8 g Total Fat; 31 g Carbohydrate; 516 mg Sodium; 2 g Dietary Fiber

Pictured on page 151.

Broccoli Salad

This is one you'll serve often. Very colorful.

Broccoli florets	5 cups	1.25 L
Diced red onion	½ cup	125 mL
Grated medium Cheddar cheese	½ cup	125 mL
Roasted and salted sunflower seeds (optional but good)	¼ cup	60 mL
Bacon slices, diced	6	6
Dressing:		
Granulated sugar	2 tbsp.	30 mL
White vinegar	2 tbsp.	30 mL
Light salad dressing (or mayonnaise)	6 tbsp.	100 mL

Combine broccoli, red onion, cheese and sunflower seeds in large bowl.

Cook bacon in non-stick frying pan. Drain well. Cool. Add to broccoli mixture.

Dressing: Mix all 3 ingredients well in small bowl. Add to broccoli mixture just before serving. Toss together. Makes 5 cups (1.25 L) salad.

1 cup (250 mL) salad: 180 Calories; 7 g Protein; 12.4 g Total Fat; 12 g Carbohydrate; 344 mg Sodium; 1 g Dietary Fiber

Pictured below.

BROCCOLI SLAW: Substitute 1 bag 16 oz., 454 g, broccoli slaw for the broccoli florets. Color will be lighter.

Top: Pasta Salad Oriental, page 150
Bottom: Broccoli Salad, above

Bean Salad

Bean Salad

Pineapple makes this different from the usual bean salad. Dressing has a good bite to it.

Canned kidney beans, drained	14 oz.	398 mL
Canned pinto (or white) beans, drained	14 oz.	398 mL
Canned cut green beans, drained	14 oz.	398 mL
Sliced celery	1 cup	250 mL
Canned pineapple chunks, drained, juice reserved	14 oz.	398 mL
Dressing:		
Cornstarch	1 tbsp.	15 mL
Reserved pineapple juice		
Lemon juice	1 tsp.	5 mL
Red wine vinegar	¼ cup	60 mL
Cooking oil	2 tbsp.	30 mL
Water	2 tbsp.	30 mL
Dry mustard	2 tsp.	10 mL
Granulated sugar	2 tsp.	10 mL
Salt	½ tsp.	2 mL
Dill weed	½ tsp.	2 mL
Pepper	¼ tsp.	1 mL
Dried whole oregano	¼ tsp.	1 mL
Garlic powder	¼ tsp.	1 mL
Onion powder	¼ tsp.	1 mL

Combine first 5 ingredients in large bowl.

Dressing: Mix cornstarch, reserved pineapple juice and lemon juice in small saucepan.

Add remaining 11 ingredients. Heat and stir until boiling and slightly thickened. Pour over vegetables in bowl. Stir. Cover. Refrigerate for 24 hours, stirring occasionally. Makes 6 cups (1.5 L) salad.

1 cup (250 mL) salad: 208 Calories; 7 g Protein; 5.4 g Total Fat; 35 g Carbohydrate; 493 mg Sodium; 6 g Dietary Fiber

Pictured above.

Top: Bacon And Pea Salad, this page
Bottom: Noodle Slaw, below

Noodle Slaw

A good way to doctor a store-bought salad.

Bag of shredded cabbage with carrot	1 lb.	454 g
Instant Chinese noodles with chicken-flavored packet, crumbled, chicken-flavored packet reserved	3 oz.	85 g
Dressing:		
Reserved chicken-flavored packet	1	1
Soy sauce	2 tbsp.	30 mL
Cooking oil	2 tsp.	10 mL
Granulated sugar	2 tsp.	10 mL
Pepper	¼ tsp.	1 mL
Toasted sesame seeds	4 tsp.	20 mL

Combine cabbage mixture and Chinese noodles in large bowl.

Dressing: Stir all 6 ingredients together in small bowl. Just before serving, pour over salad. Toss together well. Makes 7½ cups (1.8 L) salad.

1 cup (250 mL) salad: 87 Calories; 3 g Protein; 2.4 g Total Fat; 14 g Carbohydrate; 379 mg Sodium; 2 g Dietary Fiber

Pictured above.

Bacon And Pea Salad

A good addition to a lunch whether eating inside or out. Garnish with slices of red pepper.

Bacon slices, diced	5	5
Frozen peas, thawed	3 cups	750 mL
Green onions, sliced	4	4
Light sour cream	⅓ cup	75 mL
Dill weed	¼ tsp.	1 mL
Salt	½ tsp.	2 mL
Pepper, sprinkle		

Cook bacon in non-stick frying pan. Drain. Transfer to medium bowl.

Add peas, green onion, sour cream, dill weed, salt and pepper. Stir. Chill until serving time. Makes 3¼ cups (810 mL) salad.

½ cup (125 mL) salad: 94 Calories; 6 g Protein; 3.5 g Total Fat; 10 g Carbohydrate; 371 mg Sodium; 3 g Dietary Fiber

Pictured on this page.

Variation: Omit green onions and add ¼ cup (60 mL) slivered red onion.

Dilled Onions

Make your own quantity according to how much pickle juice you have.

Medium onions, thinly sliced and separated into rings	2	2
Dill pickle juice	1 cup	250 mL
Light sour cream	½ cup	125 mL
Celery seed	⅛ tsp.	0.5 mL

Combine onion rings and dill pickle juice in medium bowl. Cover and marinate in the refrigerator for at least 2 days. Drain well.

Add sour cream to onion rings. Mix well. Sprinkle with celery seed. Makes 2½ cups (625 mL) onion.

½ cup (125 mL) onion: 39 Calories; 1 g Protein; 1.8 g Total Fat; 5 g Carbohydrate; 419 mg Sodium; 1 g Dietary Fiber

Pictured on page 153.

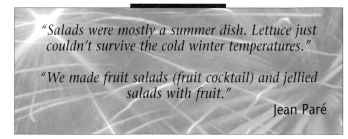

"Salads were mostly a summer dish. Lettuce just couldn't survive the cold winter temperatures."

"We made fruit salads (fruit cocktail) and jellied salads with fruit."

Jean Paré

Left: Spinach Mushroom Salad, below

Top Right: Dilled Onions, page 152
Bottom Right: Tomato Mushroom Salad, below

Spinach Mushroom Salad

Salad and dressing can be made ahead of time and tossed together at the last minute. Dressing is tangy.

Salad:

Bunch of fresh spinach leaves	1	1
Sliced fresh mushrooms	2 cups	500 mL
Sliced green onion	1/3 cup	75 mL
Bacon slices, cooked crisp and crumbled	6	6

Dressing:

Cooking oil	2 tbsp.	30 mL
Lemon juice	2 tbsp.	30 mL
Egg yolk (large)	1	1
Salt	3/4 tsp.	4 mL
Pepper	1/8 tsp.	0.5 mL
Granulated sugar	1/2 tsp.	2 mL

Salad: Combine all 4 ingredients in large bowl. Cover. Refrigerate until ready.

Dressing: Whisk all 6 ingredients together in small bowl. Pour over spinach mixture. Toss to coat. Serves 8.

1 serving: 84 Calories; 4 g Protein; 6.7 g Total Fat; 4 g Carbohydrate; 372 mg Sodium; 2 g Dietary Fiber

Pictured above.

Tomato Mushroom Salad

A terrific blend of flavors. A brightly colored salad.

Firm medium tomatoes, cut into 8 wedges each	3	3
Thickly sliced fresh mushrooms	3 cups	750 mL
Medium red onion, thinly sliced	1	1
Slivered green pepper (optional)	1/2 cup	125 mL

Dressing:

Cooking oil	1/4 cup	60 mL
Red wine vinegar	1/4 cup	60 mL
Granulated sugar	1 1/2 tsp.	7 mL
Salt	1 tsp.	5 mL
Parsley flakes	1/2 tsp.	2 mL
Dried sweet basil	1/2 tsp.	2 mL
Lemon pepper	1/4 tsp.	1 mL
Garlic powder	1/8 tsp.	0.5 mL

Put tomato wedges, mushrooms, red onion and green pepper into large bowl.

Dressing: Stir all 8 ingredients in small bowl until sugar is dissolved. Pour over tomato mixture. Stir well. Let stand for at least 1 hour before serving. Makes 8 cups (2 L) salad.

1 cup (250 mL) salad: 91 Calories; 1 g Protein; 7.6 g Total Fat; 6 g Carbohydrate; 345 mg Sodium; 1 g Dietary Fiber

Pictured above.

Potato Raita

Pronounced RI-tah. This potato salad has a different taste than most. The yogurt, ginger paste and coriander give this its East Indian flavor.

Medium potatoes, with skin	4	4
Boiling water, to cover		
Plain yogurt	½ cup	125 mL
Lemon juice	1 tsp.	5 mL
Granulated sugar	½ tsp.	2 mL
Salt	½ tsp.	2 mL
Ginger paste (available in Asian section of grocery stores)	¼ tsp.	1 mL
Chopped fresh coriander (cilantro)	1 tbsp.	15 mL

Cook potatoes in boiling water in medium uncovered saucepan until tender. Drain and cool. Remove skin, if desired. Dice into ³⁄₈ inch (1 cm) cubes.

Mix remaining 6 ingredients in small bowl. Add to potato. Stir well. Makes a generous 4 cups (1 L) salad.

1 cup (250 mL) salad: 141 Calories; 4 g Protein; 0.6 g Total Fat; 30 g Carbohydrate; 368 mg Sodium; 2 g Dietary Fiber

Pictured on this page.

Sweet Wheat Salad

Fruit, grain and dairy— all this in a mouth-watering salad. Also makes a good dessert.

Wheat (available at grocery and health food stores)	1 cup	250 mL
Boiling water, to cover		
Cream cheese, softened	8 oz.	250 g
Canned crushed pineapple, with juice	14 oz.	398 mL
Instant vanilla pudding powder (4 serving size)	1	1
Lemon juice	2 tbsp.	30 mL
Frozen whipped topping (in a tub), thawed	4 cups	1 L
Maraschino cherries, for garnish (optional)		

Cook wheat in boiling water in small saucepan for 1 hour until tender. Drain. Cool.

Beat cream cheese and pineapple with juice in medium bowl until mixed.

Beat in pudding powder and lemon juice. Add wheat. Stir.

Fold in whipped topping. Turn into serving bowl.

Garnish with cherries. Makes 8 cups (2 L) salad.

½ cup (125 mL) salad: 196 Calories; 3 g Protein; 10.7 g Total Fat; 24 g Carbohydrate; 71 mg Sodium; 2 g Dietary Fiber.

Pictured on this page.

Orange Lettuce Salad

Most attractive. A hint of both sweet and sour in the dressing.

Mixture of cut or torn greens, lightly packed	6 cups	1.5 L
Canned mandarin orange segments, drained (use all or part)	10 oz.	284 mL
Sliced almonds, toasted in 350°F (175°C) oven for 5 to 8 minutes	¼ cup	60 mL
Bacon slices, cooked crisp and crumbled (optional)	6	6
Dressing:		
White vinegar	3 tbsp.	50 mL
Granulated sugar	¼ cup	60 mL
Prepared mustard	½ tsp.	2 mL
Paprika	½ tsp.	2 mL
Cooking oil	1 tbsp.	15 mL

Place first 4 ingredients in large bowl.

Dressing: Stir vinegar, sugar, prepared mustard and paprika together well in small bowl until sugar dissolves.

Drizzle cooking oil over greens mixture. Toss well. Add dressing. Toss again. Makes 8 cups (2 L) salad.

1 cup (250 mL) salad: 73 Calories; 1 g Protein; 3.5 g Total Fat; 11 g Carbohydrate; 10 mg Sodium; 1 g Dietary Fiber

Pictured below.

Top: Potato Raita, this page   Center: Orange Lettuce Salad, above
Bottom: Sweet Wheat Salad, this page

Caesar-Dressed Salad

Contains extras such as bacon, green onion and tomato.

Large head of romaine lettuce, cut or torn	1	1
Bacon slices, cooked crisp and crumbled	5	5
Chopped green onion	3 tbsp.	50 mL
Grated Parmesan cheese	3 tbsp.	50 mL
Croutons (or more)	½ cup	125 mL
Pepper	¼ tsp.	1 mL
Dried whole oregano	⅛ tsp.	0.5 mL
Creamy Caesar salad dressing	⅔ cup	150 mL
Medium tomatoes, cut into 6 wedges each	2	2

Combine first 7 ingredients in large bowl.

Add dressing shortly before serving. Toss.

Set tomato wedges on top. Serves 6.

1 serving: 193 Calories; 5 g Protein; 14.1 g Total Fat; 11 g Carbohydrate; 371 mg Sodium; 2 g Dietary Fiber

Pictured on this page.

Caesar-Dressed Salad

Poppy Seed Salad

Poppy Seed Salad

Have dressing made ahead and waiting in refrigerator. Toss together at the last minute.

Dressing:		
Granulated sugar	½ cup	125 mL
White vinegar	6 tbsp.	100 mL
Cooking oil	2½ tbsp.	37 mL
Onion flakes	1 tsp.	5 mL
Dry mustard	½ tsp.	2 mL
Salt	½ tsp.	2 mL
Paprika	¼ tsp.	1 mL
Poppy seeds	2½ tsp.	12 mL
Salad:		
Head of lettuce, chopped (about 8 cups, 2 L)	1	1
Green onions, sliced	3	3
Radishes, sliced	8	8
Green pepper strips	⅓ cup	75 mL

Dressing: Measure all 8 ingredients into small bowl. Beat together well. Let stand in refrigerator overnight. Makes about ⅔ cup (150 mL) dressing.

Salad: Combine all 4 ingredients in large bowl. Pour dressing over top. Toss well. Serves 8.

1 serving: 108 Calories; 1 g Protein; 4.9 g Total Fat; 16 g Carbohydrate; 178 mg Sodium; 1 g Dietary Fiber

Pictured on this page.

Springtime Salad

Actually, delicious in all four seasons.

Fresh spinach (or romaine) leaves, torn and lightly packed	4 cups	1 L
Medium red pepper, slivered	½	½
Small red onion, thinly sliced and separated into rings	½	½
Croutons	½ cup	125 mL
Sunflower seeds	¼ cup	60 mL
Italian dressing	⅓ cup	75 mL

Combine spinach, red pepper and red onion rings in large bowl. Cover. Refrigerate until ready.

Add croutons, sunflower seeds and Italian dressing just before serving. Toss well. Serves 4.

1 serving: 222 Calories; 5 g Protein; 19.4 g Total Fat; 10 g Carbohydrate; 410 mg Sodium; 3 g Dietary Fiber

Pictured on page 158.

FIDDLEHEAD SALAD: Cook and drain 10 oz. (284 g) frozen fiddleheads. Cool. Add to salad along with more dressing if needed.

Cherry Cola Salad

Cola adds flavor, yet it doesn't taste like cola. A dusty rose-colored jellied salad. Garnish with whipped topping.

Envelope unflavored gelatin	1 × ¼ oz.	1 × 7 g
Water	¼ cup	60 mL
Cherry-flavored gelatin (jelly powder)	1 × 3 oz.	1 × 85 g
Canned crushed pineapple, with juice	8 oz.	227 mL
Light cream cheese, diced	4 oz.	125 g
Cola soft drink	1½ cups	375 mL
Finely chopped walnuts (or pecans)	¼ cup	60 mL

Sprinkle gelatin over water in medium saucepan. Let stand for 1 minute.

Add cherry gelatin and pineapple with juice. Heat and stir until both gelatins are dissolved.

Add cream cheese. Stir, whisking if needed, until cream cheese is melted and smooth. Remove from heat.

Add soft drink and walnuts. Stir. Pour into 4 cup (1 L) mold that has been lightly sprayed with cooking spray. Chill, stirring occasionally as it becomes syrupy so walnuts are evenly distributed. Chill until firm. Unmold onto serving plate. Makes 3½ cups (875 mL) salad.

½ cup (125 mL) salad: 191 Calories; 6 g Protein; 8.3 g Total Fat; 25 g Carbohydrate; 345 mg Sodium; 1 g Dietary Fiber

Pictured below.

Top: Cherry Cola Salad, above   Bottom: Egg Salad Mold, this page

Egg Salad Mold

A pretty yellow color. Especially good served with cold cuts and buns. Garnish with salad dressing and parsley.

Boiling water	1 cup	250 mL
Lemon-flavored gelatin (jelly powder)	1 × 3 oz.	1 × 85 g
Light salad dressing (or mayonnaise)	⅔ cup	150 mL
White vinegar	1 tbsp.	15 mL
Finely chopped celery	½ cup	125 mL
Chopped green onion	¼ cup	60 mL
Salt	½ tsp.	2 mL
Large hard-boiled eggs, mashed with fork	2	2

Stir boiling water into gelatin in medium bowl until dissolved. Chill until syrupy. Stir and scrape down sides often until beginning to thicken.

Fold in salad dressing. Add remaining 5 ingredients. Stir. Turn into 3 cup (750 mL) mold. Chill for at least 2½ hours until firm. Unmold onto serving plate. Makes 2⅔ cups (650 mL) salad.

½ cup (125 mL) salad: 182 Calories; 4 g Protein; 10 g Total Fat; 20 g Carbohydrate; 575 mg Sodium; trace Dietary Fiber

Pictured on this page.

Avocado Mold

A smooth texture with a pleasing tang. Best served same day.

Envelope unflavored gelatin	1 × 1¼ oz.	1 × 7 g
Lime-flavored gelatin (jelly powder)	1 × 3 oz.	1 × 85 g
Boiling water	1 cup	250 mL
Mashed avocado (about 1 large)	1 cup	250 mL
Sour cream	1 cup	250 mL
Mayonnaise	1 cup	250 mL
Salt	½ tsp.	2 mL
Onion powder	¼ tsp.	1 mL
Mayonnaise, for garnish	2 tbsp.	30 mL
Paprika, sprinkle, for garnish		

Stir both gelatins in medium bowl. Stir in boiling water until dissolved.

Add avocado, sour cream, first amount of mayonnaise, salt and onion powder. Whisk until smooth. Turn into 4 cup (1 L) mold. Chill until firm.

Unmold salad onto serving plate. Put dollop of second amount of mayonnaise on top in center. Sprinkle paprika over mayonnaise. Makes 4 cups (1 L) salad.

½ cup (125 mL) salad: 291 Calories; 4 g Protein; 24.1 g Total Fat; 17 g Carbohydrate; 411 mg Sodium; 1 g Dietary Fiber

Pictured on page 157.

Cranberry Jelly Salad,
this page

Cranberry Jelly Salad

Three fruits combine to make this jellied salad.
Excellent with turkey.

Envelope unflavored gelatin	1 × ¼ oz.	1 × 7 g
Cherry-flavored gelatin (jelly powder)	1 × 3 oz.	1 × 85 g
Boiling water	1¼ cups	300 mL
Canned crushed pineapple, with juice	14 oz.	398 mL
Canned whole cranberry sauce	14 oz.	398 mL
Finely diced red apple, with peel	½ cup	125 mL

Stir both gelatins in medium bowl. Stir in boiling water until dissolved.

Stir in pineapple with juice, cranberry sauce and apple. Chill, stirring occasionally, until syrupy. Pour into 4½ to 5 cup (1.1 to 1.25 L) mold. Chill for 2 to 3 hours until firm. Makes 4½ cups (1.1 L) salad.

½ cup (125 mL) salad: 148 Calories; 2 g Protein; 0.1 g Total Fat; 37 g Carbohydrate; 43 mg Sodium; 1 g Dietary Fiber

Pictured above.

Avocado Mold,
page 156

"I used to iron the clothes and sheets with an iron that had to be heated on the wood stove. It had two bases but only one handle that fit into each of them. One base would be heating while I ironed with the other. When it cooled, I'd put it back on the stove and move the handle to the hot one."

Jean Paré

1. Springtime Salad, page 155
2. Pecan Dressing, page 159
3. Cooked Salad Dressing, page 159
4. Sunny Dressing, page 159
5. Coleslaw Dressing, page 159
6. Tomato Relish Dressing, page 159

Pecan Dressing

Fast and fabulous for yogurt lovers. Use regular or low-fat yogurt. Serve with fruit salads.

Mayonnaise	1/3 cup	75 mL
White corn syrup	1/4 cup	60 mL
Chopped pecans, toasted in 350°F (175°C) oven for 8 to 10 minutes	1/3 cup	75 mL
Vanilla yogurt	1 cup	250 mL

Stir mayonnaise, corn syrup and pecans well in small bowl.

Fold in yogurt. Cover and chill. Makes 1 2/3 cups (400 mL) dressing.

2 tbsp. (30 mL) dressing: 67 Calories; 1 g Protein; 3.8 g Total Fat; 7 g Carbohydrate; 63 mg Sodium; trace Dietary Fiber

Pictured on page 158.

Sunny Dressing

So smooth and special drizzled over a fresh fruit salad.

Cream cheese, softened	8 oz.	250 g
Prepared orange juice	1/4 cup	60 mL
Granulated sugar	1/4 cup	60 mL

Beat all 3 ingredients together in small bowl until creamy. Makes about 1 1/3 cups (325 mL) dressing.

2 tbsp. (30 mL) dressing: 100 Calories; 2 g Protein; 7.9 g Total Fat; 6 g Carbohydrate; 67 mg Sodium; trace Dietary Fiber

Pictured on page 158.

FLUFFY DIP: Thaw 2 cups (500 mL) frozen whipped topping. Fold into Sunny Dressing.

Coleslaw Dressing

Just like you get in a fast-food outlet. Keeps well in the refrigerator for several weeks.

Cooking oil	1/2 cup	125 mL
White vinegar	2/3 cup	150 mL
Salad dressing (or mayonnaise)	2 1/4 cups	560 mL
Granulated sugar	3/4 cup	175 mL
Salt	2 tsp.	10 mL
Minced onion	1/3 cup	75 mL
Drops of green food coloring, enough to make pale green		

Measure all 7 ingredients into blender. Process until smooth. Makes 4 cups (1 L) dressing.

2 tbsp. (30 mL) dressing: 133 Calories; trace Protein; 11.7 g Total Fat; 7 g Carbohydrate; 268 mg Sodium; trace Dietary Fiber

Pictured on page 158.

TIME-HONORED RECIPE

Cooked Salad Dressing

From a way, way back. This has a lot of zip to it. A little goes a long way.

Granulated sugar	1/2 cup	125 mL
All-purpose flour	2 tbsp.	30 mL
Dry mustard	1 tbsp.	15 mL
Salt	1 tsp.	5 mL
Large eggs	3	3
Milk	1 cup	250 mL
White vinegar	1/2 cup	125 mL
Water	1/2 cup	125 mL

Put sugar, flour, dry mustard and salt in top of double boiler. Stir until flour is mixed in well. Beat in eggs, 1 at a time.

Stir in milk, vinegar and water. Cook over boiling water, stirring often, until thickened. Pour into container. Cover and refrigerate. Makes about 2 1/2 cups (625 mL) dressing.

2 tbsp. (30 mL) dressing: 41 Calories; 2 g Protein; 1 g Total Fat; 7 g Carbohydrate; 146 mg Sodium; trace Dietary Fiber

Pictured on page 158.

Tomato Relish Dressing

This will remind you of a well-known salad dressing.

Hard margarine (or butter)	1/4 cup	60 mL
All-purpose flour	1/4 cup	60 mL
Water	1 cup	250 mL
Ketchup	1 cup	250 mL
White vinegar	1/2 cup	125 mL
Granulated sugar	1 cup	250 mL
Celery salt	1 tsp.	5 mL
Onion powder	1 tsp.	5 mL
Salt	1 tbsp.	15 mL
Pepper	1/2 tsp.	2 mL
Sweet pickle relish	1/2 cup	125 mL

Melt margarine in medium saucepan. Add flour. Mix.

Stir in water, ketchup and vinegar until boiling and thickened.

Add remaining 6 ingredients. Stir until sugar is dissolved. Makes 4 cups (1 L) dressing.

2 tbsp. (30 mL) dressing: 54 Calories; trace Protein; 1.5 g Total Fat; 10 g Carbohydrate; 421 mg Sodium; trace Dietary Fiber

Pictured on page 158.

Variation: For a less sweet dressing omit ketchup. Add 5 1/2 oz. (156 mL) tomato paste.

Soups

Once upon a time our grandmothers and great-grandmothers had farms and vegetable gardens to create fresh and hearty soups. The arrival of quick and convenient canned, frozen, dried and freeze-dried soups was not until the mid-twentieth century. Today, many of us rely on the good old can opener to provide us with an instant, warm meal. Here is a variety of recipes for soups that use the convenience of canned goods, and some that employ fresh ingredients for a that homemade touch.

Top: Lentil Spinach Soup, this page   Bottom: Garbanzo Soup, this page

Garbanzo Soup

A soft yellow-colored broth with diced potato, ham and chick peas. Hearty.

Lean meaty ham bone (about 2 cups, 500 mL, meat), see Note	1	1
Water, to cover, approximately	6 cups	1.5 L
Medium onion, finely chopped	1	1
Garlic clove, minced (or ¼ tsp., 1 mL, powder)	1	1
Bay leaves	2	2
Medium potatoes, diced	2	2
Paprika	½ tsp.	2 mL
Salt	¼ tsp.	1 mL
Pepper	¼ tsp.	1 mL
Canned chick peas (garbanzo beans), with liquid, slightly mashed	19 oz.	540 mL

Combine first 5 ingredients in large pot or Dutch oven. Cover. Boil for about 2 hours. Discard bay leaves. Remove ham bone. Chop ham and return to pot. Discard bone.

Add remaining 5 ingredients. Cover. Cook until potato is tender. Serve hot. Makes 7½ cups (1.8 L) soup.

1 cup (250 mL) soup: 228 Calories; 13 g Protein; 9.3 g Total Fat; 23 g Carbohydrate; 734 mg Sodium; 3 g Dietary Fiber

Pictured on this page.

Note: If there is not much meat, add I can, 6.5 oz., 184 g, flakes of ham, drained and broken up.

Lentil Spinach Soup

Full-bodied soup. Freezes well. May be halved if desired.

Water	10 cups	2.5 L
Green lentils	2 cups	500 mL
Medium onion, chopped	1	1
Celery ribs, chopped	2	2
Chicken bouillon powder	¼ cup	60 mL
Pepper	¼ tsp.	1 mL
Frozen chopped spinach, thawed and chopped more	10 oz.	300 g
Grated medium Cheddar cheese, for garnish		

Combine first 6 ingredients in large pot or Dutch oven. Cover. Simmer for about 45 minutes until lentils are soft.

Add spinach. Cook for 5 minutes. Taste for salt, adding a bit if needed.

Sprinkle cheese over each serving. Makes 12 cups (3 L) soup.

1 cup (250 mL) soup: 61 Calories; 5 g Protein; 0.7 g Total Fat; 10 g Carbohydrate; 676 mg Sodium; 2 g Dietary Fiber

Pictured on this page.

Onion Soup

With just enough red wine to taste.

Ingredient	Imperial	Metric
Halved and thinly sliced onion	3 cups	750 mL
All-purpose flour	2 tbsp.	30 mL
Granulated sugar	1 tsp.	5 mL
Hard margarine (or butter)	2 tbsp.	30 mL
Water	4 cups	1 L
Liquid beef bouillon	1/4 cup	60 mL
Red (or alcohol-free red) wine	1/2 cup	125 mL
Worcestershire sauce	1/2 tsp.	2 mL
Salt, sprinkle		
Pepper, sprinkle		
Baguette, cut into 1 inch (2.5 cm) thick slices (see Note)	1/2	1/2
Grated mozzarella cheese	1 cup	250 mL
Grated Swiss cheese	1 cup	250 mL
Grated Parmesan cheese	2 tbsp.	30 mL

Toss onion, flour and sugar together well in medium bowl.

Melt margarine in non-stick frying pan or saucepan. Add onion mixture. Cook, stirring often, for 15 to 20 minutes until onion is very soft and starting to brown.

Add next 6 ingredients. Cover. Simmer over medium-low for 20 minutes.

Cut each baguette slice into quarters. Spread in ungreased 9 x 13 inch (22 x 33 cm) pan. Broil in center of oven, stirring twice, until dried and turning golden.

Combine mozzarella cheese and Swiss cheese in medium bowl. Sprinkle evenly over bread cubes. Broil until cheese is melted. Ladle soup into 6 bowls. Divide cheese and croutons into 6 portions. Place on top of each serving of soup.

Sprinkle 1 tsp. (5 mL) Parmesan cheese over each bowl. Serves 6.

1 serving: 363 Calories; 16 g Protein; 16.4 g Total Fat; 34 g Carbohydrate; 1658 mg Sodium; 2 g Dietary Fiber

Pictured below.

Note: Browned bread cubes may be put into each bowl of soup. Sprinkle with cheese. Bake in 450°F (230°C) oven until cheese is melted and golden. Be sure to use ovenproof bowls.

Onion Soup

Potato Soup

Creamy and cheesy. Good soup.

Hard margarine (or butter)	1 tbsp.	15 mL
Chopped onion	1 cup	250 mL
All-purpose flour	2 tbsp.	30 mL
Chicken bouillon powder	1½ tbsp.	25 mL
Water	4 cups	1 L
Bay leaf	1	1
Salt	½ tsp.	2 mL
Pepper	¼ tsp.	1 mL
Diced potato	4 cups	1 L
Half-and-half	1 cup	250 mL
Grated sharp Cheddar cheese	1 cup	250 mL

Melt margarine in non-stick frying pan. Add onion. Sauté until soft.

Mix in flour and bouillon powder. Stir in water until boiling and slightly thickened.

Add remaining 6 ingredients. Cover. Simmer for about 30 minutes until potato is cooked. Discard bay leaf. Run whole mixture through blender. Reheat if needed. Makes 6 cups (1.5 L) soup.

1 cup (250 mL) soup: 259 Calories; 9 g Protein; 13.4 g Total Fat; 26 g Carbohydrate; 885 mg Sodium; 2 g Dietary Fiber

Pictured on page 163.

Cream Of Garlic Soup

A creamy foolproof version of an unusual soup. For garlic lovers. Add as many garlic cloves as you dare. Garnish with chopped chives.

Garlic cloves, minced	4-8	4-8
Hard margarine (or butter)	3 tbsp.	50 mL
All-purpose flour	3 tbsp.	50 mL
Condensed chicken broth	2 × 10 oz.	2 × 284 mL
Soup cans of milk	2 × 10 oz.	2 × 284 mL
Paprika	½ tsp.	2 mL

Sauté garlic in margarine in medium saucepan until golden.

Mix in flour. Add chicken broth, stirring until boiling and thickened. Add milk and paprika. Gently simmer for about 5 minutes until garlic is cooked. Makes about 4½ cups (1.1 L) soup.

1 cup (250 mL) soup: 190 Calories; 11 g Protein; 10.7 g Total Fat; 12 g Carbohydrate; 996 mg Sodium; trace Dietary Fiber

Pictured on page 163.

Pumpkin Soup

A thick hearty soup. Delicious served with a fresh dinner roll.

Chopped onion	1 cup	250 mL
Green onions, chopped	4	4
Hard margarine (or butter)	¼ cup	60 mL
All-purpose flour	2 tbsp.	30 mL
Salt	½ tsp.	2 mL
Pepper	⅛ tsp.	0.5 mL
Ground ginger	¼ tsp.	1 mL
Chicken stock	1 cup	250 mL
Chicken stock	3 cups	750 mL
Canned pumpkin, without spices	14 oz.	398 mL
Light cream	½ cup	125 mL

Sauté onion and green onion in margarine in large saucepan. Sauté until soft.

Mix in flour, salt, pepper and ginger. Add first amount of chicken stock, stirring until boiling and thickened. Process in blender to smooth.

Stir in second amount of chicken stock, pumpkin and cream. Heat through. Makes a generous 6 cups (1.5 L) soup.

1 cup (250 mL) soup: 171 Calories; 6 g Protein; 11.6 g Total Fat; 12 g Carbohydrate; 883 mg Sodium; 2 g Dietary Fiber

Pictured below.

Left: Pumpkin Soup, above

Avocado Cucumber Soup

Medium thickness. Serve small portions of this elegant cold soup.

Medium very ripe avocados, peeled and cut into chunks	2	2
Medium English cucumber, peeled	1	1
Condensed chicken broth	10 oz.	284 mL
Light sour cream	1/2 cup	125 mL
Lemon juice	1 tbsp.	15 mL
Onion powder	1/16 tsp.	0.5 mL
Cayenne pepper	1/16 tsp.	0.5 mL
Chopped fresh parsley (or chives), for garnish		

Put avocado into blender.

Cut cucumber in half lengthwise. Remove seeds. Cut into chunks. Put into blender with avocado.

Add next 5 ingredients. Process until smooth. Chill.

Garnish with parsley. Makes about 4¼ cups (1 L) soup.

¾ cup (175 mL) soup: 159 Calories; 5 g Protein; 13 g Total Fat; 9 g Carbohydrate; 352 mg Sodium; 2 g Dietary Fiber

Pictured below.

Crab Bisque

An elegant first course. Doubles easily.

Condensed tomato soup	10 oz.	284 mL
Condensed pea soup	10 oz.	284 mL
Condensed beef consommé	10 oz.	284 mL
Skim evaporated milk	1 cup	250 mL
Cooked fresh (or frozen or imitation) crab, broken up fine	1/2 lb.	225 g
Sherry (or alcohol-free sherry or white wine)	2 tbsp.	30 mL

Empty all 3 soups into large saucepan.

Add evaporated milk, crab and sherry. Heat, stirring often, until very hot but not boiling. Makes 6 cups (1.5 L) soup.

¾ cup (175 mL) soup: 180 Calories; 15 g Protein; 2.4 g Total Fat; 24 g Carbohydrate; 1188 mg Sodium; 2 g Dietary Fiber

Pictured on page 164.

Center: Avocado Cucumber Soup, above   Top Right: Potato Soup, page 162   Bottom Right: Cream of Garlic Soup, page 162

Fresh Pea Soup

Cream Of Mushroom Soup

Creamy with lots of mushrooms. Just like it should be. Garnish with fresh parsley and sliced fresh mushrooms.

Hard margarine (or butter)	1 tbsp.	15 mL
Chopped fresh mushrooms	4½ cups	1.1 L
Chopped onion	½ cup	125 mL
Water	1 cup	250 mL
All-purpose flour	6 tbsp.	100 mL
Condensed chicken broth	2 × 10 oz.	2 × 284 mL
Pepper	⅛ tsp.	0.5 mL
Paprika, sprinkle		
Skim evaporated milk	13½ oz.	385 mL

Melt margarine in non-stick frying pan. Add mushrooms and onion. Sauté until onion is soft and moisture is evaporated. This may need to be done in 2 batches. Turn into large saucepan.

Whisk water into flour in small bowl until smooth. Add chicken broth, pepper and paprika. Whisk. Add to mushroom mixture. Heat and stir until boiling and thickened.

Add evaporated milk. Heat through. Makes 7 cups (1.75 L) soup.

1 cup (250 mL) soup: 129 Calories; 10 g Protein; 3 g Total Fat; 16 g Carbohydrate; 630 mg Sodium; 1 g Dietary Fiber

Pictured below.

TIME-HONORED RECIPE

Fresh Pea Soup

Gram made this after Sunday School—summer and winter. Garden-fresh color, with a hard-to-beat fresh garden flavor. Garnish with fresh parsley.

Chopped onion	½ cup	125 mL
Hard margarine (or butter)	2 tbsp.	30 mL
All-purpose flour	¼ cup	60 mL
Chicken stock (see Note)	4 cups	1 L
Fresh (or frozen) peas	2½ cups	625 mL

Sauté onion in margarine in medium saucepan until soft and clear. Do not brown.

Add flour. Mix in. Stir in chicken stock until boiling and thickened.

Add peas. Simmer for 5 minutes. Run through blender. Return to saucepan until ready to serve. Makes a generous 4 cups (1 L) soup.

1 cup (250 mL) soup: 234 Calories; 15 g Protein; 8.8 g Total Fat; 23 g Carbohydrate; 1574 mg Sodium; 5 g Dietary Fiber

Pictured above.

Note: Use fresh chicken stock or 3 × 10 oz., 3 × 284 mL cans chicken broth, plus water to make 4 cups (1 L).

Top: Cream Of Mushroom Soup, above
Bottom: Crab Bisque, page 163

Oyster Soup

A family favorite from the Maritimes. Mom made this when I was a youngster. Oysters were expensive and we only had this on rare occasions. Quick to prepare. Garnish with fresh parsley.

Milk	4 cups	1 L
Soda cracker crumbs	½ cup	125 mL
Salt	1 tsp.	5 mL
Pepper	¼ tsp.	1 mL
Small fresh (or frozen or canned) oysters (about 24), with juice, cut up	2 cups	500 mL
Hard margarine (or butter)	1 tbsp.	15 mL

Combine milk, cracker crumbs, salt and pepper in large saucepan. Heat until just boiling.

Add oysters with juice and margarine. Bring to a boil. Simmer for about 5 minutes until edges of oysters curl. Makes about 4½ cups (1.1 L) soup.

1 cup (250 mL) soup: 242 Calories; 17 g Protein; 9.2 g Total Fat; 22 g Carbohydrate; 982 mg Sodium; trace Dietary Fiber

Pictured on this page.

Shrimp and Mushroom Soup

A delicious combination of shrimp and mushrooms. Makes a great starter soup for a sit-down dinner. Garnish with shrimp.

Hard margarine (or butter)	1 tbsp.	15 mL
Finely chopped onion	⅓ cup	75 mL
Chopped fresh mushrooms	2 cups	500 mL
All-purpose flour	¼ cup	60 mL
Salt	½ tsp.	2 mL
Dry mustard	½ tsp.	2 mL
Garlic salt	¼ tsp.	1 mL
Pepper	⅛ tsp.	0.5 mL
Skim evaporated milk	13½ oz.	385 mL
Milk	1⅓ cups	325 mL
Water	1 cup	250 mL
Sherry (or alcohol-free sherry), optional	1 tbsp.	15 mL
Canned broken (or cocktail) shrimp, with liquid	2 × 4 oz.	2 × 113 g

Melt margarine in non-stick frying pan. Add onion and mushrooms. Sauté until onion is soft and moisture is evaporated.

Mix in next 5 ingredients.

Stir in both milks and water until boiling and thickened. Add sherry. Stir.

Add shrimp with liquid. Heat through. Makes about 5 cups (1.25 L) soup.

1 cup (250 mL) soup: 206 Calories; 20 g Protein; 4.4 g Total Fat; 21 g Carbohydrate; 577 mg Sodium; 1 g Dietary Fiber

Pictured on this page.

Squares

Squares have become very popular over the past two centuries. Because they are faster to make and often fancier than cookies, squares remain the preferred sweet to make for a special occasion. Chinese Chews, Brownies, Nut Smacks and Mystery Squares are oldies but goodies, and will probably continue to be favorites for years to come. When hosting a luncheon or having friends over for tea, squares are always welcome because of their small size and irresistible richness. They are also a good alternative to large, heavy desserts and offer the perfect sweet finale to any meal.

Tropical Squares

A pineapple and coconut topping. More moist the second day.

Bottom Layer:

All-purpose flour	1 cup	250 mL
Granulated sugar	1 tbsp.	15 mL
Hard margarine (or butter), softened	¼ cup	60 mL
Baking powder	¼ tsp.	1 mL
Large egg, fork-beaten	1	1

Top Layer:

Large eggs, fork-beaten	2	2
Medium or flake coconut	2 cups	500 mL
Granulated sugar	1 cup	250 mL
Canned crushed pineapple, drained	14 oz.	398 mL
Hard margarine (or butter), melted	1 tbsp.	15 mL
Lemon juice	1 tsp.	5 mL

Bottom Layer: Mix first 4 ingredients in small bowl.

Add egg. Mix lightly. Press in ungreased 9 × 9 inch (22 × 22 cm) pan.

Top Layer: Combine all 6 ingredients in small bowl. Mix well. Spoon and spread over bottom layer. Bake in 350°F (175°C) oven for about 40 minutes. Cool. Cuts into 36 squares.

1 square: 97 Calories; 1 g Protein; 5.5 g Total Fat; 11 g Carbohydrate; 27 mg Sodium; trace Dietary Fiber

Pictured on page 166/167.

Brownies

An old family recipe. Great with or without icing.

Hard margarine (or butter)	½ cup	125 mL
Unsweetened chocolate baking squares, cut up	2 × 1 oz.	2 × 28 g
Brown sugar, packed	1½ cups	375 mL
Large eggs, fork-beaten	2	2
Vanilla	1 tbsp.	15 mL
All-purpose flour	1 cup	250 mL
Chopped walnuts	¾ cup	175 mL

Chocolate Icing:

Hard margarine (or butter), softened	3 tbsp.	50 mL
Icing (confectioner's) sugar	1⅓ cups	325 mL
Cocoa	⅓ cup	75 mL
Hot prepared coffee	1½ tbsp.	25 mL

Melt margarine and chocolate in medium saucepan over low, stirring often. Remove from heat.

Stir in brown sugar. Add eggs and vanilla. Stir vigorously.

Add flour and walnuts. Stir just to moisten. Turn into greased 9 × 9 inch (22 × 22 cm) pan. Bake in 350°F (175°C) oven for about 25 minutes until wooden pick inserted in center comes out clean. Do not overbake. Cool.

Chocolate Icing: Beat all 4 ingredients together in small bowl until smooth. Add more icing sugar or prepared coffee if needed to make proper spreading consistency. Spread over cooled brownies in pan. Cuts into 36 squares.

1 iced square: 130 Calories; 1 g Protein; 6.5 g Total Fat; 18 g Carbohydrate; 50 mg Sodium; 1 g Dietary Fiber

Pictured on page 166.

Mystery Squares

A shortbread base with a chewy coconut filling.
Good with or without icing.

Bottom Layer:

All-purpose flour	1 cup	250 mL
Hard margarine (or butter), softened	½ cup	125 mL
Granulated sugar	2 tbsp.	30 mL

Second Layer:

Large eggs, fork-beaten	2	2
Brown sugar, packed	1 cup	250 mL
Vanilla	½ tsp.	2 mL
Salt	⅛ tsp.	0.5 mL
Medium coconut	½ cup	125 mL
All-purpose flour	2 tbsp.	30 mL
Baking powder	1 tsp.	5 mL

White Icing:

Icing (confectioner's) sugar	1½ cups	375 mL
Hard margarine (or butter), softened	3 tbsp.	50 mL
Vanilla	½ tsp.	2 mL
Milk	2 tsp.	10 mL

Bottom Layer: Mix flour, margarine and sugar in small bowl until crumbly. Press in ungreased 9 × 9 inch (22 × 22 cm) pan. Bake in 350°F (175°C) oven for 10 minutes.

Second Layer: Combine eggs, brown sugar, vanilla and salt in medium bowl. Beat well. Stir in coconut, flour and baking powder. Pour over bottom layer. Bake for about 25 minutes until browned. Cool.

White Icing: Beat all 4 ingredients in small bowl, adding more icing sugar or milk for proper spreading consistency. Spread over cooled squares in pan. Cuts into 36 squares.

1 iced square: 108 Calories; 1 g Protein; 4.9 g Total Fat; 16 g Carbohydrate; 60 mg Sodium; trace Dietary Fiber

Pictured on page 167.

New Magic Squares

Chocolate base with a nutty topping.

First Layer:

Hard margarine (or butter)	⅓ cup	75 mL
Chocolate wafer crumbs	1½ cups	375 mL

Second Layer:

Flake coconut	1 cup	250 mL
Sliced almonds (or walnuts or pecans), toasted in 350°F (175°C) oven for 5 to 8 minutes	⅔ cup	150 mL
Semisweet chocolate chips	⅔ cup	150 mL

Third Layer:

Sweetened condensed milk	11 oz.	300 mL

Fourth Layer:

Sliced almonds, toasted in 350°F (175°C) oven for 5 to 8 minutes (optional)	¼ cup	60 mL

First Layer: Melt margarine in small saucepan. Stir in wafer crumbs. Press in 9 x 9 inch (22 x 22 cm) foil-lined pan. Bake in 350°F (175°C) oven for 10 minutes.

Second Layer: Sprinkle with coconut, almonds and chocolate chips. Press down firmly.

Third Layer: Drizzle condensed milk over top.

Fourth Layer: Sprinkle with almonds. Bake in 350°F (175°C) oven for 25 to 30 minutes. Cool. Cuts into 36 squares.

1 square: 104 Calories; 2 g Protein; 6.9 g Total Fat; 10 g Carbohydrate; 39 mg Sodium; 1 g Dietary Fiber

Pictured below.

TIME-HONORED RECIPE

Matrimonial Squares

Favorite date squares that are not nearly as messy to eat as some others. These crumbs hold together well.

Oatmeal Layers:

All-purpose flour	1¼ cups	300 mL
Quick-cooking rolled oats (not instant)	1½ cups	375 mL
Brown sugar, packed	1 cup	250 mL
Baking soda	1 tsp.	5 mL
Salt	½ tsp.	2 mL
Hard margarine (or butter), softened	1 cup	250 mL

Date Filling:

Chopped dates	1½ cups	375 mL
Granulated sugar	½ cup	125 mL
Water	⅔ cup	150 mL

Oatmeal Layers: Measure flour, rolled oats, brown sugar, baking soda, salt and margarine into large bowl. Cut in margarine until crumbly. Press a generous ½ of crumbs in greased 9 x 9 inch (22 x 22 cm) pan.

Date Filling: Combine dates, sugar and water in small saucepan. Bring to a boil. Simmer until mushy. If mixture becomes too dry before dates have softened, add more water. If you find you have too much water, simmer until some is evaporated. Spread over bottom layer of crumbs. Sprinkle second ½ of crumbs over top. Press down with your hand. Bake in 350°F (175°C) oven for 30 minutes until golden brown. Cool. Cuts into 36 squares.

1 square: 131 Calories; 1 g Protein; 5.7 g Total Fat; 20 g Carbohydrate; 142 mg Sodium; 1 g Dietary Fiber

Pictured below.

New Magic Squares, above

Matrimonial Squares, above

Brazil Bars

A nutty buttery bar. Almost a shortbread.

Butter (not margarine), softened	6 tbsp.	100 mL
Brown sugar, packed	¾ cup	175 mL
Large egg	1	1
Vanilla	½ tsp.	2 mL
All-purpose flour	1½ cups	375 mL
Salt	¼ tsp.	1 mL
Sliced or chopped Brazil nuts	¾ cup	175 mL

Cream butter and brown sugar together in medium bowl. Beat in egg and vanilla.

Add flour, salt and Brazil nuts. Stir just to moisten. Pack in greased 9 x 9 inch (22 x 22 cm) pan. Bake in 350°F (175°C) oven for 20 to 25 minutes until edges are starting to brown. Cool. Cuts into 36 bars.

1 bar: 73 Calories; 1 g Protein; 3.7 g Total Fat; 9 g Carbohydrate; 45 mg Sodium; trace Dietary Fiber

Pictured below.

TIME-HONORED RECIPE

Nut Smacks

Butterscotch flavor, rich with nuts and brown sugar. An old family favorite.

Bottom Layer:		
Brown sugar, packed	½ cup	125 mL
Egg yolks (large)	2	2
Vanilla	1 tsp.	5 mL
Hard margarine (or butter), softened	½ cup	125 mL
Salt	¼ tsp.	1 mL
All-purpose flour	1½ cups	375 mL
Baking powder	1 tsp.	5 mL
Second Layer:		
Egg whites (large), room temperature	2	2
Brown sugar, packed	1 cup	250 mL
Chopped walnuts	1 cup	250 mL

Bottom Layer: Combine all 7 ingredients in large bowl. Mix until crumbly. Press firmly in ungreased 9 x 9 inch (22 x 22 cm) pan.

Second Layer: Beat egg whites in medium bowl until frothy. Add brown sugar ⅓ at a time, beating until stiff. Fold in walnuts. Spoon over bottom layer, spreading evenly. Bake in 350°F (175°C) oven for about 25 minutes until golden. Cool. Covering pan allows meringue to soften for easier cutting. Cuts into 36 squares.

1 square: 109 Calories; 1 g Protein; 5.3 g Total Fat; 14 g Carbohydrate; 58 mg Sodium; trace Dietary Fiber

Pictured above.

Chip Bars

The flavor of toffee. These do a disappearing act fast.

Bottom Layer:		
Hard margarine (or butter), softened	½ cup	125 mL
Brown sugar, packed	¾ cup	175 mL
All-purpose flour	1½ cups	375 mL
Second Layer:		
Butterscotch chips	2 cups	500 mL
Corn syrup	½ cup	125 mL
Cooking oil	2 tbsp.	30 mL
Peanuts, whole or chopped (bars are easier to cut when nuts are chopped)	2 cups	500 mL

Bottom Layer: Mix margarine, brown sugar and flour well in small bowl. Press in ungreased 9 x 13 inch (22 x 33 cm) pan. Bake in 375°F (190°C) oven for about 10 minutes.

Second Layer: Combine butterscotch chips, corn syrup and cooking oil in small saucepan. Heat over low, stirring constantly, until butterscotch chips are melted.

Add peanuts. Stir. Spoon over bottom layer. Bake in 375°F (190°C) oven for about 6 minutes. Cool. Cuts into 54 bars.

1 bar: 116 Calories; 2 g Protein; 5.5 g Total Fat; 16 g Carbohydrate; 29 mg Sodium; 1 g Dietary Fiber

Pictured below.

Top: Chip Bars, above
Bottom: Brazil Bars, page 170

Chinese Chews

TIME-HONORED RECIPE

Chinese Chews

I remember Grandad making these after Gram died. They are moist and therefore can last quite awhile.

Granulated sugar	1 cup	250 mL
Chopped dates	1 cup	250 mL
Baking powder	1 tsp.	5 mL
Salt	¼ tsp.	1 mL
Chopped walnuts	½ cup	125 mL
All-purpose flour	¾ cup	175 mL
Large eggs	2	2
Icing (confectioner's) sugar, to cover	2 tbsp.	30 mL

Mix first 6 ingredients in medium bowl.

Beat eggs in small bowl until light in color and thickened. Pour over flour mixture. Stir until well moistened. Scrape batter into greased 9 x 9 inch (22 x 22 cm) pan. Bake in 350°F (175°C) oven for about 25 minutes until wooden pick inserted in center comes out clean. Cool.

Cut into small squares and roll in icing sugar while still warm, or cool and sift icing sugar over top. Cuts into 36 squares.

1 square: 57 Calories; 1 g Protein; 1.5 g Total Fat; 12 g Carbohydrate; 23 mg Sodium; 1 g Dietary Fiber

Pictured above.

Caramel Chocolate Squares

Rich chocolate flavor covers a shortbread base.

Hard margarine (or butter), softened	½ cup	125 mL
All-purpose flour	1¼ cups	300 mL
Brown sugar, packed	⅓ cup	75 mL
Light cream cheese, softened	4 oz.	125 g
Large egg	1	1
Caramel ice cream topping	¾ cup	175 mL
Vanilla	1 tsp.	5 mL
Chopped walnuts (or pecans)	½ cup	125 mL
Milk chocolate chips	1 cup	250 mL

Mix margarine, flour and brown sugar in small bowl until crumbly. Reserve ⅔ cup (150 mL). Press remainder in ungreased 9 x 9 inch (22 x 22 cm) pan.

Beat cream cheese and egg in medium bowl. Add caramel topping and vanilla. Beat. Stir in reserved crumb mixture.

Add walnuts. Stir. Spoon over crust. Bake in 375°F (190°C) oven for 30 to 35 minutes.

Sprinkle with chocolate chips. Let stand until melted. Spread over all. Cool. Cuts into 36 squares.

1 square: 104 Calories; 2 g Protein; 5.9 g Total Fat; 12 g Carbohydrate; 71 mg Sodium; trace Dietary Fiber

Pictured on page 173.

"We had two desserts every day. Our biggest dessert (pie or pudding) was at dinner (noontime). A smaller dessert of cake or brownies and fruit, or cookies and fruit, was served at supper."

Jean Paré

Chocolate Goodies

Rich chocolate taste. Soft and gooey.

Hard margarine (or butter), softened	½ cup	125 mL
Brown sugar, packed	1 cup	250 mL
Large egg	1	1
Vanilla	1 tsp.	5 mL
All-purpose flour	1¼ cups	300 mL
Quick-cooking rolled oats (not instant)	1½ cups	375 mL
Baking soda	½ tsp.	2 mL
Salt	½ tsp.	2 mL
Sweetened condensed milk	⅔ cup	150 mL
Semisweet chocolate chips	1 cup	250 mL
Hard margarine (or butter)	2 tbsp.	30 mL
Vanilla	1 tsp.	5 mL
Salt	¼ tsp.	1 mL

Cream first amount of margarine and brown sugar together in large bowl. Beat in egg and first amount of vanilla.

Add flour, rolled oats, baking soda and first amount of salt. Mix. Pack ⅔ of oat mixture in greased 9 x 9 inch (22 x 22 cm) pan.

Heat and stir remaining 5 ingredients in small saucepan until chocolate chips are melted. Spread over bottom layer. Drop remaining rolled oat mixture in little dabs over top. Spread as best you can. Don't be concerned if a few spaces aren't covered. Bake in 350°F (175°C) oven for 20 to 25 minutes. Cool. Cuts into 36 squares.

1 square: 127 Calories; 2 g Protein; 5.8 g Total Fat; 18 g Carbohydrate; 127 mg Sodium; 1 g Dietary Fiber

Pictured on page 173.

Chocolate Mince Squares

Moist, mildly spiced. Good texture.

Hard margarine (or butter), softened	½ cup	125 mL
Granulated sugar	1 cup	250 mL
Large eggs	2	2
Mincemeat	1 cup	250 mL
Chopped pecans (or walnuts)	½ cup	125 mL
Vanilla	1½ tsp.	7 mL
All-purpose flour	1¼ cups	300 mL
Cocoa	¼ cup	60 mL
Salt	½ tsp.	2 mL
Caramel Icing:		
Brown sugar, packed	½ cup	125 mL
Milk	3 tbsp.	50 mL
Hard margarine (or butter)	¼ cup	60 mL
Icing (confectioner's) sugar	1½ cups	375 mL

Cream margarine and sugar together well in large bowl. Beat in eggs, 1 at a time. Add mincemeat, pecans and vanilla. Stir.

Add flour, cocoa and salt. Mix well. Spread in greased 9 x 9 inch (22 x 22 cm) pan. Bake in 350°F (175°C) oven for 30 to 35 minutes. Cool.

Caramel Icing: Heat and stir brown sugar, milk and margarine in small saucepan until boiling. Boil for 2 minutes. Remove from heat. Cool.

Add icing sugar. Beat until smooth. Add a bit more milk or icing sugar if needed to make proper spreading consistency. Makes about ⅞ cup (200 mL) caramel icing. Spread over cooled squares in pan. Cuts into 36 squares.

1 square (with icing): 141 Calories; 1 g Protein; 5.8 g Total Fat; 22 g Carbohydrate; 107 mg Sodium; 1 g Dietary Fiber

Pictured on page 173.

Peanut Butter Squares

Yummy taste. Soft in consistency. Thin like a candy bar.

Hard margarine (or butter)	½ cup	125 mL
Smooth peanut butter	½ cup	125 mL
Icing (confectioner's) sugar	1¼ cups	300 mL
Graham cracker crumbs	1 cup	250 mL
Milk chocolate chips	1 cup	250 mL

Melt margarine and peanut butter in small saucepan, stirring constantly, until smooth. Remove from heat.

Add icing sugar and graham crumbs. Mix well. Pack in greased 9 x 9 inch (22 x 22 cm) pan.

Sprinkle with chocolate chips. Heat in 200°F (95°C) oven for about 5 minutes to soften. Spread evenly over top. Cool. Cuts into 36 squares.

1 square: 96 Calories; 2 g Protein; 6.2 g Total Fat; 10 g Carbohydrate; 75 mg Sodium; trace Dietary Fiber

Pictured on page 167.

Top: Chocolate Mince Squares, page 172
Bottom Left: Chocolate Goodies, page 172
Bottom Right: Caramel Chocolate Squares, page 172

"When electric mix masters replaced manual beaters, it took Gram a while to get used to the different, lighter texture of cakes."

"Most of Gram's recipes never had any amounts for any of the ingredients—and yet everything always turned out!"

Jean Paré

Pumpkin Cheesecake Squares, below

Frosted Pumpkin Squares, below

Pumpkin Cheesecake Squares

A moist, spiced-just-right treat.

All-purpose flour	1 cup	250 mL
Brown sugar, packed	⅓ cup	75 mL
Hard margarine (or butter), softened	6 tbsp.	100 mL
Finely chopped pecans	½ cup	125 mL
Filling:		
Light cream cheese, softened	8 oz.	250 g
Granulated sugar	¾ cup	175 mL
Canned pumpkin, without spices	½ cup	125 mL
Ground cinnamon	1½ tsp.	7 mL
Ground allspice	1 tsp.	5 mL
Vanilla	1 tsp.	5 mL
Large eggs	2	2

Measure flour, brown sugar and margarine into small bowl. Mix in margarine until crumbly.

Stir in pecans. Reserve ¾ cup (175 mL) for topping. Press remaining crumbs in ungreased 8 x 8 inch (20 x 20 cm) pan. Bake in 350°F (175°C) oven for 15 minutes. Cool slightly.

Filling: Beat cream cheese and sugar in small bowl. Add pumpkin, cinnamon, allspice and vanilla. Beat. Add eggs, 1 at a time, beating just to blend after each addition. Spread over crust. Sprinkle with reserved crumbs. Bake for 30 to 35 minutes. Cool. Cuts into 36 squares.

1 square: 88 Calories; 2 g Protein; 4.6 g Total Fat; 10 g Carbohydrate; 94 mg Sodium; trace Dietary Fiber

Pictured above.

Frosted Pumpkin Squares

A cake-type square. Cut in larger pieces for dessert.

Large eggs, fork-beaten	4	4
Granulated sugar	2 cups	500 mL
Canned pumpkin, without spices	1 cup	250 mL
Cooking oil	⅔ cup	150 mL
Ground cinnamon	2 tsp.	10 mL
Salt	½ tsp.	2 mL
All-purpose flour	2 cups	500 mL
Baking powder	1 tsp.	5 mL
Baking soda	1 tsp.	5 mL
Raisins	1 cup	250 mL
Frosting:		
Light cream cheese, softened	4 oz.	125 g
Hard margarine (or butter)	6 tbsp.	100 mL
Icing (confectioner's) sugar	2½ cups	625 mL
Vanilla	1 tsp.	5 mL
Milk, if needed	2 tsp.	10 mL

Combine eggs, sugar and pumpkin in large bowl. Beat well. Add cooking oil, cinnamon and salt. Beat to mix.

Add flour, baking powder and baking soda. Stir. Add raisins. Stir. Turn into greased and floured 10 x 15 inch (25 x 38 cm) jelly roll pan. Bake in 350°F (175°C) oven for 20 to 25 minutes until wooden pick inserted in center comes out clean.

Frosting: Beat cream cheese, margarine, icing sugar and vanilla on low just to moisten. Beat on medium to fluff up. Add milk, 1 tsp. (5 mL) at a time if needed to thin frosting. Spread while squares are still slightly warm. Cuts into 72 squares.

1 square (with frosting): 94 Calories; 1 g Protein; 3.5 g Total Fat; 15 g Carbohydrate; 70 mg Sodium; trace Dietary Fiber

Pictured above.

Vegetables

In the late nineteenth and early twentieth centuries, boiling, baking and frying vegetables were the preferred methods of cooking. Seasoning at this time was not yet a common practice. By World War I however, most cookbooks suggested the use of butter, salt, pepper or white sauce over vegetables. It wasn't until the mid-twentieth century that vegetable casseroles became popular. Canned vegetables came into use during the nineteenth century, and frozen and dehydrated vegetables, including instant potatoes, in the twentieth century. During the 1940s and 1950s, baking soda was often added to the cooking water of green vegetables such as green beans, asparagus, broccoli and spinach, to keep them bright green until it was discovered that the vitamin C was destroyed. Today, we have become more creative than ever in how we prepare and serve vegetables.

Beets And Onions

Good way to enjoy beets. They cook worry-free in the oven.

Peeled and grated raw beet (food processor works well)	4½ cups	1.1 L
Very finely chopped onion	¼ cup	60 mL
Salt	½ tsp.	2 mL
Pepper, sprinkle		
Hard margarine (or butter), melted (optional)	1 tbsp.	15 mL

Combine beet and onion in ungreased 1½ quart (1.5 L) casserole. Sprinkle with salt and pepper. Cover. Bake in 350°F (175°C) oven for about 1 hour.

Drizzle with margarine. Makes 5 cups (1.25 L) vegetables.

½ cup (125 mL) vegetables: 41 Calories; 1 g Protein; 1.3 g Total Fat; 7 g Carbohydrate; 196 mg Sodium; trace Dietary Fiber

Pictured on page 176.

TIME-HONORED RECIPE

Tomato Dumplings

For something different, try this old classic.

Canned tomatoes, with juice	28 oz.	796 mL
Granulated sugar	1 tsp.	5 mL
Finely chopped onion	¼ cup	60 mL
Finely chopped celery	2 tbsp.	30 mL
Water	½ cup	125 mL
Salt	½ tsp.	2 mL
All-purpose flour	1 cup	250 mL
Baking powder	2 tsp.	10 mL
Granulated sugar	1 tsp.	5 mL
Salt	½ tsp.	2 mL
Shortening	1 tbsp.	15 mL
Milk	½ cup	125 mL

Combine tomatoes with juice, sugar, onion, celery, water and first amount of salt in large pot or Dutch oven. Bring to a boil.

Combine flour, baking powder, sugar and second amount of salt in medium bowl. Cut in shortening until crumbly. Add milk. Stir to mix. Drop by spoonfuls over boiling tomatoes. Cover. Boil for 15 minutes. Serves 6.

1 serving: 145 Calories; 4 g Protein; 2.9 g Total Fat; 26 g Carbohydrate; 691 mg Sodium; 2 g Dietary Fiber

Pictured on page 176.

TIME-HONORED RECIPE

Bubble And Squeak

An old recipe from the British Isles.
Cabbage adds to appearance and to texture.

Mashed potato	4 cups	1 L
Cooked cabbage, chopped	4 cups	1 L
Salt	1 tsp.	5 mL
Pepper	¼ tsp.	1 mL
Hard margarine (or butter)	2 tbsp.	30 mL

Mix first 4 ingredients in large bowl. Shape into patties.

Melt margarine in non-stick frying pan. Brown patties on both sides. Makes 8 large or 16 medium patties.

1 large patty: 160 Calories; 3 g Protein; 3.3 g Total Fat; 31 g Carbohydrate; 394 mg Sodium; 3 g Dietary Fiber

Pictured on page 176.

Variation: This may all be browned in 1 big patty, turned out onto plate then eased back into pan to brown other side. This may also be scramble-fried instead of made into patties.

Zucchini Casserole

Golden brown crumbly topping over melted cheese. Green and red show up from the vegetables. Doubles easily.

Medium zucchini, with peel, quartered lengthwise and sliced	2 cups	500 mL
Salt, sprinkle		
Medium onion, sliced	1	1
Hard margarine (or butter)	1 tsp.	5 mL
Large tomato, sliced	1	1
Salt, sprinkle		
Pepper, sprinkle		
Dried sweet basil, sprinkle		
Medium zucchini, with peel, quartered lengthwise and sliced	2 cups	500 mL
Salt, sprinkle		
Process cheese slices	6	6
Topping:		
Hard margarine (or butter)	2 tbsp.	30 mL
Dry bread crumbs	½ cup	125 mL

Layer first amount of zucchini in greased 1 quart (1 L) casserole. Sprinkle with salt.

Sauté onion in margarine in non-stick frying pan until soft. Scatter over zucchini.

Add layer of tomato slices, overlapping if necessary. Sprinkle with salt, pepper and basil. Scatter second amount of zucchini over top. Sprinkle with salt. Lay cheese slices over top.

Topping: Melt margarine in small saucepan. Stir in bread crumbs. Sprinkle over cheese. Bake, uncovered, in 350°F (175°C) oven for about 40 minutes. Serves 4.

1 serving: 275 Calories; 11 g Protein; 17.7 g Total Fat; 20 g Carbohydrate; 642 mg Sodium; 4 g Dietary Fiber

Pictured on page 176.

Elegant Squash

With carrot and a seasoned crumb topping.

Grated carrot	1 cup	250 mL
Finely chopped onion	½ cup	125 mL
Cooking oil	1 tsp.	5 mL
Condensed cream of chicken soup	10 oz.	284 mL
Light sour cream	1 cup	250 mL
Cooked and mashed yellow squash (such as butternut)	2 cups	500 mL
Salt	1 tsp.	5 mL
Pepper	¼ tsp.	1 mL
Brown sugar, packed	1 tbsp.	15 mL
Large eggs, fork-beaten	2	2
Topping:		
Hard margarine (or butter)	2 tbsp.	30 mL
Dry bread crumbs	½ cup	125 mL
Poultry seasoning	¼ tsp.	1 mL
Parsley flakes	½ tsp.	2 mL

Sauté carrot and onion in cooking oil in non-stick frying pan until soft.

Add next 7 ingredients. Stir well. Turn into ungreased 1½ quart (1.5 L) casserole.

Topping: Melt margarine in small saucepan. Add bread crumbs, poultry seasoning and parsley. Stir. Sprinkle over top. Bake, uncovered, in 350°F (175°C) oven for about 1 hour until set. Serves 6.

1 serving: 238 Calories; 7 g Protein; 13.1 g Total Fat; 25 g Carbohydrate; 1011 mg Sodium; 3 g Dietary Fiber

Pictured on page 176.

Turnip Bake

A really delicious dish. Garnish with fresh tomato slices.

Yellow turnip, cut up	3 lbs.	1.4 kg
Water, to cover		
Large eggs, fork-beaten	2	2
Brown sugar, packed	1 tbsp.	15 mL
Salt	½ tsp.	2 mL
Pepper	⅛ tsp.	0.5 mL
All-purpose flour	2 tbsp.	30 mL
Baking powder	1 tsp.	5 mL
Topping:		
Hard margarine (or butter)	2 tbsp.	30 mL
Soda cracker crumbs	½ cup	125 mL

Cook turnip in water in large saucepan until very soft. Drain well. Mash.

Combine next 6 ingredients in small bowl. Mix. Add to turnip. Beat well. Turn into ungreased 2 quart (2 L) casserole.

Topping: Melt margarine in small saucepan. Stir in cracker crumbs. Sprinkle over top. Bake, uncovered, in 350°F (175°C) oven for 30 to 35 minutes until set. Makes 5 cups (1.25 L) turnip.

½ cup (125 mL) turnip: 97 Calories; 3 g Protein; 4 g Total Fat; 13 g Carbohydrate; 301 mg Sodium; 2 g Dietary Fiber

Pictured on page 178.

Top: Baked Onions, below
Bottom: Turnip Bake, page 177

Corn Scallop

Makes a nice vegetable dish. More special than many.

Skim evaporated milk	½ cup	125 mL
All-purpose flour	2 tbsp.	30 mL
Chopped green pepper	2 tbsp.	30 mL
Finely chopped onion	¼ cup	60 mL
Soda cracker crumbs	¼ cup	60 mL
Parsley flakes	½ tsp.	2 mL
Salt	½ tsp.	2 mL
Pepper	¼ tsp.	1 mL
Ground marjoram, just a pinch		
Canned cream-style corn	2 × 10 oz.	2 × 284 mL
Grated medium Cheddar cheese	¾ cup	175 mL
Topping:		
Hard margarine (or butter)	2 tbsp.	30 mL
Dry bread crumbs	½ cup	125 mL
Onion powder	⅛ tsp.	0.5 mL
Grated medium Cheddar cheese	⅓ cup	75 mL

Whisk evaporated milk into flour in medium bowl until smooth. Add next 9 ingredients. Mix well. Turn into ungreased 1 quart (1 L) casserole.

Topping: Melt margarine in small saucepan. Stir in bread crumbs, onion powder and cheese. Sprinkle over top. Bake, uncovered, in 350°F (175°C) oven for about 45 minutes until bubbling. Serves 6.

1 serving: 279 Calories; 11 g Protein; 12.5 g Total Fat; 34 g Carbohydrate; 833 mg Sodium; 2 g Dietary Fiber

Pictured on page 179.

Baked Onions

A nice onion flavor. Not overbearing because the rice is cooked with the onion.

Hard margarine (or butter)	2 tbsp.	30 mL
Chopped onion	6 cups	1.5 L
Uncooked long grain white rice	½ cup	125 mL
Salt	¼ tsp.	1 mL
Skim evaporated milk	⅔ cup	150 mL
Grated Muenster cheese	1 cup	250 mL

Melt margarine in non-stick frying pan. Add onion, rice and salt. You will need to do this in batches. Sauté until onion is soft. Turn into large bowl.

Add evaporated milk and cheese. Stir well. Turn into greased 1½ quart (1.5 L) casserole. Cover. Bake in 350°F (175°C) oven for 55 minutes. Remove cover. Bake for 5 minutes until browned. Makes about 5 cups (1.25 L) onion.

½ cup (125 mL) onion: 153 Calories; 6 g Protein; 6.2 g Total Fat; 19 g Carbohydrate; 195 mg Sodium; 2 g Dietary Fiber

Pictured above.

Glazed Onions

Makes an excellent side dish with a roast or pork chops.

Sliced onion (4 large)	6 cups	1.5 L
Water	1 cup	250 mL
Hard margarine (or butter)	2 tbsp.	30 mL
Granulated sugar	3 tbsp.	50 mL

Cook onion in water in covered non-stick frying pan for about 20 minutes. Drain.

Add margarine and sugar. Heat and stir until margarine is melted. Cook, uncovered, stirring often, for 10 to 15 minutes until golden brown and water is evaporated. Makes 2 cups (500 mL) onion.

½ cup (125 mL) onion: 117 Calories; 1 g Protein; 6 g Total Fat; 16 g Carbohydrate; 71 mg Sodium; 1 g Dietary Fiber

Pictured on page 179.

Stuffing Balls

Especially handy for freezing ahead.
Simply heat as few or as many as needed.

Hard margarine (or butter)	2 tbsp.	30 mL
Chopped onion	¾ cup	175 mL
Chopped celery	½ cup	125 mL
Large eggs, fork-beaten	2	2
Frozen kernel corn	1 cup	250 mL
Milk	1 cup	250 mL
Dry bread crumbs	3 cups	750 mL
Poultry seasoning	1½ tsp.	7 mL
Parsley flakes	1½ tsp.	7 mL
Salt	¾ tsp.	4 mL
Pepper	¼ tsp.	1 mL
Hard margarine (or butter), melted	¼ cup	60 mL

Melt first amount of margarine in non-stick frying pan. Add onion and celery. Sauté until soft.

Combine next 8 ingredients in large bowl. Add onion and celery. Mix well. Shape into 14 balls using ¼ cup (60 mL) for each one. Add water if needed to hold together. Arrange in small greased roaster or baking dish large enough to hold in single layer.

Drizzle second amount of margarine over top. Cover. Bake in 350°F (175°C) oven for about 35 minutes. Makes about 14 stuffing balls.

1 stuffing ball: 174 Calories; 5 g Protein; 7.1 g Total Fat; 23 g Carbohydrate; 407 mg Sodium; 1 g Dietary Fiber

Pictured below.

Wild Rice Stuffing

A good stuffing for Cornish hens, chicken or whole salmon.

Wild rice	½ cup	125 mL
Brown rice	½ cup	125 mL
Water	3 cups	750 mL
Chicken bouillon powder	1 tbsp.	15 mL
Hard margarine (or butter)	2 tbsp.	30 mL
Chopped onion	1 cup	250 mL
Chopped fresh mushrooms	3 cups	750 mL
Chopped celery	¼ cup	60 mL
Parsley flakes	1 tsp.	5 mL
Dried thyme	¼ tsp.	1 mL
Ground marjoram	¼ tsp.	1 mL
Chopped pecans	½ cup	125 mL

Combine first 4 ingredients in large saucepan. Cook for about 45 minutes until rice is tender and water is absorbed.

Melt margarine in non-stick frying pan. Add onion, mushrooms and celery. Sauté until soft.

Stir in parsley, thyme, marjoram and pecans. Add to rice mixture. Stir well. Makes 4 cups (1 L) stuffing.

½ cup (125 mL) stuffing: 180 Calories; 4 g Protein; 9 g Total Fat; 22 g Carbohydrate; 285 mg Sodium; 2 g Dietary Fiber

Pictured below.

Left: Glazed Onions, page 178   Top Center: Corn Scallop, page 178   Bottom: Center: Stuffing Balls, this page   Right: Wild Rice Stuffing, above

2000 Cake

What a terrific centerpiece for the big event! This 2000 cake leaves no doubt in people's mind what the celebration is all about. To actually see the numbers as you count down, gives a visual element to the moment that will become a part of your guests' millennium memories.

We have chosen to show you one way that you can decorate the cakes. However, the choice is yours. Decide ahead of time what color icing you would like. The White Decorator Frosting, page 181, can be tinted using food coloring or icing colors from concentrated paste (available at craft stores or wedding specialty stores). The pastes come in a wide variety of colors, making it easy to match tablecloth colors or create other desired shades. The piping is not as difficult as it looks and the piping kits are readily available in stores. However, if you choose not to, use your spreading knife to make decorative swirls in the frosting and stop at Step 3.

Make four 9 x 13 inch (22 x 33 cm) cakes, either from a recipe or a mix, in whatever flavor you like. Be sure to line your pan with foil for easy removal of cake when it's cooled. Wash and re-line pan for each cake. When the cakes have cooled, you are ready to begin. Follow the instructions below for making the number patterns (see Step 1). And don't forget to save the cut away pieces of cake for Irish Cream Trifle on page 181. It's a heavenly dessert that would be wonderful on New Year's Day. Or freeze the leftover pieces for a later date. The cakes may be frozen before cutting, just after cutting, or after they have been iced. They are easiest to cut when completely thawed and at room temperature. But icing them will be less crumby if they are partially frozen. For a final touch, add candles or sparklers to really make the cake a focal point at midnight.

For the 2000 Cake, shown on this page and on pages 10 and 11, you will need:

4 chocolate cake mixes, 2 layer size each
4 batches White Decorator Frosting
   (see recipe, page 181)
4 foiled 10 x 12 inch (25 x 30 cm) cake boards
   (available at most craft or wedding specialty stores)
1 serrated knife
1 spreader knife
2 piping bags
   (one fitted with straight wedge tip, one fitted with star tip)

To create patterns:

1 square = 1 square inch

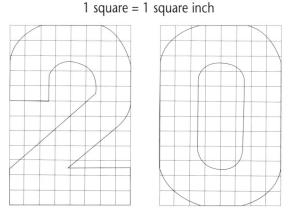

To make one number cake:

1 Using legal-size paper, draw 2 rectangles, 8 x 12 inches (20 x 30 cm) each. Make a grid of horizontal and vertical lines, 1 inch (2.5 cm) apart, inside each rectangle. Using the guidelines on this page, draw the numbers 2 and 0. Cut out each number pattern.

To make number cakes:

2 Turn out 1 cooled cake onto cutting board or countertop. Place number 2 pattern on top of cake, centering to fit. Place one hand gently on pattern to hold in place (or use sewing pins). Using the serrated knife, and keeping it straight up and down, use a sawing motion to cut out the cake. Carefully remove excess pieces of cake. (Note: Use leftover cake in Irish Cream Trifle, page 181). Gently remove pattern. Using metal spatula and pancake lifter, carefully lift and move number cake onto foiled board, centering it before removing lifters.

3 Take 1 batch of White Decorator Frosting and divide equally into 2 bowls. Completely ice the top and sides of cake, using the frosting in 1 bowl.

4 Before the frosting has had a chance to set, take a decorator comb and drag it gently through the surface of the frosting to create a pattern.

5 Take the remaining frosting and divide it again equally into 2 bowls. Tint each half a different color.

Using the piping bag fitted with the flat wedge design tip, pipe first color around the bottom sides, about ½ inch (12 mm) up from base. Repeat around top of cake, about ½ inch (12 mm) in from edge. Using piping bag fitted with the star tip, pipe second color right below first, all around very bottom edge of cake. Repeat around top of cake, along outer edge.

Irish Cream Trifle,
this page

White Decorator Frosting

Good consistency for decorating. Enough to ice top and sides, plus piping decoration as shown, for one of the number cakes. Make four batches to cover "2000" cake.

Solid white vegetable shortening (such as Crisco), room temperature	1½ cups	375 mL
Icing (confectioner's) sugar	8 cups	2.1 L
Light cream or evaporated milk	6½ tbsp.	107 mL
Vanilla (clear is best)	1 tbsp.	15 mL
Icing (confectioner's) sugar	½-1 cup	125-250 mL

Beat shortening on high until fluffy. Gradually add first amount of icing sugar, 1 cup (250 mL) at a time, beating continually until mixture becomes very stiff.

Add cream and vanilla. Beat well.

Add second amount of icing sugar, ¼ cup (60 mL) at a time, to make creamy and smooth for spreading. Makes 6½ cups (1.6 L) frosting.

2 tbsp. (30 mL) frosting: 129 calories; trace Protein; 6 g Total Fat; 19 g Carbohydrate; 1 mg Sodium; 0 g Dietary Fiber

Pictured on page 180 and 181.

Irish Cream Trifle

Irish Cream liqueur and coffee for adult tastes only! Chocolate-covered coffee beans or chocolate curls make a nice garnish.

Instant vanilla pudding powders (4 serving size)	2	2
Milk	4 cups	1 L
Leftover chocolate cake, cut into 1 inch (2.5 cm) cubes	12 cups	3 L
Irish Cream liqueur	½ cup	125 mL
Whipping cream (or frozen whipped topping, thawed)	2 cups	500 mL
Irish Cream (or Cappuccino) flavored instant coffee beverage mix	⅓ cup	75 mL
Cocoa powder, for garnish	1 tsp.	5 mL

Mix pudding powders and milk as directed on package. Pour 1 cup (250 mL) pudding into bottom of 14 cup (3.5 L) glass serving bowl or large trifle dish. Arrange ⅓ of cake cubes over top. Drizzle with about 3 tbsp. (50 mL) liqueur.

Whip cream and beverage mix together until stiff. Spread ⅓ of cream mixture over cake cubes. Repeat layers twice more, piping remaining cream mixture decoratively over cake cubes.

Sift cocoa powder over top. Makes 12 to 14 cups (3 to 3.5 L) trifle. Serves 16 to 20.

1 serving: 347 calories; 5 g Protein; 18.9 g Total Fat; 40 g Carbohydrate; 217 mg Sodium; trace Dietary Fiber

Pictured on this page.

What's Next?

Who truly knows what we can expect in future years? Changes are happening incredibly fast, with obsolescence hot on the heels of new and improved. But it can be fun to speculate.

Food shopping and food preparation have reached the age of cyberspace. Order your groceries over the internet. Or have your computer create your grocery list after you punch in your selection of recipes for the upcoming week.

Many see nutrition in the next millennium as a paradox of sophistication and simplicity. Research will continue to uncover the powerful link between nutrition and health and will add meaning to the nineties phrase "you are what you eat." High tech discoveries in the areas of nutrition and health research will translate into simple messages: "Eat your veggies," "An apple a day keeps the doctor away," and "Breakfast is the most important meal of the day." Research will prove that Grandma was right!

Plants will be a huge area of research. Thousands of phytochemicals (phyto means "plants"), naturally occurring substances in plants, have been discovered in the last few years and are only the tip of the iceberg! They have been shown to protect the body from the development of certain types of cancer, from heart disease, and from diseases of aging such as cataracts. We will be encouraged to eat more foods of plant origin in order to reap the rewards of nature's medicine. Fruits, vegetables, legumes, grain products, seeds, etc. will be on our plates in greater quantities. This trend has already been reflected in the most recent Food Guides in both Canada and the United States.

The demand for more nutritious and delicious fruits and vegetables will fuel research in genetic engineering. Scientists will be able to alter the genetic makeup of foods to harness certain preferred characteristics such as taste, nutritional value, size or temperature resistance. For example, the gene that ripens tomatoes can be reversed, resulting in a tomato that can ripen on the vine, have vine-ripened juiciness, but that can stay at its peak for several weeks—during transportation, grocery store display and finally in your home.

Will breakfast, lunch and dinner as we know them, become obsolete? Will "snacktime" replace "mealtime"? Will we pop breakfast into the microwave on the dashboard of our car? Will we have supersize vegetables containing mega nutrients? Will nutriceuticals, functional foods, and flavanoids become common, everyday words for the consumer? Only time will tell.

Special thanks to Joanne McIvor, B.Sc., Registered Dietician, for sharing with me her insights into the next millennium.

Bibliography

Anderson, Jean. *American Century Cookbook*. New York: Clark & Potter, 1997.

Canada's Food Guide Handbook. Ottawa: The Minister of National Health and Welfare, Revised Edition, 1983.

Dale, Rodney & Weaver, Rebecca. *Machines In The Home*. Toronto: Oxford University Press, 1992.

Ferguson, Carol. *A Century of Canadian Home Cooking*. Scarborough: Prentice-Hall Canada, 1992.

Panati, Charles. *Panati's Extraordinary Origins of Everyday Things*. New York City: Harper & Row, 1987 (Revised in 1989).

Stewart, Katie. *The Joy Of Eating*. Owings Mills: Stemmer House Publishers, 1977.

The Development Of Canada's Food Guide To Healthy Eating: Notes On Consumer Research. Ottawa: Health and Welfare Canada, June 11, 1993.

The Horizon Cookbook and Illustrated History of Eating and Drinking Through the Ages. New York: American Heritage, 1968.

USDA's Food Guide - Background and Development. Hyattsville: Publication Number 1514.

Using The Food Guide. Ottawa: The Minister of National Health and Welfare, 1992.

Wallace, Lilly Haxworth. *The Lily Wallace New American Cookbook*. New York City: Books Inc., 1946.

Wright, Lawrence. *Home Fires Burning: The History of Domestic Heating And Cooking*. London: Routledge & Kegan Paul Ltd., 1968.

Measurement Tables

Throughout this book measurements

are given in Conventional and Metric measure.

To compensate for differences between the two

measurements due to rounding, a full metric measure

is not always used. The cup used is the standard

8 fluid ounce. Temperature is given in degrees

Fahrenheit and Celsius. Baking pan measurements

are in inches and centimetres as well as quarts

and litres. An exact metric conversion is

given on this page as well as the working

equivalent (Standard Measure).

Oven temperatures

Fahrenheit (°F)	Celsius (°C)
175°	80°
200°	95°
225°	110°
250°	120°
275°	140°
300°	150°
325°	160°
350°	175°
375°	190°
400°	205°
425°	220°
450°	230°
475°	240°
500°	260°

Pans

Conventional Inches	Metric Centimetres
8x8 inch	20x20 cm
9x9 inch	22x22 cm
9x13 inch	22x33 cm
10x15 inch	25x38 cm
11x17 inch	28x43 cm
8x2 inch round	20x5 cm
9x2 inch round	22x5 cm
10x4¹/₂ inch tube	25x11 cm
8x4x3 inch loaf	20x10x7.5 cm
9x5x3 inch loaf	22x12.5x7.5 cm

Spoons

Conventional Measure	Metric Exact Conversion Millilitre (mL)	Metric Standard Measure Millilitre (mL)
¹/₈ teaspoon (tsp.)	0.6 mL	0.5 mL
¹/₄ teaspoon (tsp.)	1.2 mL	1 mL
¹/₂ teaspoon (tsp.)	2.4 mL	2 mL
1 teaspoon (tsp.)	4.7 mL	5 mL
2 teaspoons (tsp.)	9.4 mL	10 mL
1 tablespoon (tbsp.)	14.2 mL	15 mL

Cups

¹/₄ cup (4 tbsp.)	56.8 mL	60 mL
¹/₃ cup (5¹/₃ tbsp.)	75.6 mL	75 mL
¹/₂ cup (8 tbsp.)	113.7 mL	125 mL
²/₃ cup (10²/₃ tbsp.)	151.2 mL	150 mL
³/₄ cup (12 tbsp.)	170.5 mL	175 mL
1 cup (16 tbsp.)	227.3 mL	250 mL
4¹/₂ cups	1022.9 mL	1000 mL (1 L)

Dry measurements

Conventional Measure Ounces (oz.)	Metric Exact Conversion Grams (g)	Metric Standard Measure Grams (g)
1 oz.	28.3 g	28 g
2 oz.	56.7 g	57 g
3 oz.	85.0 g	85 g
4 oz.	113.4 g	125 g
5 oz.	141.7 g	140 g
6 oz.	170.1 g	170 g
7 oz.	198.4 g	200 g
8 oz.	226.8 g	250 g
16 oz.	453.6 g	500 g
32 oz.	907.2 g	1000 g (1 kg)

Casseroles (Canada & Britain)

Standard Size Casserole	Exact Metric Measure
1 qt. (5 cups)	1.13 L
1¹/₂ qts. (7¹/₂ cups)	1.69 L
2 qts. (10 cups)	2.25 L
2¹/₂ qts. (12¹/₂ cups)	2.81 L
3 qts. (15 cups)	3.38 L
4 qts. (20 cups)	4.5 L
5 qts. (25 cups)	5.63 L

Casseroles (United States)

Standard Size Casserole	Exact Metric Measure
1 qt. (4 cups)	900 mL
1¹/₂ qts. (6 cups)	1.35 L
2 qts. (8 cups)	1.8 L
2¹/₂ qts. (10 cups)	2.25 L
3 qts. (12 cups)	2.7 L
4 qts. (16 cups)	3.6 L
5 qts. (20 cups)	4.5 L

Index

G

H

I

J

K

L

M

Denotes previously published recipe